555841

D0297214

796 ⟨⟩ ⟨⟩L

WITHDRAWN FROM LIBRARY STOCK

Training Professionals in the Practice of Sport Psychology

Training Professionals in the Practice of Sport Psychology

John M. Silva III
The University of North Carolina—Chapel Hill

Jonathan N. Metzler
Georgia Southern University

Bart Lerner
Argosy University

Fitness Information Technology
A Division of the International Center for Performance Excellence
262 Coliseum, WVU-PE
P. O. Box 6116
Morgantown, WV 26506-6116

Copyright © 2007, by West Virginia University

All rights reserved.

Reproduction or use of any portion of this publication by any mechanical, electronic, or other means is prohibited without written permission of the publisher.

Library of Congress Card Catalog Number: 2006939830

ISBN: 9781885693761

Cover photographs courtesy of: Carolina Panthers, Jenn Cook, Jim Burgess, and Atlanta
    Falcons. Photograph on page 213 courtesy of Dan Sears.
Cover design: Scott Lohr, 40 West Studios
Printed by Sheridan Books

12 11 10 09 08 07   1 2 3 4 5

Fitness Information Technology
A Division of the International Center for Performance Excellence
West Virginia University
262 Coliseum, WVU-PE
PO Box 6116
Morgantown, WV 26506-6116
800.477.4348 (toll free)
304.293.6888 (phone)
304.293.6658 (fax)
Email: icpe@mail.wvu.edu
Website: www.fitinfotech.com

SOUTHAMPTON SOLENT
UNIVERSITY LIBRARY
SUPPLIER DAWSONL
ORDER No
DATE 20/10/09

Any accomplishment, big or small is dedicated to my parents.
To the late John M. Silva Jr.: I love you, Dad, and will
never forget everything you did for me and for our family.
To my mom, Jennie M. Silva: I love you, Mom.
Your ability to give without measure is unmatched.
Every soul should be so fortunate to have a mom and dad like mine.

Chris, Mom Maki, Taylor, Tally, Buddie, Coco, Sandy,
Jersey, Patches, and Cleo, always lots of love!
—JMS

To my family—Heidi, Mom, Dad, & Brad, and John,
Vicki, and Haley, who have continually supported me
throughout my professional pursuits.
—JNM

To my wife, Deb, the love of my life.
You are my inspiration.
—Bart

CONTENTS

FOREWORD

The contents of this book are truly unique, as no other resource of its kind exists. *Training Professionals in the Practice of Sport Psychology* makes a significant contribution for those who are or will be involved in the practice of sport psychology. Academic graduate sport psychology programs offer the substance of research and professional articles and inform students about the psychological and mental areas related to achieving in sport and the challenges that athletes face. Typically what is missing in this education are knowledge and experience in preparing students to actually *practice* and apply their knowledge in real settings.

Putting it simply, the contents of this book educate would-be practicing sport psychologists about how to develop effective consulting skills. The book is targeted to understanding and exploring the consulting process. Dimensions include the role as a counselor in helping athletes to cope with personal issues impeding success, as well as how to deliver performance-enhancement techniques that might improve concentration, mental preparation, and many other processes related to accomplishing. Dr. Silva is well recognized internationally and nationally for his expertise as a university professor teaching graduate courses and mentoring students, as a scholar, and as a practicing sport psychologist for over 30 years. He is the lead contributor in organizing and framing the contents on the book and has selected colleagues whose practical experiences provide substantial contributions to the text.

Included in the book are many examples and practical situations that will prepare the sport psychologist for the effective delivery of consulting services. As such, it should be used as a resource in graduate programs with sport psychology specializations. It is also useful for sport psychologists already working in applied settings. The book provides the reader with background information on the application of sport psychology as well as how to actually structure and conduct experiences that will enhance the skills of counselors-in-training, and in turn, the performance of athletes and teams.

The contents presented represent a synthesis of relevant information from general psychology, counseling psychology, clinical psychology, and sport psychology. This integration serves as the basis of the book in providing practical knowledge and practical applied skills. Many of us who have taught applied sport psychology graduate courses and worked with athletes would have benefited considerably if such a text had existed previously. Fortunately, it does now. And, fortunately, sport psychologists with interests in directly applying their knowledge to athletes will benefit considerably in the present and the future.

Robert N. Singer
Professor Emeritus
Department of Applied Physiology
 and Kinesiology
University of Florida

PREFACE

The genesis for writing this book on training professionals in the practice of sport psychology was initiated in the mid 1980s. Within the exciting sport psychology graduate program at The University of North Carolina-Chapel Hill, there was no shortage of creative ideas or constructive criticism on the state of the *profession and practice* of sport psychology. In the 1980s and 1990s part of every student's education involved healthy discussions on how to change the sport psychology world for the better, especially in the applied or practice aspect of the field. In the midst of these discussions, a "mini-boom" in the practice of sport psychology was accelerated when the United States Olympic Committee (USOC) demonstrated a genuine interest in sport psychology services during the 1984 Los Angeles Olympics.

But where did these new service providers receive their training in sport psychology? Where could one find the gold standard programs for training aspiring sport psychology service providers? How could professionals provide applied services when there were less than a handful of graduate programs training individuals to practice sport psychology?

In an attempt to address this "blind spot" and contribute to the development of the profession and practice of sport psychology, the graduate program at North Carolina was built around a science and practice model. Students received a rigorous course of study in the science of sport psychology and conducted high-level research projects that were often published in refereed journals. But there was more to experience in this program. Students were offered a series of course experiences, as well as hands-on practicum experiences that provided the opportunity to engage in directly supervised clinics focused on counseling collegiate athletes.

As a teacher of these courses and as a supervisor of the clinics, I found textbooks on the practice of sport psychology nonexistent. Although over a decade had passed since my own 1970s graduate experience, I was forced to patch together readings just as my mentors had been forced to do. There was no "go to" book on how to educate a sport psychology counselor-in-training. I often found that colleagues offering practice experiences encountered the same challenge. We would put together readings from a collection of four to five books from related fields. But none of these books specifically addressed sport psychology training or issues unique to the practice of sport psychology. There was much jumping from book to book and flipping from chapter to chapter-it was applied sport psychology gymnastics! This exercise demonstrated to both professors and students that there was a significant lack of attention directed to the training and development of individuals interested in the practice of sport psychology. Over the years I collected ideas, information, and most importantly years of hands on experiences working with athletes and mentoring students in clinic settings that focused on the practice of sport psychology. It was obvious to many of us in applied sport psychology that a text that focused on training professionals in the practice of sport psychology was long overdue.

As a first effort to synthesize the many elements required of both the supervisor and the counselor-in-training we hope to reduce that blind spot in graduate applied sport psychology. We also hope that other colleagues who spend a significant amount of their graduate teaching in the applied area will produce similar texts focused on the training and development of practicing sport psychologists. In this spirit, we welcome comments, criticisms, and real-life experiences from coaches, athletes, students, and colleagues who share our interest and passion in the advancement of applied sport psychology. While this text may be a first, it should certainly not be the last!

John M. Silva III
Chapel Hill, NC

ACKNOWLEDGMENTS

I would like to gratefully acknowledge my wife, Christine, for her support of all my endeavors from writing books to running marathons to coaching Carolina Team Handball to spending countless hours at the office: You have always let me pursue my ambitions without restraint.

I am also grateful to all the Carolina sport psychology graduate students with whom I have worked over the years and all the graduate students from various programs who have spoken with me and challenged me and my colleagues to enhance the preparation experiences we offer to aspiring sport psychology practioners.

And to Dr. Burris Husman who guided me when I was a graduate student-what a remarkable job you did! With virtually no sport psychology specific texts or resources you made the practice of sport psychology come alive. You always stimulated me to look toward the future, to contemplate what this great field can be to those of us who live it every day in our work and in our play.

Finally, I would like to acknowledge Drs. Andy Ostrow and Bob Singer. Andy, thank you for having the insight and courage to publish this first-of-a-kind book focused on how to train professionals in the practice of sport psychology. I hope it will help energize colleagues to produce more texts that will fill a significant need for ideas and information in the area of sport psychology graduate training. Bob, thank you for always being a great global ambassador for the field of sport psychology, and for your valuable insights and friendship over the past thirty years, Thanks also for writing the foreword for this text and for your benevolence on the racquetball courts and the pool table!

—JMS

I would like to acknowledge the contributions of my coauthors for not only this text but for their contributions to my professional development and understanding of graduate training in sport psychology. I am particularly appreciative of John "Doc" Silva whose passion for sport psychology as a profession and science is unparalleled and inspirational. I am grateful for the opportunities and mentorship he has afforded me throughout the years—pushing me to always consider the question, "What would Larry do?"

Many of the thoughts and philosophies regarding education subtly reflected in my contributions to this text must be appropriately attributed to my undergraduate mentors at Concordia University-Portland. Several colleagues have had particular influence on my understanding of graduate training and/or sport psychology (Camille Cassidy, David Conroy, Erik Dunlap, Angie Fifer, Scott Kretchmar, Mike Navarre, Artur Poczwardowski, Jason Willow, Dave Yukelson). To my present colleagues at Georgia Southern, specifically Dan Czech and Barry Joyner, thank you for the opportunity to carry out my dream of advancing the science and practice of sport psychology. I look forward to many productive and collegial years. Special thanks to my students who have rejuvenated my passion for developing future scientist-practitioners. Lastly, I am indebted to family, friends, clients, coaches, classmates, teammates, and opponents over the years who have provided support, opportunity, challenge, and growth for me in sport and in life. Each of you has impacted me in a positive way that continues to resonate throughout each day of my life.

—JNM

I appreciate the opportunity to be an author of this book. I would like to thank all my students who helped contribute to this book. Your valuable insight, input, and work were nothing short of spectacular. You are all very special to me, and I am proud to have the ability to be a part of your lives.

My family is very exceptional. My heart is full of love for you all. Thanks to my mom and dad for continued guidance and encouragement throughout my educational accomplishments. My three children, Matthew, David, and Sara, are the light of my life. You bring me joy and happiness every time I see your smiling faces. My wife, Deb, is my true partner in life. You have always been there to support me in my life aspirations. I love you very much. Forever and always,

—Bart

CHAPTER 1

The Emergence of Applied Sport Psychology

This chapter lays the foundation for further discussion of training aspects designed to assist individuals in practicing applied sport psychology. To establish a context for understanding sport psychology as a discipline and a practice, the authors provide a brief summary of the origins, history, and development of applied sport psychology. The significance of integrating science and practice is emphasized throughout the chapter. The scientist-practitioner model has its roots in psychology, where it has flourished as a philosophy resulting in sophisticated advancement of training. The chapter accentuates the relevance of applied sport psychology training grounded in this science-practice model.

Upon reading the chapter, sport psychology consultants will have an appreciation for developing a working knowledge of theoretical principles and supporting research so that they can utilize interventions based on sound science. The chapter will aid developing professionals in understanding the important role scientific methodology plays in objectifying and replicating the effectiveness of intervention. Additionally, readers will learn that theoretical knowledge combined with scientific thinking provides a base for professional integrity in sport psychology; however, development of competence in applied sport psychology also requires consulting athletes under supervision. The chapter culminates by describing the role professional organizations play in monitoring professional integrity through certification, ethical decision making, and accreditation of training programs.

Twenty-five years ago, the publication of a text focused on the training of professionals in the practice of sport psychology would have generated the interest of a dedicated but small group of practitioners. As the first decade of the millennium passes, the field of sport psychology continues to experience a growing interest in the training necessary to practice sport psychology. The emergence of applied sport psychology in the past 25 years has been fairly rapid and a very positive professional development worldwide. The accomplishments of the Soviet Union from the 1960s through the early 1980s in applying sport psychology is well documented (Silva, 2002). It was, however, the period around the 1984 Los Angeles Olympics that initiated a landmark period in the growth, visibility, status, and practice of sport psychology in North America. The media visibility provided to the sport sciences and to sport psychology during and after the 1984 Olympics set the stage for unparalleled interest and growth in the application of sport psychology. By the 1990s, interest in the practice and application of sport psychology with individuals and teams evolved rapidly and is now global.

The traditional educational and training model in sport psychology focused on the discipline (research) and the teaching of sport psychology. Today, many graduate students specializing in sport psychology are eager to train and find the experiences necessary to become practitioners of sport psychology. Given the continued growth in the professional practice of sport psychology, this text is targeted toward both established and emerging young professionals interested in developing or enhancing a professional practice in sport psychology. Many established professionals with a background in sport psychology research, clinical, or counseling psychology have demonstrated an interest in expanding their career options to include the practice of sport psychology.

The information in this text is based on current research and over 50 years of combined experience in the practice of sport psychology by the authors. These experiences include counseling individual athletes, collegiate, Olympic and professional athletes, and working with teams at all competitive levels. The authors also have considerable experience supervising sport psychology graduate students, structuring and engaging in peer supervision, establishing and conducting sport psychology clinics, as well as developing and directing graduate programs in the practice of sport psychology. The information in this text can facilitate personal professional development, and the development of graduate program curriculum. A major objective of the text is to provide information on the educational and training experiences needed to prepare for professional practice sport psychology. By so doing, the text will fill an obvious informational void, and graduate training in the practice of sport psychology will be advanced to the benefit of both the client and the practitioner.

Specificity of Training in the Practice of Sport Psychology

In the United States, the 1960s and 1970s were characterized by a tremendous growth in sport psychology research. Following successful International Sport Psychology Congresses in Rome (1965) and Washington, D.C. (1968), a dramatic emergence and proliferation of research-based graduate programs took place in the United States. This surge of interest in sport psychology research was followed by a second wave of interest in the application and practice of sport psychology, which came about in the 1980s and continues into the present. Unfortunately, to date this second wave has not spawned "new" graduate programs specifically designed to prepare emerging professionals in the practice of sport psychology. The interest in the practice has far outdistanced the infrastructure in place in colleges and universities to properly educate and train practicing professionals in sport psychology.

A model designed to prepare one to be capable in science and practice requires specificity and cross-discipline training. Unfortunately, few senior faculty members in sport psychology are trained in a scientist-practitioner model. A model of graduate education focusing on sport psychology research continues to dominate graduate training in this area. The lack of developed programs and specificity in training has significantly impacted the preparation of future professionals and slowed expansion in the practice of sport psychology. This is unfortunate since many young professionals have entered graduate education in sport psychology with an interest in gaining competence in the research, teaching, and the practice of sport psychology.

As the visibility and acceptability of practicing sport psychology evolved in the 1980s, many professionals saw the practice itself as an opportunity for personal satisfaction and intrinsically rewarding experiences. Often sport psychology professionals work with highly motivated, achievement-oriented individuals of all ages and competitive levels. The attractiveness of sport psychology as a practice has tempted many individuals to "visit" the discipline and leave after a very short stay. Unfortunately, untrained or poorly trained individuals who practice sport psychology often experience frustration and marginal results as they attempt to navigate and frame athlete concerns. With no formal experience or training to provide guidance and structure, this can be a difficult task, since the practice is reduced to a trial and error process, something that is not tolerated in most professional fields. Without a sound knowledge base and an understanding of the sport subculture, many practitioners lose the athlete's interest, since an athlete can quickly tire of "teaching the teacher." Athletes who are in season can hardly afford this misuse of time as they need to benefit from every interaction they have with the clinician. Lack of proper preparation becomes a legitimate public and community concern when an athlete, organization, or parent is paying for services from an individual claiming to be a "professional."

Proper training in graduate programs and proper retooling by interested professionals currently practicing in related helping professions will reduce the likelihood of the trial and error experience and the potential legal implications of such a practice. Certainly, graduate students interested in the practice of sport psychology should receive a systematic education and training in application during their graduate program. Such specificity in course work and in supervised counseling experiences prepares the aspiring practitioner for practice and specialization certification. Andersen, Van Raalte, and Brewer (1994) stated that a high level of program development and the opportunity for supervision in professional practice was not commonly available for those interested in the practice of sport psychology. Apparently, the lack of structured programs and the opportunity for formal training experiences in sport psychology has not improved dramatically since the 1990s (Silva, 2001a).

Given the program and preparation limitations noted, one of the major objectives of this text is to provide recommendations and guidance on how to educate and train an individual interested in practicing sport psychology. The content, perspectives, and experiences offered in this text should prove useful to graduate students interested in practicing, to retooling professionals, and to current faculty adjusting their graduate curriculum to address application and practice issues. While sport psychology has been characterized by the development of a notable scientific discipline, the nurturing and maturing of the professional practice of sport psychology has lagged behind and is in need of systematic attention and professional commitment by interested individuals and professional organizations. There appears to be a need for a more inclusive view of graduate education and training in sport psychology.

Toward Integration of Academic Aims and Knowledge Types

The maturation of graduate training focused on sport psychology as a profession should not supplant or supersede existing research-based models. Too often thinking in academia has narrowed, establishing more boundaries rather than expanding horizons. Regarding physical activity, Newell (1990) described three related academic program aims: disciplinary, professional, and performance-oriented. Rather than integrating these aims into education, programs have more frequently decided on one particular academic aim, which stimulates an unfortunate hierarchical value structure. Programs with disciplinary (i.e., science-based) aims often undervalue professional and performance endeavors. This is largely due to the fact that university success, and thus faculty promotion and tenure, is based upon external research funding received and contributions made to the body of knowledge. The expanding interest in sport psychology service should be perceived as an opportunity for the value of professional academic aims to increase independent of the value of disciplinary aims. In other words, the development of professional interests should not devalue or decrease the frequency of disciplinary training.

Many scholars erroneously assume that types of knowledge relating directly to academic programmatic aims are, in general, mutually exclusive. Disciplinary training is thought to require development of theoretical knowledge whereas little value is placed on gaining professional or procedural knowledge (i.e., knowing how to do something). In reality, theoretical, practical, and procedural knowledge domains are intertwined; each informs the other. According to Newell (1990), integration of theoretical, practical, and procedural knowledge for the purposes of disciplinary or professional development is a realistic vision for academic training in the sport sciences. Regardless of academic priority, integration of knowledge domains can produce greater breadth in training. Research-focused graduate students in sport psychology would benefit from exposure to applied sport psychology practice just as practice-oriented graduate students would benefit from exposure to systematic theory testing. Moreover, if the Eastern European model were followed, each would benefit from experiencing procedural knowledge in sport (i.e., learning how to play tennis, football, etc.). Adopting a philosophy of integrating science and practice is beneficial in that it broadens the scope of training in sport psychology and reduces inequities in the value placed on either disciplinary or professional training. Given that sport psychology has predominantly focused on developing the body of knowledge, equal integration of science and practice requires an increased emphasis on the value of practical knowledge and professional training without undermining the importance of theoretical knowledge and disciplinary training.

Origins of Applied Sport Psychology

The genesis of applied sport psychology can be found in the work of Coleman R. Griffith[g1] in the 1920s (Wiggins, 1984). In addition to being an accomplished researcher and writer, Griffith also applied and practiced sport psychology. While he adhered to a scientist-practitioner model, the development of the profession and practice of sport psychology did not evolve directly from his pioneering efforts. The interface of motor learning and sport psychology in the 1940s and 50s resulted in more of a laboratory/research orientation than a professional practice orientation. From the time Griffith began his work in the 1920s on into the late 1970s, the term *applied sport psychology* was virtually unknown. As recent as the late 1980s, some professors of sport psychology were opposed to the application of sport psychology information with coaches or athletes (Kaplan, 1988). This type of thinking functions more subtly today, yet it has a powerful impact on how graduate curriculum is developed and how students are prepared. Although interest in the practice of sport psychology is considerable, systematic training models and organizational standards regarding education and training, as well as program accreditation, are conspicuously absent in present day sport psychology. Students often attempt to patch together advanced degree programs emphasizing the practice of sport psychology since few sport psychology programs exist today with a systematic focus on practice.

The concern over the lack of professional development has been discussed in the literature (Andersen & Williams-Rice, 1996; Silva, 1984a, 1989, 1992, 1996a, 1996b). The field of sport psychology needs to develop and revise educational and training programs to reflect the interest in practice. As noted, practice models will not replace traditional research models. They will, however, provide another viable option that stresses science and the proper preparation for practice. This would be a timely addition to the sport psychology research models that have existed as the only advanced degree option since the 1950s. Scientist-practitioner models and purely professional models of training in sport psychology will develop. This is a critical aspect of the evolution of sport psychology that should have occurred more than two decades ago during the 1980s, when a proliferation of practitioners untrained in sport psychology entered the field.

With a minimal level of systematic marketing, sport psychology services could be made available on a wide scale to the recreational public, the scholastic and collegiate athlete, as well as the Olympic and professional athlete. Would the field have a sufficient number of properly trained and certified practicing professionals to meet such a demand? Do sport psychology graduate programs currently provide proper training for future generations of practicing sport psychologists? As a field, sport psychology has an obligation to properly identify modes of training for those who wish to practice it. What should this model look like? Many professionals maintain that the scientist-practitioner model can provide the balanced training and education necessary to address the demands often placed upon the contemporary sport psychologist.

The Evolution of the Scientist-Practitioner Model in Psychology

The end of World War II signaled the beginning of the modern era of training in clinical psychology. The war boosted demand for mental health services, resulting in a "large number of budgeted but unfilled positions open for members of the mental hygiene professions" (Raimy, 1949, p. 20). Many universities in the United States were scrambling to produce graduates to fill these positions. The demand for quality service provision from the US government compelled the leadership of the American Psychological Association (APA) to examine the training mechanism required to produce quality graduates for clinical positions. In the mid-1940s, APA's then-president Carl Rogers appointed the Committee on Training in Clinical Psychology and charged the group with accrediting universities that train clinical psychologists. In 1947, this committee issued what became known as the **Shakow**

Report (APA, 1947), which established the guidelines by which programs were judged in consideration for APA approval. More importantly, however, the Shakow Report served as a foundation for some of the more formal training principles that were to emerge in this rapidly developing field (Routh, 1994).

In 1949, the APA hosted the **Conference on Graduate Training in Psychology** at the University of Colorado at Boulder in an effort to follow up on the work begun by the Shakow Report. Seventy-one professionals participated in this conference, which lasted from August 20, 1949, to September 3, 1949 (Raimy, 1949). While this conference was based on the body of work generated by the Committee on Training in Clinical Psychology, the APA Board of Directors wisely decided to appoint a Conference Executive Committee with representatives from all of the bodies involved in graduate training. With this in mind, the committee was composed of representatives from the United States government, the APA, and representatives of the departments that had been credited initially by the Committee on Training in Clinical Psychology. Several critical tasks were accomplished at this conference:

- First, participants defined the societal needs that the field of clinical psychology could and was being expected to satisfy.

- Having defined these needs, participants then assembled a core curriculum that formed the basis for training in clinical psychology and enhanced the likelihood of professionals meeting society's needs for service provision.

- Perhaps most importantly, however, the Conference produced a model for graduate education based in both science and practice. This model has since come to be known as the **Boulder Model.**

The Boulder Model was conceived to satisfy societal needs for clinical psychology through a combination of research and professional practice. The first and most well-known of these needs involved the treatment and remediation of psychological ills or maladjustments. Clinical psychology, however, also sought to develop methods for preventing maladjustment and develop a "Mental Health Model." This model emphasizes "maximum development of an individual's potentialities rather than barely adequate adjustment" (Raimy, 1949, p. 21). The applied nature of these needs clearly demonstrates the necessity of a practice component to training. The Boulder Model also advocates training in science and research, since many clinical psychologists find themselves in positions where they either conduct and/or supervise research or evaluate research into the effectiveness of applied techniques (Raimy, 1949). As clinical psychology became entrenched in the societal mainstream, expectations from society grew, and the scientist-practitioner training model has been successful in many health provision fields.

Ogilvie (1979) and Singer (1993) have noted similarities and differences in the training and practice of clinical, counseling, and sport psychology. This perspective was also noted in a report on the status of graduate training in sport psychology submitted to the Executive Board of the Association for the Advancement of Applied Sport Psychology (Silva, 2001b). The report suggested that the graduate training model for the practice of sport psychology would benefit from a scientist-practitioner model similar to those commonly found in many related helping professions. The report also noted that graduate program accreditation in sport psychology was overdue and needed to provide structure and validity to the advancement of applied sport psychology and the practice of it as well.

The Scientist-Practitioner Model and Sport Psychology

Sport psychology underwent significant self-examination from the mid-1980s through the 1990s (Feltz, 1987; Rejeski & Brawley, 1988; Silva, 1984a, 1984b, 1992, 1996a, 1996b). Many professionals attempted to clarify the definition of the field as well as discuss models best suited for training professionals interested in the emerging discussion about the practice of sport psychology. Concurrent with this examination, the United States Olympic Committee (USOC) designated the service roles within the field of sport psychology as clinical, educational, and research (USOC, 1983). The USOC's interest in the practice of sport psychology played a positive role in enhancing the interactions between a professional organization such as AAASP and an organization with teams and athletes potentially seeking applied sport psychology service. Equally important, this interest enhanced interaction among professionals from psychology and the exercise sciences. As this interaction increased, it became obvious that the academic disciplines of counseling, exercise science, and psychology were all essential in providing the cross-pollination and training needed to enhance preparation for the practice of sport psychology.

Application based on science. Scientists and practitioners subscribe to the notion that application should be based on research and good science. Operating without a science base and a theoretical background can leave the practitioner without structure or confidence in techniques. When consulting with athletes, applied sport psychologists should implement theory-based and empirically tested interventions. In addition to using these interventions, the practice of sport psychology provides ample opportunity for novel yet systematic approaches to intervention. In these cases, the scientist-practitioner strives to document approach and methods and to develop objective means for assessing resultant change.

Objectification of results. Applied research must be objective in order to contribute to science. Without objective results, the interpretability of a finding is limited to speculation and subjective interpretation. Great care must be taken when designing studies that examine intervention techniques. Without well-defined methodologies, sound assessment procedures, and appropriate analyses, fellow professionals will be unable to benefit from research efforts or replicate existing research. Without attention to these details, the exact source of any change cannot be precisely identified or determined. It is not enough to say an intervention works because "we think it works"!

Yet, how does a practicing sport psychologist objectify results? This task is as difficult as it is important. Applied research examining intervention effectiveness presents many difficult and problematic situations. The behavior targeted for modification must be quantified and measured in a pre- and post-intervention manner and some type of control group should be established. Objective measurement can be accomplished by having the participant serve as a control in a repeated-measures-type design or by teammates not receiving the treatment serving as a control group. In the reality of working in the field with a team or a coach, these standards of science may be difficult to put into place. This is a difficult challenge because without attention to result objectification, there is no scientific evidence to confirm the efficacy of the intervention. A scientist-practitioner model must advance the knowledge base of practice through an objective process. One of the greatest challenges in objectifying results is determining which characteristics should be measures and how they should be measured. Sometimes interventions can begin under the appearance of one problem and then the intervention leads to more self-revelation as the counseling relationship grows. In these cases, the scientist-practitioner is faced with getting a baseline measure even though a counseling relationship has developed and perhaps an intervention has been initiated. A conscientious effort must be made to gain a valid and reliable pre-intervention measure for comparison to a post-intervention measure.

Beyond the challenges of objectifying results, it is also difficult to determine whether any psychological change in an athlete is actually the result of the intervention or whether it is a secondary gain resulting from physical or skill improvements over the same period of time. Some results may even be a manifestation of a Hawthorne effect. One way to distinguish "real" results from the intervention from secondary training gains or placebo effects is through statistical confirmation across time and samples. Awareness of these factors benefits the practitioner and the athlete receiving services designed to enhance one's performance or well-being. Although objectifying intervention results is a difficult challenge, its importance is well understood by the practicing sport psychology professional trained in the scientist-practitioner model.

Replication. Science is less about truth and more about fact. Facts are liquid, they change. This is a strength of the scientist-practitioner model-as science changes, practice based upon that science should change. This is the norm in most fields of practice such as medicine, optometry, and dentistry. The change, however, is a careful and logical one since one study alone is not a "proof." New techniques and methods are often based on the results of interventions replicated with different samples, in different situations and across time. The stability and the generalizability of the intervention must be established. The effectiveness of an intervention should not be idiosyncratic to the practitioner utilizing the intervention. While effectiveness may certainly vary as a function of clinical expertise, competent practitioners should be able to demonstrate the efficacy of the intervention itself. Thus, different practitioners should be able to replicate intervention effectiveness and experience similar success if the intervention is a powerful tool. Idiographic methodologies provide very effective tools for examining intervention effectiveness and, although causation is often difficult to infer from the techniques used in a particular intervention, valid and reliable conclusions can be drawn regarding the structure and effectiveness of the intervention. For example, early applied intervention research has demonstrated the effectiveness of a three-stage cognitive-behavior modification program consisting of problem identification, cognitive restructuring, and covert conditioning (e.g., Kirschenbaum & Wittrock, 1984; Meichenbaum, 1977; Silva, 1982). These studies utilized a similar method with three different clinicians who were addressing different client concerns. This form of replication demonstrates the robustness of the cognitive behavioral technique by accounting for both clinician variance and client variance.

Professional integrity. Scientist-practitioner training emphasizes the importance of practicing only in areas in which the practitioner has developed and exhibited competence. Some in the field of sport psychology subscribe to the notion, "I will get competent as I practice." Professional integrity is defined in part by how students are trained, how sport psychology is practiced and promoted, and how the field is regulated. Professional integrity is characterized by an intimate familiarity with a subculture's unique dynamics and the environmental demands presented in a specific practice setting. Would a professional trained in marriage counseling feel comfortable "learning on the job" to counsel prison inmates? Would a professional trained in child psychology feel comfortable moving his or her practice to industrial and organizational intervention without engaging in retooling? It is essential to question why some individuals feel that psychological training generalizes to the specific practice of sport psychology but not to other specializations within psychology. A lack of knowledge or familiarity with the cognitive, emotional, motoric, physiological, and social aspects of sport can limit a clinician's ability to offer effective, performance-enhancing counsel. In some instances, the "trial and error" and "learning on the job" approach can actually impair rather than enhance athlete or team performance. Most contemporary clinicians practicing sport psychology agree that training in general counseling is necessary but insufficient when it comes to the actual practice. Without a proper body of knowledge and supervised practicum experiences involving athletes, clinicians will have no criteria to judge whether they are practicing effectively.

Supervised practice experience. The opportunity and importance of having a series of supervised practice experiences would provide one of the most important educational and training experiences for aspiring sport psychology practitioners. These structured experiences provide a "safe" environment for learning not only about the practice of sport psychology but about one's ability to interact during counsel, manage difficult and unpredictable client situations, and adjust techniques based on supervisor and peer feedback. Furthermore, these structured experiences often help develop confidence in the novice clinician's ability to go from "classroom knowledge" to "working knowledge." Experienced practitioners in any field understand that application requires a different set of skills than those that make up one's knowledge base.

A considerable amount of this text is targeted toward how to structure the supervised practice experience. This experience often provides in-vivo experience for novice consultants. They also provide an opportunity to self assess whether one's initial interests and motivation to practice sport psychology are realized in the skill and ability as a clinician. Supervised practice and organizational guidance for the structuring of these essential educational and training experiences are two central aspects in the practice of sport psychology in need of systematic address by the field. Practicing sport psychology without having the opportunity to experience direct and indirect supervisory feedback from an experienced professional is akin to a dentist practicing without appropriate apprentice and mentoring experiences. The fact that this situation exists today in sport psychology accentuates the need for professional leadership and organizational guidance in the development of the profession and practice of the discipline.

The Role of Academic and Professional Organizations in the Practice of Sport Psychology

The most effective means of reinforcing principles and beliefs designed to encourage and guide scientific and practical conduct within sport psychology is through professional organizations. Historically, no group or organization has advocated the professional development of sport psychology. Commonly recognized organizations such as the American Alliance for Health, Physical Education, Recreation and Dance (AAPHERD), the American College of Sports Medicine (ACSM), the International Society for Sport Psychology (ISSP), and the North American Society for the Psychology of Sport and Physical Activity (NASPSPA) have focused on research and research dissemination.

The lack of advocacy for the professionalization of sport psychology is both concerning and problematic. The lack of organizational and professional involvement in the practice was brought to a head in 1984 when NASPSPA voted not to address the critical professional issues confronting the field (Magill, 1984). This statement was from the only major sport psychology-related organization in North America at that time. The lack of interest in professional issues by NASPSPA motivated the formation of an organization focused upon addressing these concerns. **The Asso-**

ciation for the Advancement of Applied Sport Psychology (AAASP) was founded in 1985 in Chapel Hill, NC. One of the first agenda items for AAASP was to develop and recognize a set of minimum competencies and experiences for professional colleagues interested in the practice of sport psychology. The AAASP Certification document was the first formal step toward recognizing individuals who are sufficiently trained to apply and supervise the application of sport psychology principles with athletes and athletic groups (AAASP, 1991). The USOC adopted the AAASP certification guidelines in 1996 (S. McCann & K. Peterson, personal communication, September 14, 2004). Adoption by the USOC was historical, for one, because a major sports organization had finally recognized the necessity of a professional credential to practice with athletes and teams under the jurisdiction of the USOC. One can only imagine the practice opportunities that would become available if other sport organizations such as Major League Baseball, Major League Soccer, the Women's National Basketball and Men's National Basketball Associations, and other professional leagues required an AAASP certification in order to practice with their respective organizations.

AAASP and, more recently, **Division 47 of the APA** are the only professional organizations in North America to address professional issues such as training, certification, ethics, and accreditation. AAASP and APA Division 47 have generated interest and national communication about the professionalization and practice of sport psychology. A document has been jointly developed by these two organizations and the NASPSPA addressing prospective students' question about career paths and training opportunities in sport psychology (APA, AAASP, NASPSPA, 1994). These three organizations have joined with the ISSP to form the Sport Psychology Council, which has the potential to be a major vehicle that can address, on an international level, many applied issues that confront the field of sport psychology today and will confront it in the future.

Summary

Applied sport psychology has experienced tremendous growth since the early 1980s. Many individuals seeking careers in sport psychology today desire applied skills in addition to the research and teaching skills they developed during their graduate education. Unfortunately, few advancements have been made in the training model used to prepare future sport psychology students. Many students aspiring to practice sport psychology are confronted with a significant deficit in their applied practice and supervised experiences (Silva, Conroy, & Zizzi, 1999). The scientist-practitioner model commonly used in the field of clinical psychology and other health-related fields is proposed as an appropriate model for graduate training in programs preparing students to practice sport psychology. Academic and professional organizations, such as AAASP, APA Division 47, and the Sport Psychology Council, are excellent vehicles for promoting and developing the practice of sport psychology. These entities need to increase their leadership role in order for the advancement of professional aspects of sport psychology to evolve in an orderly and timely manner.

References

American Psychological Association. (1947). Committee on training in clinical psychology: Recommended graduate training programs in clinical psychology. *American Psychologist, 2,* 539–558.

American Psychological Association Division of Exercise and Sport Psychology, Association for the Advancement of Applied Sport Psychology, & North American Society for the Psychology of Sport and Physical Activity. (1994). *Graduate training possibilities in exercise and sport psychology.* Washington, DC: Author.

Andersen, M. B., Van Raalte, J. L., & Brewer, B. W. (1994). Assessing the skills of sport psychology supervisors. *The Sport Psychologist, 8,* 238–247.

Andersen, M. B., & Williams-Rice, B. T. (1996). Supervision in the education and training of sport psychology service providers. *The Sport Psychologist, 10,* 278–290.

Association for the Advancement of Applied Sport Psychology (1991). *Certified Consultant, Association for the Advancement of Applied Sport Psychology.* Chapel Hill, NC: Author.

Feltz, D. L. (1987). The future of graduate education in sport and exercise science: A sport psychology perspective. *Quest, 39,* 217–223.

Kaplan, R. (Executive Producer). (1988, February 17). *Nightline* [Television broadcast]. New York: American Broadcasting Corporation.

Kirschenbaum, D. S., & Wittrock, D. A. (1984). Cognitive behavioral interventions in sport: A self-regulatory perspective. In J. M. Silva & R. S. Weinberg (Eds.), *Psychological foundations of sport* (pp. 81–97). Champaign, IL: Human Kinetics.

Magill, R. (1984, Fall). President's Message *North American Society for the Psychology of Sport and Physical Activity Newsletter,* 1

Meichenbaum, D. (1977). *Cognitive-behavior modification: An integrative approach.* New York: Plenum Press.

Newell, K. M. (1990). Physical activity, knowledge types, and degree programs. *Quest, 42,* 243–268.

Ogilvie, B. C. (1979). The sport psychologist and his professional credibility. In P. Klavora & J. V. Daniel (Eds.), *Coach, athlete, and the sport psychologist* (pp. 44–55). Champaign, IL: Human Kinetics.

Raimy, V. C. (1949). *Training in clinical psychology.* New York: Prentice-Hall.

Rejeski, W. J., & Brawley, L. R. (1988). Defining the boundaries of sport psychology. *The Sport Psychologist, 2,* 231–242.

Routh, D. K. (1994). *Clinical psychology since 1917: Science, practice and organization.* New York: Plenum.

Silva, J. M. (1982). Competitive sport environments: Performance enhancement through cognitive intervention. *Behavior Modification,* 6, 443–463.

Silva, J. M. (1984a). The emergence of applied sport psychology: Contemporary trends-future issues. *International Journal of Sport Psychology,* 15, 40–51.

Silva, J. M. (September, 1984b). The status of sport psychology: A national survey of coaches. *Journal of Physical Education, Recreation and Dance,* 55, 46–49.

Silva, J. M. (1989). Establishing professional standards and advancing applied sport psychology research. *Journal of Applied Sport Psychology,* 1, 160–165.

Silva, J. M. (1992). On advancement: An editorial. *Journal of Applied Sport Psychology,* 4, 1-9.

Silva, J. M. (1996a). Current issues confronting the advancement of applied sport psychology. *Journal of Applied Sport Psychology,* 8, S50–S52.

Silva, J. M. (1996b). A second move: Confronting persistent issues that challenge the advancement of applied sport psychology. *Journal of Applied Sport Psychology,* 8, S52.

Silva, J. M. (2001a). Future directions in sport psychology. In R. N. Singer, H. A. Hausenblaus, & C. M. Janelle (Eds.), *The Handbook of Sport Psychology* (2nd ed., pp. 823-832). New York, NY: John Wiley & Sons.

Silva, J. M. (2001b). Sport psychology graduate training committee: Final report. Association for the Advancement of Applied Sport Psychology, September 25.

Silva, J. M. (2002). The evolution of sport psychology. In J.M. Silva & D.E. Stevens (Eds.), *Psychological foundations of sport* (pp. 1–26). Needham, MA: Allyn & Bacon.

Silva, J. M., Conroy, D. E., and Zizzi, S. J. (1999). Critical issues confronting the advancement of applied sport psychology. *Journal of Applied Sport Psychology,* 11, 298–320.

Singer, R. N. (1993). Ethical issues in clinical services. *Quest,* 45, 88–105.

United States Olympic Committee (1983). US Olympic Committee establishes guidelines for sport psychology services. *Journal of Sport Psychology,* 5, 4–7.

Wiggins, D. K. (1984). The history of sport psychology in North America. In J. M. Silva & R. S. Weinberg (Eds.), *Psychological foundations of sport* (pp. 9–22). Champaign, IL: Human Kinetics.

CHAPTER 2

Preparing to Practice
Sport Psychology

I n this chapter, a number of issues relevant to preparation for the practice of sport psychology are introduced to the reader. The way in which the sport environment is unique and may provide difficult challenges to those not trained specifically within the sport context is addressed and discussed. Additionally, the importance of gaining a broad range of theoretical knowledge from coursework in exercise science, psychology, and counseling is highlighted. Indeed, development of competence specifically in sport psychology should be a priority and may be best approached systematically through a progression of interdisciplinary coursework and practice experiences within the sport environment. The authors discuss several professional mechanisms that have been developed to ensure minimum competencies are met by professionals. Upon reading the chapter, developing professionals will be able to differentiate between these credentials and understand that accredited programs in psychology and counseling may not provide opportunities required for certification as an applied sport psychology consultant. The chapter also discusses the history and potential future of accreditation of programs that lead specifically to AAASP certification. The latter part of the chapter is dedicated to discussing the state of the profession in terms of job market and technology. Readers will appreciate the opportunity, challenge, and responsibility they have as developing young professionals in applied sport psychology.

All academic disciplines and practicing professions go through a series of experiences that can best be described as "growing pains." Psychology spent years attempting to break away from the restraints of medicine (Cook et al., 1958). Given the relative youth of sport psychology, it is not surprising that several important issues continue to confront the field. These issues range from designing appropriate counselor training experiences and determining counselor competence, to establishing graduate program accreditation and enhancing applied job opportunities with individual athletes and organized sport groups. Advancement in applied aspects of sport psychology has taken place through discussion and the implementation of initiatives such as AAASP certification, certification options for those with a master's degree, and the movement toward applied sport psychology program accreditation. Although it may be deemed "human nature" or "polite politics" to avoid challenging issues, such an approach slows the progression of professional aspects of sport psychology. Many fundamental issues, such as graduate education and training models, availability of retooling experiences, and establishment of educational opportunities to facilitate the development of sport psychology counseling competence, have not been addressed in a meaningful manner.

Why Is Specificity Needed in Sport Psychology Training?

Like most people in achievement-oriented endeavors, athletes are under tremendous pressure to perform at consistently high levels. Unlike many other fields of endeavor, athletes are held accountable daily. They are exposed to many more public criticisms than high-profile players in other fields, such as business, art, or music. A few years ago, a couple of Los Angeles Lakers high-profile basketball players were suspended for their behavior. Lakers' general manager Jerry West explained, "When you lose in this game we're all held up to a higher authority and that's the news media. And no one wants to fail in those people's eyes" ("Give It a Rest," 1996). As West noted and as we have witnessed many times in recent media reports, athletes face many performance-related pressures that are unique to high-level sport. Research has shown that athletes experience stress from the demands of participation, fear of failure, feelings of inadequacy, guilt, loss of control, parental involvement, performance achievement, personal struggles, reward structures, sibling rivalry, significant other relationships, social evaluation, media scrutiny, team climate, team rejection, unsportsmanlike conduct, and even bad "luck" (Gould, Horn, & Spreemann, 1983; Kroll, 1979; Scanlan & Passer, 1979; Silva, Cornelius, Conroy, Petersen, & Finch, 1996).[g1] Given the wide variety of potential stressors in sport, it is clear that athletes are extremely susceptible to stress in both private, team-only communications and in public situations, such as through media exposure.

With more athletes going to professional sport right out of high school, many athletes are not prepared to deal with the emotional burden that often accompanies sport achievement. Few professions thrust such high visibility and responsibility on the young and unprepared as does competitive sport. Imagine the pressures placed upon a college graduate if his or her performance were to determine the success or failure of a large organization, such as a Fortune 500 company. This is the situation many athletes are placed in at the age of 18 to 21. Young athletes are offered tremendous opportunities through sport, yet they are simultaneously confronted with extraordinary challenges. Oftentimes, these athletes are ill-equipped to manage and cope with the obstacles in a positive manner. Adding to the pressure, the adjustment from high-school star to college athlete to professional hopeful often is played out in the media.

In addition to the high visibility an athlete must come to terms with, the coach-athlete relationship has its own stresses. Coaches wield unparalleled influence and control over athletes' lives. At the college level, coaches often determine an athlete's scholarship status, playing time, class schedule, diet, body weight, and physical training program. Such involvement can have a significant impact on an athlete's perception of self-worth. The sheer physical demands of high-level training regulate many of the other, everyday functions of athletes such as what, when, and how much they can eat, how often they must study, and even what they can do in their free time. The influence of coaches at the professional level is also powerful since, except for the franchise-caliber player, these coaches determine or have a large voice in the athlete's career development through their control of the athlete's playing time, role on the team, and input to management concerning player salary. There are few interpersonal relationships that are characterized by the power imbalance that exists in the common coach-athlete relationship. If a coach chooses to abuse his or her power over an athlete, the athlete has few choices but to accept the coach's behavior, even if the behavior places the athlete at risk. These situations are more widespread than most people care to imagine, and an athlete's only real alternative to accepting the behavior and suffering inwardly is exiting the relationship. This option, however, creates a real conflict for athletes when they consider their history of investment and commitment to the sport. Without a strong understanding of the dynamics of this relationship, a sport psychologist will not be able to assist either coaches or athletes. The skills required to effectively intervene require years of experience working in this environment and understanding the unique contingencies that operate in it. Without direct experience in this setting, the clinician is ill-prepared for the dynamics and the intensity that separate the sports environment from virtually all other counseling and consulting environments.

In view of the unique challenges presented by the sport environment, it is surprising that there is continued debate over the need for specific training. Naive counselors and psychologists, without specific training in performance enhancement, would argue that training in counseling or clinical psychology is a sufficient qualification to work with athletes on performance-related issues. Some have argued that it is improper for individuals with specialized training in sport psychology to work with athletes since their degree is not from the counseling or psychology departments. **In reality, the focus of sport psychology is not the remediation of pathological states. Sport psychologists are concerned with assisting athletes to reach their human potential and to maximize their athletic performance.** Sport psychologists should be capable of identifying the warning signs and symptoms of psychopathology and should tactfully refer those cases to appropriately trained mental health professionals. This referral system does not mean that sport psychologists should avoid discussing personal, non-sport-related issues with clients. Any attempt to dichotomize the issues in an athlete's life into sport-related and non-sport-related will be artificial and can make the interaction between the client and clinician awkward. Athletes are people, and their lives off the field are going to directly impact their ability to perform on the field, particularly in high-pressure, competitive situations. A sport psychologist must help the athlete come to terms with his or her emotional state, cope with the stress, and understand how personal stress can debilitate athletic performance.

A license to practice clinical or counseling psychology does not mean that an individual is skilled in the practice of sport psychology. Counseling and clinical psychology recognize the need for specificity within their own fields. For example, it is widely recognized that school psychologists require specialized training that is different from the specialized training needed to practice family and marriage counseling or substance abuse counseling. Why does this same logic not hold true for sport psychology? Performance enhancement in sport is a specialization and requires specific training. Until this fact is widely recognized and accepted by practitioners, the service population of athletes and coaches will be at risk of receiving inadequate, and potentially harmful, service provision.

Training and the Development of Counselor Competence

How far has sport psychology developed in providing formal educational and training opportunities for individuals who wish to practice sport psychology? In the 1950s through the 1980s, very little formal training designed to develop counselor competence existed. Graduate students were trained in physical education departments that emphasized research, but offered little in the way of applied training and experiences. Virtually no retooling opportunities existed for established professionals looking to add to their areas of practice. Has this situation changed significantly since the1980s? Apparently not. Although some graduate programs have expanded their course offerings in sport psychology to include applied courses, few programs have developed systematic course offerings in professional aspects of sport psychology (Burke, Sachs, & Smisson, 2004). Even fewer opportunities exist for supervised practicum experiences for graduate students and novice practitioners.

It is extremely difficult for a sport psychology student to gain experience and learn sound techniques and intervention skills without supervised experiences. Without an experienced sport psychologist to supervise and guide the student, how do novice counselors know when they are making errors or not picking up on significant client concerns shared by athletes in their own language? Some graduate programs advise students to find their own athlete or team to work with and to develop a consulting relationship. The student makes contact with the athlete or coach of a team and initiates the consultation process. Once a week, the supervising faculty member meets with the student to discuss the nature of the interaction and how the relationship is progressing. This is a common approach in many sport psychology programs, but is this indirect supervision approach a satisfactory model? There can be dramatic differences in the quality of what transpires when the supervising faculty member is present during the sessions versus simply being informed about the student counselor's perceptions of a session. *This is particularly notable when the counselor-in-training is inexperienced.*

A Progression for Practice Experiences

A beneficial supervisory progression would initiate with a sequence of applied sport psychology **coursework.** Embedded in the advanced courses would be structured opportunities for **role playing** as an individual athlete, as well as small group intervention. Courses would then move to a more practical format, with novice practitioners **observing** an experienced counselor engaged with an individual athlete, over a period of at least one academic semester. This experience would then be followed by **direct supervision** of the novice counselor conducting intervention for approximately one hundred hours. The novice counselor would receive direct verbal and written feedback from the supervisor and a peer observer during these experiences. The sequence would be culminated with **indirect supervisory experiences.** It should be noted that this approach emphasizes that the novice practicing professionals would receive specific classroom training on the nature of intervention and the consultant's role in the intervention process prior to any direct contact with a client. This sequence of coursework, role playing, observation, direct supervision, and indirect supervision would supply the novice counselor with the knowledge and skills to recognize when and how to apply them.

The difficulty in the development of applied counseling skills in sport psychology should not be underestimated. The challenge is not in *becoming* a sport psychology counselor; the challenge is in *being an effective* sport psychology counselor. The sport subculture is unique. Applied skill is developed over time and enhanced through the feedback of an experienced supervisor, peer feedback, and evaluation of videotaped sessions. A similar practicum sequence should be established for small-group and team-related interventions, as these interventions present unique challenges and dynamics different from the individual intervention setting.

The course and supervision sequence noted above represents a logical and orderly progression of courses in a science practice graduate program. This progression is designed to educate and train individuals in sport psychology practice as well as in sport psychology research. Supervisors can establish the intervention sessions for student athletes as voluntary and consented sport psychology clinic experiences. The student athlete receives counsel, and in return, permits one or more novice counselors to sit in as observers. This sport psychology clinic approach has been employed successfully at the University of North Carolina-Chapel Hill for more than 15 years. While the novice practitioner is in the observer role, there should be post-session dialogue between the experienced counselor and the observer(s). All observers are encouraged to take notes during the sessions, and the primary observer maintains a casebook of the entire intervention program. Following successful participation in the observational practicum, the novice practitioner should be provided with directly supervised, "hands-on" sport psychology clinical experiences. These intervention experiences will provide the novice practitioner with the leadership role in the intervention process.

It is extremely beneficial for the student clinician to submit a pre-plan for each session and a post-session self-evaluation to the supervising professional. The supervisor should provide feedback to the novice practitioner about the pre-plan, prior to the actual session with the athlete, so that suggestions can be reflected upon and implemented by the supervisee. The post-session self-evaluation should focus on both the dynamics of the session itself and the strengths and weaknesses exhibited by the student clinician in that session. This type of self-reflection is a tremendous learning experience for the novice practitioner since it requires an objective and constructive review of the intervention process and the work completed in each session. Only after several direct supervision experiences is the supervisor able to determine if the professional development of the supervisee warrants indirect supervisory experiences. Both the supervisor and supervisee should document all supervised hours carefully so that these experiences can be credited as practicum documentation in the AAASP certification process.

Traditionally, sport psychology graduate students interested in practice have been forced to learn "on the fly" with little or no direct supervision of their work. Would this model be acceptable in any other branch of practicing psychology? Why is it promoted in sport psychology as a substitute for a major learning experience necessary for those who wish to practice? From the consumer's perspective, untrained or unsupervised clinicians should not be learning by trial and error with an unsuspecting client. Unfortunately, this has been the norm in the field. Many sport psychology graduate students who graduate with minimal applied experiences often end up initiating practice experiences with individual athletes and teams. In the past, clinicians from other specializations of psychology have failed to retool in sport psychology, choosing to generalize their consulting skills to various aspects of human behavior and performance. With the adoption of ethical principles by AAASP (AAASP, 1996) it is important that all professionals interested in the practice of sport psychology be mindful of practicing in areas where competence can be demonstrated.

Practicing in Areas of Competence

Silva (1989) has written that if training in the practice of sport psychology evolves in a positive manner, the academic department a student graduates from (e.g., counseling, exercise science, psychology) should be less relevant than the course of study and practicum experiences provided to the student. To date, no discipline has made significant advances in developing well-conceived training models for graduate students interested in practicing sport psychology. Unfortunately, what has continued is the ongoing debate relating to what a person trained in an exercise science program specializing in sport psychology can practice versus what a person trained in counseling or clinical psychology can practice. Some professionals (e.g., Weinberg & Gould, 1999) promote psychological skills as a practice model. Exactly what is a psychological skills model? Generally, this approach is presented as a sort of package to the athlete. The athlete is trained in various psychological skills that are believed to enhance athletic performance. The psychological skills may include relaxation training, imagery, goal setting, time management, stress management, and concentration training. Although these skills may have relevance, they are sometimes taught to athletes, with little regard for the specific performance concerns the athlete may be experiencing, in what is called a "cookbook approach."

Underlying dysfunctional thoughts, irrational beliefs, and conditioned psychological responses that interfere with optimal performance are often not addressed in this psychological skills approach. The clinician essentially becomes a technician who teaches a set of psychological skills to the athlete. While such skills no doubt have a role to play in the performance enhancement process, presenting them to an athlete without identifying if there are any psychological concerns or dysfunctional thought patterns is addressing only symptoms and does not address underlying causes of performance difficulties.

Not surprisingly, some practicing professionals seem happy with this approach. It allows them to practice tangible skills that are believed to improve athletic performance. Some psychologists are comfortable with non-licensed individuals practicing these skills since the clinician seldom interacts with the athlete in a manner that addresses the psychological underpinnings of the performance concern. The skills or techniques taught to the athlete do not require a license, and realistically they can be taught to an athlete by anyone. Psychological skills should not be used in a psycho-social environmental vacuum. If psychological factors that underlie performance issues are unresolved, old habits can resurface and the athlete may question the superficiality presented by a psychological approach.

A professional practicing sport psychology should be more than a mere technician. Students who are properly trained in sport psychology and counseling techniques through course work and supervised experiences should be prepared to work with athletes within the framework of a systematic intervention program. There are several intervention orientations or structures, such as rational emotive behavior therapy (REBT; Ellis, 1962), cognitive-behavioral therapy (CBT; Meichenbaum, 1973), behavioral approaches (Skinner, 1953), psychoanalytic models (Adler, 1958; Freud, 1900), Rogerian approach (Rogers, 1951), Gestalt techniques (Perls, Hefferline, & Goodman, 1951) and reality therapy (Glasser, 1965), to name a few. The fit between cognitive-behavioral approaches (i.e., REBT, CBT) and task demands in sport has facilitated the wide use of cognitive based intervention by sport psychology consultants. Whatever intervention model a clinician chooses to follow, minimum training requirements for the practice of sport psychology need to be established and met by both new and retooled professionals.

Training and Counselor Competence

More interdisciplinary graduate programs need to be developed that expose students to the multi-faceted, interdisciplinary aspects of sport psychology. Recently, increased attention has been paid to applied sport psychology, which has led to discussions in the literature concerning who should be able to practice sport psychology (Petrie & Watkins, 1994). In particular, professionals have discussed whether licensure, certification, or either should be required for sport psychology practice. They have also debated training and preparation models for students pursuing a career within the field of sport psychology. Further, the literature (e.g., Howard, 1993; Petrie & Watkins, 1994) has usually shown that many of the courses in counseling psychology can add significant value to applied sport psychology training by introducing counseling theories, counseling practica, and counseling techniques. An interdisciplinary program that involves sport science and counseling will help further integrate these two fields of study, in terms of obtaining a specific degree. As previously noted, a degree that facilitates one to become licensed will further define the role of a practicing sport psychologist (e.g., one who is interested in the practice aspects of sport psychology).

Until only recently, professionals who entered the field of sport psychology either brought an emphasis in sport and a minor training emphasis in psychology/counseling or brought a primary training focus in psychology with little formal education in the sport sciences. Obviously, the different types of training these individuals receive contribute to divergent perspectives on issues that continue to confront the field. Although most professionals associated with sport psychology agree that a better training model is needed, there is still disagreement regarding which model to adopt. In addition, individuals who have had years of experience in the field are not eager to admit that they may be inadequately trained or currently unqualified to provide services to athletes and coaches.

If sport psychology is to advance, it must continue to be interdisciplinary in nature, requiring expertise and training in the sport sciences, counseling, and the psychological sciences. Traditionally, sport psychologists have been trained in exercise science or kinesiology departments in specialized graduate programs. These specialized programs require a broad and in-depth background in the sport sciences (e.g., statistics, research methods, exercise physiology, motor learning, and biomechanics). Students may also be required to establish a program of psychology courses (e.g., social, developmental, clinical, and counseling), identify one or more psychology department faculty members to serve on the dissertation committee, and establish a program of research that is psychological in nature.

A fundamental problem associated with the delivery of certain services (e.g., counseling and psychological skills training) is that the majority of sport psychologists today are inadequately trained in either counseling/psychology or the sport sciences. More often than not, they are ill-prepared to serve the public. In particular, exercise science graduates generally lack the broad-based clinical training and experience of counselors, whereas counselors commonly lack an understanding of the unique nature and requirements of sport performance that exercise scientists possess (Fisher, 1982). Frequently, sport psychologists are not the products of accredited doctoral programs in counseling/psychology. It is uncommon for a sport psychology graduate student to receive formal training in counseling skills and obtain extensive practical experience applying such knowledge with an athlete in a supervised setting. Therefore, the roles and training currently needed to function as a sport psychologist are undetermined, and "it remains unclear who sport psychologists are in terms of formal training and allegiance" (Harrison & Feltz, 1979, p. 182).

While the field continues to move slowly toward the resolution of these important training issues, it is important to recognize that opportunities are opening for the provision of professional services. Practitioners must offer services consistent with externally imposed and internally generated codes of ethics. AAASP certification is fundamental to maintaining the integrity of sport psychology and protecting the consumer. The field would be professionally negligent if it did not engage in this process of self-definition. Those who wish to affiliate themselves with the field of sport psychology should be encouraged to demonstrate they are indeed specialists in this field. Thus, certification can facilitate the structuring of graduate programs and is a logical first step to the accreditation process at an institutional level.

The Case for Interdisciplinary Training

As with the field of psychology in general, sport psychology tends to separate into two general orientations: professionals with a primary emphasis in research, and professionals with a primary emphasis in education and practice. Over the years, professionals have argued that an interdisciplinary approach is needed to develop an adequate base of knowledge that incorporates the exercise sciences and psychology/counseling (Alderman, 1980; Martens, 1980; Silva, 1989). At the same time, demand has increased for applied sport psychologists, and this demand should continue to increase, especially in the private sector. Feltz (1987) suggested that graduate training for sport psychologists, within exercise science, has clearly changed. She addressed the need for interdisciplinary work, which will merge exercise science and psychology/counseling programs. As the field has moved toward more application, Feltz (1987) has suggested the resources of psychology/counseling programs be better utilized to take advantage of that expertise. Without an interdisciplinary emphasis, sport psychology graduate students within exercise science programs will lack sufficient exposure and training in psychology/counseling.

A practice that is gaining popularity among today's graduate students is receiving a master's degree in one discipline and a doctoral degree in second discipline. For example, some students acquire a master's degree in counseling and then undertake their doctoral work in sport science. Others receive a master's degree in sport science and then pursue doctoral training in psychology. Typically, the doctoral study is the area of primary interest to the student. Individuals need to have a clear understanding of their personal interests and professional goals, as well as the practical issues of graduate education, so their training will be congruent with their career aspirations and goals.

Professionals have offered different perspectives on what is appropriate training in applied sport psychology. However, the overriding theme that has emerged suggests effective training should emphasize an interdisciplinary approach that includes course work and experience in counseling and sport psychology (Brown, 1982; Dishman, 1983; Mahoney, 1987; Nideffer, Feltz, & Salmela, 1982; Petrie & Watkins, 1994; Singer, 1987; Silva, Conroy, & Zizzi, 1999; Taylor, 1991; Waite & Pettit, 1993).

Petrie and Watkins (1994) found the majority of programs within counseling did not offer a course in sport psychology at the undergraduate (93.8%) or graduate (92.2%) level, and none of the programs reported having future plans to offer such a course at either level. Almost half of the program directors within counseling (47.9%) indicated that sport psychology courses were offered at their respective institutions through departments of exercise and sport science. They also found that 41.1% of faculty members and 66.7% of graduate students within counseling have interests in pursuing research in the area of sport psychology. These findings suggest that, although sport psychology normally is not offered within counseling programs, there is an openness and acceptance for both students and faculty to pursue such an interest.

Further, 64.7% of the directors noted that an interdisciplinary program, rather than a program associated solely with counseling (19.6%) or sport science (7.8%), would offer the best and most comprehensive training for individuals interested in sport psychology. It would be valuable for a doctoral program to provide a balanced curriculum in the areas of specialization (i.e., counseling and sport psychology). Formal course work should include specific information and training in the areas students wish to work. For example, students should be offered training within sport science (i.e., sport psychology, exercise physiology, and motor learning), and counseling (i.e., counseling theories, counseling practica, and counseling techniques). This interdisciplinary approach can provide a more global understanding of the particular needs of athletes and an understanding of athletes in their everyday lives outside of sport.

This course work would enhance their competency in their own area of interest and enable them to recognize when clients' concerns required a referral to someone with the appropriate specialized training to address them. In addition to the clear benefits of a solid educational foundation, an interdisciplinary background might make practitioners more competitive in the job market (Taylor, 1991; Waite & Pettit, 1993).

Currently, academic positions for sport psychologists exist in exercise science/ kinesiology departments, with very few employment opportunities in other academic departments. Given this circumstance in the academic job market, applicants for sport psychology positions need formal academic course work in exercise and sport science core areas, such as sport psychology, exercise physiology, motor development, biomechanics, and sport sociology. However, in order to best provide athletes with performance enhancement and consultation, professionals should be certified/licensed within counseling or clinical psychology. Clearly, a desirable model would be an interdisciplinary program of study that offers future sport psychology practitioners course work and practical opportunities in both the sport sciences and counseling/clinical psychology.

Minimum Training Requirements and Programmatic Concerns

The type of training that an individual receives will be a significant influence on how that individual practices sport psychology. The AAASP certification process has been in place since 1992, and the criteria for individuals to identify themselves as AAASP-certified counselors are well established. The certification criteria established by AAASP should play a significant role in guiding the minimum training requirements developed by graduate programs interested in training individuals in the practice of sport psychology. Perusal of the AAASP certification standards (AAASP, 1990, 2003) indicates that specific coursework, supervised practica, other supervised experiences, and sustained involvement within the field are all requirements for certification.

As previously noted, a sport psychologist needs to be trained in an interdisciplinary manner with significant coursework in the sport sciences, counseling, and psychology. Specific coursework in the biological bases of behavior, including comparative psychology, exercise physiology, and psychopharmacology, may be a part of the minimum training requirements along with courses in the cognitive and affective bases of behavior, social bases of behavior, and individual bases of behavior.

A fundamental core of coursework should also exist in the specific sub-discipline of sport psychology. Courses should include intervention and performance enhancement, health and exercise psychology, social psychology, professional ethics within sport psychology, and research and statistical methodologies pertinent to applied sport psychology. During their training, individuals should also take support courses that provide a broad background in exercise physiology and motor learning, as well as in the sociological, historical, and philosophical bases of sport. These courses provide a firm understanding of the discipline within which a sport psychologist will be working. It is also important for the individual, in training for practice, to observe athletes' participation in their sport, including practices and competitive games. It is helpful, too, for the individual to have the opportunity to interact with athletes and coaches in order to gain insight and perspective prior to engaging in practica.

When individuals have reached the level of training at which they have a basic knowledge of counseling, psychology, sport psychology, as well as some practical experience of what the coaches' and athletes' experiences may be like, their training should then move to a level at which basic skills in counseling, learned in the classroom setting, are now developed in supervised practicum experiences. In the true development of training standards for individuals in the field, science and practice should go hand-in-hand. Sport psychologists' training should rigorously expose them to research questions that relate to practice and even the supervisory process.

In Table 2.1 a sample curriculum for a science-practice program in sport psychology is presented. Such a program provides for a diversification in the individual's training, yet allows for specificity in several important areas. Thus a balanced approach should prepare the individual for the counseling process and provide knowledge of social psychological aspects of sport, knowledge in the research in these questions, and knowledge in major professional issues and counseling issues that may confront the individual. In addition to these course requirements, the students should also be involved in supervised practicum experiences in which they receive supervision on individual and group interventions. This process should start out with the interventions being faculty-directed and -supervised and, in the advanced stages, should move more toward the interventions being conducted and led by the student, with faculty observation. The final practical experience should be an internship with a high school, college, Olympic, or professional team.

The student should have a minimum of two semesters working as a teaching assistant for an undergraduate sport psychology class, should complete a comprehensive written and oral examination, should present a formal proposal of his or

TABLE 2.1 **Suggested Coursework for Training in Applied Sport Psychology**

Sport Psychology/Psychology	**Measurement and Research**
Applied Sport Psychology	Quantitative Research Methods
Group Dynamics in Sport	Qualitative Research Methods
Social Issues in Sport	General Linear Modeling
Psychological Aspects of Injury	Multiple Regression
Theories of Personality	Applied Measurement Theory
Introduction to Clinical Psychology	Psychometrics in Sport
Personality Measurement	Test Theory and Analysis
Advanced Psychopathology	Factor Analysis
	Structural Equation Modeling
	Applied Multivariate Analysis
	Computational Statistics
Social and Developmental Psychology	**Exercise & Health Psychology**
Child Development	Exercise Adherence
Family Theory and Research	Psychosomatic Responses to Exercise
Group Dynamics	Psychology of Pain
Social Development	Addictions in Sport
Social Psychology	
Counseling and Professional Issues	**Practica in Sport Psychology**
Theories of Counseling	Practicum in Individual Interventions I
Issues in Contemporary Sport Psychology	Practicum in Individual Interventions II
Ethical Issues in Counseling	Practicum in Individual Interventions III
Professional Problems in Psychology	Practicum in Group and Team Dynamics I
Career Counseling and Development	Practicum in Group and Team Dynamics II
Group Counseling	Internship with High School or College
Rehabilitation Counseling	
Cross-Cultural Counseling	

her dissertation topic, and should complete a formal oral defense of the dissertation topic. A program such as this should increase the probability of the sport psychology doctoral student being prepared not only to practice but also to conduct research. This preparation should fit nicely with the type of jobs sought by Ph.D. students and young professionals entering the field. These jobs often require the individual to have teaching skills, counseling skills, and research skills. Individuals' ability to advance through the ranks in the system of higher education will be dependent on their ability in these three areas. Such a program will also thoroughly prepare students for an academic appointment, AAASP certification, or entry into professional practice.

In the future, a written examination may be required for a professional to receive sport psychology certification. This practice is common in many fields, including athletic training. Some specializations in sports medicine require passing practical and written exams in order to receive certification as an exercise technician. This form of testing has been common in the field of psychology and various sub-disciplines, in which a written examination is required for a person to receive certification or overall state licensure. If the field of sport psychology does, in fact, continue to evolve in this fashion, it will be essential for graduate programs to prepare sport psychology students properly so they can meet the criteria for entrance into the profession.

In 1995, the USOC recognized the AAASP certification as the one that will be required in order for individuals to work with an Olympic team. This is, of course, very beneficial to the certification process. It is incumbent upon AAASP to educate individuals in higher education, professional sports, and collegiate sports of the need for hiring certified individuals. When this educational and exposure process is brought to a higher level, the certification process will take on a higher profile and will be meaningful to collegiate and professional teams. Another way certification can be enhanced is through the job market itself. As individuals apply for jobs at institutions of higher learning, a criterion for an individual to be considered as an applicant should be a basic qualification of certification in that field. Currently, an individual who is certified must apply to be recertified every five years. The recertification process involves the following:

1. Recertification is conducted in a five-year cycle and recertification requires continuous membership in AAASP.

2. The individual must have documented attendance at three conferences in five years, at least one of which is an AAASP annual conference. The remaining two conferences may be state, regional, or national, conferences that include but are not limited to sport psychology content. For example, attendance at an American Psychological Association meeting or a behavior therapy meeting would be appropriate and could count toward the remaining two conferences required.

3. The individual must also participate in, either by conducting or attending, a workshop or course intended to upgrade knowledge or skills. The workshop must be comparable at a minimum to a six-hour AAASP pre-conference workshop.

Although certification is a step in the right direction, it has not diminished programmatic concerns about the formal preparation of sport psychology professionals. Unfortunately, most of the current graduate education models for future sport psychology professionals are not at an acceptable standard.

Accreditation of Sport Psychology Graduate Programs

The recognition of formal standards for practice in sport psychology, by AAASP and the USOC, was a significant advancement in the field. While AAASP has adopted standards for practice in applied sport psychology, the field has yet to identify which graduate programs are capable of providing students with the necessary experiences for certification upon graduation. The next logical step in the advancement of the practice of sport psychology is the development and formal recognition of programs that prepare students for sport psychology certification and successful careers in the practice of sport psychology. Although few would argue against this ideal, the topic of accreditation has been controversial in the field of sport psychology.

One of the major factors fueling this controversy is the nature of traditional graduate training programs in sport psychology. As discussed in chapter 1, many of the early sport psychology graduate programs evolved from motor learning programs, and these programs followed a research paradigm for graduate education. As the field has developed and become more applied, programs have made minimal changes in their curriculums and training procedures. Consequently, graduate training has struggled to keep pace with the changing demands and intense interest in the practice of sport psychology. This position has resulted in research-based programs that do not meet reasonable standards of education and training in the application and practice of sport psychology. Many programs do not offer applied course work, and they have not developed supervised opportunities in the sport setting where graduate students can work with athletes. Clinical psychology and counseling psychology have developed accreditation procedures to establish and maintain a standard of preparation in their fields. Enhancing graduate programs in sport psychology, to properly prepare students to practice sport psychology, has been challenging, yet it is a task that must be undertaken if sport psychology is to gain recognition as a viable area of professional practice.

A minority of graduate programs have modified their curriculum to meet the standards for AAASP certification. In fact, the AAASP certification document states that the process is designed to "provide colleges and universities with guidelines for programs, courses and practicum experiences in the field of sport psychology" (AAASP, 1990). Programs that meet student needs for certification in sport psychology should be recognized at an organizational level, and this is exactly what an accreditation procedure is designed to accomplish. Unfortunately, only a small fraction of graduate training programs in sport psychology would meet reasonable accreditation criteria at the current time. This should not stop the progress toward this important advancement in the field of sport psychology. Initial standards should be established, and programs that meet most of the criteria for certification, including criteria for supervised practicum in sport psychology, should be recognized. As more graduate programs develop to meet AAASP accreditation, the criteria for accreditation will be reviewed and revised if necessary.

Accreditation standards should not attempt to dictate the content of graduate training in sport psychology. These guidelines should outline a structure for programs to follow. As demonstrated in table 2.1, coursework can be diverse, with flexibility in the design of a program. In addition to a required number of hours in each area of preparation, accreditation should require that programs offer students experiences in supervised practica, teaching sport psychology, and research in the form of a sport psychology dissertation.

In order for science-practice training programs in sport psychology to be accredited, interdisciplinary training efforts will most likely be required. Most contemporary sport psychology graduate programs simply do not have the number and diversity of faculty in sport psychology to provide the depth and diversity of experience needed to train a student in the practice of sport psychology. A carefully designed interdisciplinary program can draw educational experiences from various specialized fields, such as psychology and counseling, and integrate these experiences into the specialized training that the practice of sport psychology requires.

Recognizing that the training requirements for future professionals can be accomplished through the accreditation, a group of faculty and students formally re-initiated discussion regarding the accreditation of sport psychology graduate programs at the 10th Annual AAASP conference in New Orleans (1995). Moved by this initiative, a new Graduate Training Committee was formed in 1998 by AAASP president, Robin Vealey. The charge of this committee was to examine graduate programs in sport psychology and examine how other helping professions regulated graduate education. After three years of systematic study, the Graduate Training Committee's final report was submitted in September 2001. The committee recommended a three to five year program recognition-accreditation process be initiated by AAASP to enhance graduate education and training in sport psychology graduate programs. The recommendations of the committee were rejected by the 2001 executive board of AAASP. Unfortunately, this action continued to leave many future professionals unsure about which institution they should attend for their doctoral experiences and training.

Because there is no standardization or minimum training requirements for graduate programs in sport psychology, many students remain confused about which graduate program will best prepare them for practice and certification in sport psychology. Obviously, greater organizational leadership is needed to address this most central issue confronting the continued development and advancement of applied sport psychology. Such leadership was exhibited in the fall of 2005 by AAASP president, Craig Wrisberg, who reassembled a committee to study the accreditation process in sport psychology.

AAASP Certification

The term certification and licensure represents that an individual is competent to practice specific interventions, and/or techniques, for a specific population. Additionally, certification and licensure allow a practitioner to adhere to a certain set of ethical guidelines established by an organization (i.e., APA, ACA, AAASP). It is important for the field of professional counseling and sport psychology to set these standards, and for individuals to achieve a credential that will ultimately protect the consumer. In 1989, AAASP created guidelines for individuals interested in becoming certified consultants in the field of sport psychology.

The course of study includes the following:

1. Professional ethics and standards—1 course

2. Sport psychology—3 courses (2 at the graduate level)

3. Biomechanical and/or physiological bases of sport (e.g., kinesiology, biomechanics, exercise physiology)—1 course

4. Historical, philosophical, social or motor behavior bases of sport (e.g., motor learning/control, motor development, sociology of sport, history and philosophy of sport/physical education)—1 course

5. Psychopathology and its assessment (e.g., abnormal psychology, psychopathology)—1 course

6. Counseling skills (e.g., graduate coursework in basic interventions in counseling, supervised practica in counseling, clinical psychology, industrial/organizational psychology)—1 course

7. Skills/techniques/analysis within sport or exercise and related experiences, such as coaching (e.g., sport skills and techniques classes, clinics, formal coaching experiences, or organized participation in sport or exercise)

8. Research design, statistics, and psychological assessment (e.g., graduate course in any of these areas)—1 course

9. Biological bases of behavior (e.g., comparative psychology, neuropsychology, physiological psychology, psychopharmacology, sensation, exercise physiology, biomechanics/kinesiology)—1 course

10. Cognitive-affective bases of behavior (e.g., cognition, emotion, learning, memory, motivation, motor development, motor learning/control, perception, thinking)—1 course

11. Social bases of behavior (e.g., cultural, ethnic, group processes, gender roles in sport, organizational and systems theory, social psychology, sociology of sport)—1 course

12. Individual behavior (e.g., developmental psychology, health psychology, individual differences, exercise behavior, personality theory)—1 course

Each course fulfills only one requirement, and up to four upper-level undergraduate courses could be implemented in the curriculum.

Additionally, 400 hours of supervised experience is needed, which usually involves the immersion with one or more teams and individual athletes. One hundred hours (25%) must be the direct contact of services provided to athletes and teams, in which performance enhancement strategies and/or interventions are utilized, and are thus eligible for inclusion. Direct services that deal with personal issues unrelated to the sport are not eligible, as they are not the purpose of a certified consultant's status and expertise. Finally, 40 hours (10%) must be spent in direct supervision with a certified consultant or an individual who is approved by the AAASP Certification Review Committee.

Previously, this certification was strictly for individuals who had obtained a doctoral degree from an accredited university. However, in 2002, certification was extended to master's level practitioners. These individuals must meet the same requirements as doctoral level consultants, and then complete a two-year "provisional" period in which they must accrue 300 hours (25% must be direct contact and 10% direct supervision). When these requirements are met, these individuals receive the title of "Certified Consultant." However, if the 300 hours are not achieved within the two-year period, then they must reapply for provisional status. When they have successfully completed all of the requirements, they maintain the distinction of Certified Consultant for five years, at which time the recertification process is implemented. Certified Consultants must maintain a certain number of continuing education requirements throughout the five years. Namely, they must maintain continuous AAASP membership, attend a minimum of three conferences (at least one AAASP conference and the other two that are related to sport psychology), and participate in a workshop or course (i.e., comparable to a 6-hour AAASP pre-conference workshop) that is of a sport psychology nature.

APA Practice Emphasis (Proficiency)

To address growing issues of specialization in professional psychology, the APA developed the Committee for the Recognition of Specialties and Proficiencies in Professional Psychology (CRSPPP) in 1995. The CRSPPP is charged with evaluating petitions for recognizing areas of specialty and proficiency for licensed psychologists. The CRSPPP defines proficiency as "a circumscribed activity in the general practice of professional psychology or one or more of its specialties. The relationship between a body of knowledge and a set of skills related to the parameters of practice specified . . . represents the most critical aspect of the definition of proficiency" (Joint Interim Committee for the Identification and Recognition of Specialties and Proficiencies, 1995, para. 2). In February 2003, the APA approved a petition put forth by Division 47 to recognize sport psychology as proficiency (American Psychological Association [APA], 2003). The APA sport psychology proficiency was developed to address two central issues in the field: public protection and appropriate training. Accordingly, individuals who receive a doctoral degree in a traditional field of psychology (e.g., clinical, social, developmental) from an APA-accredited institution, and achieve state licensure, are recommended to supplement their training with sport-specific educational experiences in the following areas:

- a knowledge of theory and research in social, historical, cultural, and developmental foundations of sport psychology
- the principles and practices of applied sport psychology, including issues and techniques of sport-specific psychological assessment and mental skills training for performance enhancement and satisfaction with participation
- clinical and counseling issues with athletes
- organizational and systemic aspects of sport consulting
- an understanding of the developmental and social issues related to sport participation
- knowledge of the biobehavioral bases of sport and exercise (e.g., exercise physiology, motor learning, sports medicine) (APA, 2003, para. 2)

Although the sport psychology proficiency is officially recognized by the APA, several challenges to ensuring adequate training and service provision are still on the horizon. First and foremost, evaluation of individuals applying for proficiency recognition has yet to be determined. As of the writing of this text, no method is currently in place for deciphering who has or has not met the recommendations for sport psychology proficiency. Currently, Division 47 considers the development of a standardized exam, as well as credential reviewing, to evaluate interested licensed psychologists (APA Division 47, 2003, para. 3). Secondly, the majority of APA-accredited psychology programs do not require coursework in sport science/kinesiology or supervised practica working specifically with athletic individuals; therefore, many licensed psychologists may need extensive supplemental education to meet proficiency recommendations. Division 47 must develop a strategy to provide considerable continuing education for interested individuals. Moreover, to be effective, Division 47 must develop strategies to encourage or implement the recommended experiences for current and future students within the infrastructure of current APA-accredited psychology programs. Lastly, given that sport psychology has traditionally been (and continues to be) housed in sport science/kinesiology departments, the APA proficiency must address concerns of exclusion in the very near future. Many current, well-established sport psychology practitioners are not licensed psychologists. The majority of future practitioners is currently being educated within sport science/kinesiology departments and may not become licensed psychologists upon degree completion. Hopefully, APA Division 47 will develop a symbiotic relationship with AAASP in order to accommodate professionals from the sport science/kinesiology and psychology academic traditions.

Counselor Certification

Each state has its own requirements for certification/licensure as a professional/ mental health counselor. As of April 10, 2003, however, 46 states, the District of Columbia, and Puerto Rico have passed counselor credentialing legislation (American Counseling Association [ACA], 2004). From this data, 45 states and the District of Columbia designate an individual who has successfully completed the state requirements as a "licensed professional counselor." Five states use the label "licensed metal health counselor"; three states distinguish the term as "certified professional counselor"; two states use "licensed clinical professional counselor"; and three different states elected the names "clinical counselor in mental health," "licensed clinical mental health counselor," and "certified mental health counselor," respectively. Two states and Puerto Rico have passed legislation but have not designated a term, and three other states have not passed legislation at this time (ACA, 2004). If an individual is interested in becoming licensed/certified in the field of professional counseling, then the first place to begin the search for requirements would be the respective state's board that oversees licensure/certification, or locate more information at www.nbcc.org.

The National Board for Certified Counselors (NBCC) has specific requirements for individuals seeking certification as a National Certified Counselor (NCC). In particular, one must possess a master's degree or higher in the field of counseling from an accredited college or university. Currently, one must complete a minimum of 48 semester or 72 quarter hours of graduate-level coursework in the following areas:

- human growth and development—an understanding of individuals at all developmental levels
- social and cultural foundations—an understanding of concerns in a multicultural and diverse society
- helping relationships—an understanding of counseling theories and techniques
- group work—an understanding of group dynamics and processes
- career and lifestyle development—an understanding of career development
- appraisal—an understanding of assessment and evaluation of individuals and groups
- research and program evaluation—an understanding of research methods, statistics, and ethical and legal issues
- professional orientation—an understanding of the history, organizational structures, ethics, standards, and credentialing in the field of counseling
- field experience—a supervised counseling experience, for at least two academic terms, that earned three semester or five quarter graduate credit hours (National Board for Certified Counselors, 2004)

Additionally, individuals who have not completed a graduate program accredited by the Council for the Accreditation of Counseling and Related Educational Programs (CACREP) must complete two years of counseling experience after the degree was conferred. This requirement includes 3000 counseling hours with 100 hours of face-to-face supervision from a professional with a master's degree or higher in counseling or a related field (i.e., psychology or social work). Finally, one must successfully pass the National Counselor Examination for Licensure and Certification, which is based on 200 multiple-choice questions. Certification as an NCC lasts for five years, in which time one must accrue 100 continuing education credit hours in order to qualify for recertification. If that does not occur, then the NCE must be taken and passed again (NBCC, 2004).

Integrating Organized Sport Groups

As a field, sport psychology has a professional responsibility to educate coaches, athletes, and sport organizations regarding the specialized training that is required to provide quality sport psychology services. This educational process needs to be directly targeted to National Governing Bodies, the National Collegiate Athletic Association, college and high school athletic directors, coaches, and youth sport organizations. Without a formal institutionalized mechanism for information dissemination, it is nearly impossible for coaches, athletes, and sport groups to make informed decisions regarding who should provide sport psychology services. Uninformed decisions are potentially dangerous since they may endanger the athlete's psychological well-being, the team's success, and the credibility of sport psychology with the service population. Sport psychology has endured public humiliations as a result of the damage perpetrated by individuals masquerading as sport psychologists. Many years ago, Hall-of-Fame football coach George Allen publicly criticized sport psychology on ABC's *Nightline*. His comments were based on his experience with an individual who provided services to the Washington Redskins under the auspices of the title "Sport Psychologist."

Unfortunately, use of this specialized title is not regulated by licensure. Until the title is regulated by law, certification standards offer the only guidance related to education and training standards for practice. With the adoption of AAASP certification standards, there is at least agreement among sport psychologists regarding the minimum qualifications necessary to practice sport psychology. Unfortunately, awareness of these qualifications is not widely known in athletic circles, or in the general public. Athletes, coaches, parents, and sport organizations are generally unaware of the AAASP certification criteria for practicing sport psychology. In order for certification to be of benefit to the practitioner and to the consumer, organizations like AAASP must bring an awareness of certification to sport organizations and parent groups. Without this communication, sport groups will not be integrated by professionals with certification in sport psychology.

Facilitating Competent Counselor Selection by Sport Organizations

Sport organizations need to be able to identify and select competent sport psychology service providers. The first step in this process is to identify the sport organizations that need information on how to select a sport psychology service provider. National Governing Bodies, professional sports leagues (i.e., Major League Baseball, National Basketball Association, National Football League, and National Hockey League), the National Collegiate Athletic Association and each of its member institutions, state high school athletic associations and athletic directors, and major youth sport leagues should all receive information on the process of selecting a sport psychology service provider. The next step is to educate these organizations on the potential roles for a sport psychologist (i.e., areas of practice) and on the suggested minimum qualifications for individuals working in the capacity of a sport psychologist. Organizations should be made aware of the highly specialized nature of sport psychology, the different qualifications of clinical, counseling, and sport psychologists, AAASP/USOC certification criteria, the role of referrals, and ethical considerations involved in service provision.

How can this be accomplished? There are a number of strategies for promoting sport psychology among sport organizations. Publishing and distributing an informational brochure on sport psychology on what to look for when selecting a sport psychologist, establishing a formal liaison between AAASP and regulatory sport bodies, and creating a formal position in a professional organization, such as AAASP, for information dissemination are all positive initiatives. These initiatives should clearly define sport psychology and its sub-specializations, as well as explicitly describe the role of a sport psychologist and the minimum qualifications for the practice of sport psychology.

Educating Coaches and Athletes Regarding Sport Psychology Services

Educating sport organizations regarding sport psychology services is an excellent start to integrating sport groups; however, it is also important to reach out to the coaches and athletes who will be receiving the services, as well. It has been estimated that over 110 million American adults participate in some form of an exercise program and over 70 million American adults participate in organized sports each year (US Bureau of Census, 1995). Additionally, the Occupational Outlook Handbook estimates that more than 280,000 people are employed as coaches in the United States (US Bureau of Labor Statistics, 1996). Given the tremendous number of coaches and athletes who participate in sports each year, the only feasible means of reaching a majority is through mass communication. One economical method for educating players and coaches about counselor competence is through the preparation of a brochure similar to the one recommended for distribution to sport organizations. This brochure could include basic information about what sport psychology is, as well as a set of recommended questions to ask potential service providers. A practicing sport psychologist should be prepared to answer questions regarding competency, similar to those in table 2.2. These responses will help athletes and coaches make educated decisions about the sport psychologist's qualifications to work with athletes, coaches, and teams. In addition to an educational brochure, the major sport psychology organizations should invest resources into publicizing the role of sport psychologists, and a list of certified sport psychology consultants should be sent yearly to athletic directors and professional sport organizations.

Another way to gain widespread exposure is by utilizing the media to the field's advantage. The major media outlets need to be provided with a list of certified sport psychology consultants who are willing to provide interviews on their specializations. The field can reduce the likelihood of misrepresentation if it provides the media with informed sources who are willing to discuss relevant issues. Additionally, workshops should be developed and presented at conferences to help sport psychologists be more comfortable when interacting with the media. These workshops could cover such topics as maintaining client confidentiality while providing an interesting and informative interview, recognizing what reporters are looking for in an interview , projecting a professional image, and any number of procedural technicalities, including how to handle being misquoted! By providing the media with reliable, informed sources, the field of sport psychology can take

---

TABLE 2.2. **Questions a Sport Psychology Service Provider Should Be Prepared to Answer**

1. What professional certifications do you hold?
2. What professional organizations do you currently belong to?
3. What is your highest degree? Do you have a specialization?
4. What sports do you primarily work with?
5. What other sports are you familiar with to be an effective counselor?
6. Have you worked directly with the sport a client is interested in?
7. Approximately how many contact hours have you had working with individual athletes?
8. Approximately how many contact hours have you had working with athletic teams?
9. Can you provide a current coach or athlete as a reference?
10. Would you be willing to provide me a copy of your vita?
11. What is your fee schedule for service provision?

advantage of the mass media and communicate with the general public. With greater efforts to integrate sport organizations, interest in sport psychology services should increase tremendously. Thousands of teams that exist throughout all competitive levels could benefit from the services of a sport psychologist in one way or another. Through greater information provided to these organizations, and through assistance in identifying who is a sport psychologist and what types of services this person may be able to provide, the job market for sport psychologists could increase dramatically.

Job Market

The job market is an interesting topic in the field of sport psychology. To some degree, there is a perception that there are no jobs for sport psychologists. Many young professionals are conflicted about specializing in the field of sport psychology because they are concerned there will be few jobs available for them upon completion of their degree. This perception has led many individuals who had the intention of being trained as sport psychologists to go into other fields or to specialize in the areas of clinical and counseling psychology. Although a degree in clinical or counseling may provide a wider variety of job opportunities, it may decrease marketability, specifically in the area of sport psychology. Many of the jobs advertised for sport psychologists are teaching-research positions at the university level. These positions often require a Ph.D. degree with specialization in sport psychology. Exercise science and kinesiology departments traditionally hire an individual with specialized qualifications and training in sport psychology. Williams and Scherzer (2003) found that the field of sport psychology graduated twenty to thirty Ph.D.s per year from 1994 to 1999. Unlike clinical and counseling psychology, sport psychology does not graduate thousands of Ph.D.s per year who are seeking job employment opportunities.

Competitive sport has experienced substantial growth over the past few decades. Among the advancements were significant increases in opportunities for women at all levels, continued expansion of professional leagues, and the addition of sports to Olympic competition. Many service-providing sport professions have experienced parallel escalation. Athletic training, strength and conditioning, sport nutrition, sport management, sport marketing, and sport journalism-each has experienced professional explosion. Indeed, in the United States, it is unlikely to find a professional team or NCAA Division I college athletic department that does not employ an individual related to each of the aforementioned specialized professions. Given the proliferation of professions centered on sport and the rising interest in sport psychology, it is not surprising that sport psychology scholars have expressed optimism regarding the expansion of career opportunities for sport psychology consultants (Silva, 1989). With 153 major professional teams, 47 Olympic sports, 1039 NCAA schools with approximately 355,000 student-athletes, as well as countless individual sport professionals (e.g., golf, tennis), minor leagues, sport clubs, and youth sport organizations in the United States alone, it is difficult not to be optimistic about the opportunity for work in applied sport psychology.

A few empirical studies have been conducted to systematically examine employment issues in applied sport psychology. Waite and Pettit (1993) contacted 55 individuals who received doctoral degrees from sport psychology programs between 1984 and 1989. Of the 34 individuals who completed the questionnaire, 27% reported not working full-time in a sport psychology related job, half of whom were not seeking such employment. The majority of graduates working in sport psychology spent over half of their time teaching at academic institutions and slightly over half (56%) reported consulting; however, only two graduates spent over 50% of their time consulting with athletes. Approximately half of individuals reported that finding sport psychology work for pay was very or moderately difficult. Anderson, Williams, Aldridge, and Taylor (1997) replicated and expanded Waite and Pettit's study by examining employment of individuals who received doctoral or master's degrees from sport psychology programs between 1989 and 1994. Of the 92 doctoral graduates who responded to the survey, 79% reported primary employment in academia (teaching and/or research) and 51% of kinesiology graduates reported consulting with athletes. Overall, only seven doctoral graduates reported spending more than half of their time consulting athletes. Anderson et al. (1997) also found that 70% of doctoral graduates reported that finding paid sport psychology work was at least moderately difficult. Three quarters of the schools contacted had provided information regarding master's graduates resulting in an underestimation of 539 total master's graduates from 1989 to 1994. Of the 332 master's graduates contacted, 162 responded; 24% reported pursuing a doctoral degree and 15% reported engaging in private consulting practice. More recently, Williams and Scherzer (2003) examined sport psychology graduates from 1994 through 1999. Based on their results, academia remains the primary career for doctoral graduates (73% of 107 doctoral graduates who responded to the survey) and 52% of doctoral graduates reported consulting with athletes. Interestingly, 51% of doctoral graduates from 1994 to 1999 reported that finding sport psychology work for pay was moderately or very difficult, a percentage smaller than the previous sample (Anderson et al., 1997). Another trend reported by Williams and Scherzer (2003) was the increase in percentage of master's graduates pursuing advanced degrees from 24% to 43% in the 1994-1999 sample. The authors suggest that the advent of AAASP certification may have had an impact on students' orientation to achieve a doctoral degree.

As a collective, the tracking of sport psychology graduates over the past 15 years highlights a few central trends in sport psychology employment. First, the number of graduates from both master's and doctoral programs continue to grow. Given that the majority of these programs exist within exercise science and kinesiology programs and that the majority of doctoral graduates are employed in academia, it appears that sport psychology as an academic discipline continues to flourish. Second, although for master's students there may be a trend toward pursuing doctoral degrees, the results raise concern regarding the number of master's students who have not been tracked. Master's graduates who participated in the studies reviewed above may not be entirely representative of the job market for master's graduates. Many master's students could not be tracked over the past 15 years. Thus, it is unclear whether these master's students have found sport psychology employment or shifted their career paths.

Studies that have emphasized employment experiences of recent graduates of sport psychology programs may be limited in their scope because recent graduates may not have established themselves in the field of applied sport psychology. To address this limitation and to expand the sample to include practitioners grounded in psychology training, Meyers, Coleman, Whelan, and Mehlenbeck (2001) invited members of APA Division 47 and AAASP to complete a sport psychology career and income survey. Of the 433 respondents, 47% reported working primarily in academia and 36% reported working in private practice. Only one respondent reported working primarily with a professional sport organization, although 26 indicated this setting as a secondary form of employment. When separated into training background, 20% of sport scientists, 87% of clinical psychologists, and 80% of counseling psychologists were employed primarily in applied settings; however, sport-science-based professionals averaged more time spent doing sport psychology related work than clinical- or counseling-based professionals. The authors conclude that training in psychology, whether clinical or counseling, lends itself to employment in applied settings. Unfortunately, sport psychology work with athletes remains a supplemental facet of this type of career path, just as it may be supplemental for academic sport psychology professionals, as well.

Using a different approach, Voight and Callaghan (2001) contacted NCAA Division I universities during the period of 1998 to 1999 to examine their use of sport psychology professionals with their student athletes. The study comprised 96 of 115 athletic departments representing, arguably, the strongest financial athletic conferences in the United States. Although more than half of the university athletic departments reported using some form of sport psychology, 19 stated that individual sport coaches hired part-time consultants, 10 departments hired part-time consultants, 7 departments employed full-time consultants, and 7 used faculty members or graduate students. Universities cited several reasons for not using sport psychology services, including lack of funding, use of university counseling centers for such services, and lack of beneficial results. On an optimistic note, approximately half of the athletic departments who did not use sport psychology services appeared receptive to the notion. This included 11 that reported being currently involved in hiring or at least discussing employing a sport psychology consultant.

Professional sport is another area where individuals are providing sport psychology services to athletes and teams. Dunlap (1999) reviewed data submitted by

64 professional sport teams that demonstrated 42 of the 64 teams (65.62%) utilize or have utilized the services of a sport psychology consultant. Interest in sport psychology services by professional teams was high, as 84.4% of the respondents indicated that they were supportive of sport psychology services, and 78.6% of the teams responding indicated that the services provided were beneficial. Teams were most interested in service provision in the areas of self-confidence, communication/team communication, performance enhancement, cohesion, and conflict resolution. Unfortunately, Dunlap's data also demonstrated that most professional teams knew very little about the qualifications, certification status, or license status of their service providers. Only 10 of the 64 teams reported that the service provider for their team had either a certification or a license. Only 3 of the 10 were able to name or specify the credential they believed the service provider held. While services are being provided to professional teams, professional sports remains an untapped market for certified sport psychology consultants. A systematic marketing effort by a reputable organization, such as AAASP, could increase the job opportunities for many certified sport consultants and bring a level of organization to service provision for professional sports that would greatly enhance the development of professional practice in the field of sport psychology.

If sport psychology organizations systematically market the professional and practice aspects of sport psychology, job opportunities for individuals with specialized training should increase. While colleges and universities have provided the major job market for individuals with specific training and specialization in sport psychology, the greatest untapped job markets for aspiring sport psychologists are clearly the area of professional sport teams and youth sport participants. While Dunlap's (1999) data demonstrated that professional teams often like to hire sport psychologists, many of these individuals are hired on a word-of-mouth basis. With a greater educational effort and more visible marketing of sport psychology opportunities with professional teams, major and minor leagues could provide a bevy of job opportunities. The field of sport psychology could quickly find itself in a very positive situation-one in which the demand for certified sport psychology service providers surpasses the ability to provide quality service providers. By preparing in an interdisciplinary manner, graduates will be competitive for entry into the job market in both the traditional university setting and in the emerging practice setting. Continued movement in the field toward interdisciplinary training, certification, and accredited programs should provide the next generation of sport psychologists greater opportunity for placement in applied jobs and in traditional teaching and research positions.

Preparing to Practice: The Role of Technology

The rapid advancement of technology has expanded opportunities and created challenges for both the science and practice of sport psychology. The heart of the technological evolution is the proliferation and exponential enhancement of computers. Significant increases in processor speed, storage capacity, networking, and mobility provide the foundation for substantial progress in the utility and efficiency of computer applications. Moreover, propagation of the Internet has transformed the landscape of interpersonal communication and relationships. Possibly the most substantial aspect of this digital revolution is that the computer interface has largely become standardized. In a Windows-based world, very little computer programming knowledge is needed to utilize the vast applications that computers afford; simply point and click. Technological advancement is gaining momentum; therefore, technological literacy is critical for sport psychology research and practice.

Given the dynamic nature and speed of advancement in technology, it is almost impossible to describe the "state of the art" in a printed text. In 1998, a standard personal desktop computer (PC) had the following specifications: Pentium II 266 megahertz processor, 4 gigabyte hard drive, 32 megabytes of RAM, CD ROM, "floppy" drive, and Windows 98 operating system. In 2004, a standard PC had a Pentium 42.66 gigahertz processor, 40 gigabyte hard drive, 128 megabytes of RAM, CD ROM (if not a CD burner), and Windows XP operating system. In 6 years (approximately the duration of graduate school), the processor speed and hard drive storage has increased tenfold and memory has quadrupled.

Significant increases in space and processing speed have naturally allowed computer software to evolve rapidly, as well, enhancing the functionality and efficiency of word processing, data management, statistical analyses, and presentation development. Moreover, previous creative sport psychology endeavors, such as creating audiotape relaxation scripts or videotape highlights for clients, can be produced entirely using digital technology. The rapid evolution of computer hardware, media, and software has reduced barriers to professional creativity. The trend does not appear to be subsiding, suggesting that individuals should not only become well versed in advancing technology, but they should adopt a philosophy of constant progress, using foreword thinking to maximize creativity and expand possibilities for the profession.

Concurrent with advancements in computer hardware, media, and software has been the rapid expansion of the Internet, the integration of computers and telecommunication. The Internet is rapidly transforming interpersonal communication, relationships, and general daily living, and will be a powerful tool for the field of sport psychology. As of August 2003, 126 million (63%) American adults were online, many of who use e-mail (93%), instant messaging (46%), and chat rooms (25%) (Pew Internet & American Life Project, 2003). From March 2000 to September 2002, Americans who used the Internet to check sports scores and information grew from 30 million to 52 million users, pointing toward a vast online interest in sport. Current technologies, such as, e-mail, instant messaging (i.e., America Online Instant Messenger [AIM], ICQ), chat rooms, dynamic web pages, and videoconferencing (via personal web cameras), may provide new opportunities for both the science and practice of sport psychology. Of course, use of the Internet for research and consulting does create unique challenges that must be navigated.

Web-based empirical research has several distinct advantages over traditional research procedures, which are often laden with very practical inconveniences:

1. Internet research actually democratizes data collection (Kraut et al., 2004, p. 106). Researchers need not be limited solely to local samples. Participants can be recruited from anywhere throughout the world, thus expanding research possibilities for individual scholars and facilitating research with rural samples, or more directly stated, non-university samples.

2. Although there are initial costs incurred for set-up of Internet research, costs per participant are drastically reduced in Internet research. Cobanoglu, Warde, and Moreo (2001) estimated a cost of $1.93 per participant for postal mail surveys, which places a ceiling on the potential size of sample due to financial constraints. Consequently, the scalability of Internet assessment is much greater than traditional paper-and-pencil assessment (Naglieri et al., 2004). Research protocols implemented on the Internet have minimal, if any, cost per participant allowing for substantially larger sample sizes.

3. Data collection and management on the Internet can be entirely automated, thus minimizing human error. Challenges of paper-and-pencil assessment, such as interpreting written responses (e.g., distinguishing a "2" from a "5") and optical scanning problems (e.g., stray pencil marks, poor erasing, inadequately darkened answers), can be overcome with computer assessment. Moreover, the removal of data entry and automation of data management allow for feedback to be provided instantly to respondents, if desired. For instance, clients of sport psychology science-practitioners could rate the intensity of their emotions using the Individual Zones of Optimal Functioning (Hanin, 2000) or Profile of Mood States (McNair, Lorr, & Droppleman, 1992) on the Internet 30 minutes before competition and receive instant feedback regarding their precompetitive emotional arousal. Although this example may seem absurd from a logistical standpoint (specifically, who has Internet capability in competition?), Internet access in college athletes' lockers (Clark, 2003), as well as the proliferation of handheld devices linked to the Internet (e.g., PDAs, web-capable cellular phones), make this seemingly distant endeavor a possibility in the present.

4. Internet research increases the flexibility of research protocols. Internet researchers are able to individualize instructions, stimuli, or questions based on responses made by respondents. Research may also be truly randomized using computer technology to randomly order scenario or questionnaire presentation.

5. Research conducted on the Internet or using computer automation allows for recording detailed respondent behavior during assessment. Data that is often difficult or impossible to obtain, including time spent on items or frequency and direction of changes made to responses, can be captured rather easily using computer technology.

Although research conducted on the Internet has several clear and compelling advantages over traditional methodologies; several preconceptions exist regarding the validity of data collected in cyberspace. Gosling,Vazire, Srivastava, and John, (2004) found many of the concerns about Internet research to be unsubstantiated. Much more research is needed regarding Internet methods, particularly given that little has been done in sport psychology. In general, many initial concerns regarding evolving technology appear unfounded; however, three central principles remain related to the security of Internet data: confidentiality, integrity, and authentication (Howard, Paridaens, & Gramm, 2001).

The expansion of Internet technology has the potential to impact the provision of sport psychology services, too. In general, psychology and behavioral health care terms, such as online counseling (Alleman, 2002), telehealth (Nickelson, 1998), e-therapy (Manhal-Baugus, 2001), and Behavioral eHealth (Maheu & Gordon, 2000), have been coined by scholars to describe the evolution of psychological services offered by practitioners with computer technology. Using Google and Netscape search engines, Heinlen, Welfel, Richmond, and O'Donnell (2003) identified 44 Web sites that offered some form of e-therapy by licensed psychologists. The majority of these sites utilized asynchronous (time-delayed; see Suler, 2000) e-mail technology; however, practitioners also provided real-time services via individual chat, group chat, or video conferencing. Although video conferencing appears to be the most similar to traditional face-to-face therapy, only four of the websites surveyed provided this service. No research has been conducted specifically regarding the prevalence of sport psychology services provided via Internet technology. Given the relative youth of sport psychology as a profession, it is not preposterous to assume that the use of Internet technology is significantly less prevalent in sport psychology compared to psychology in the main.

E-consulting may provide several advantages over traditional face-to-face consulting. Manhal-Baugus (2001) described four distinct advantages of general e-therapy that are particularly relevant for sport psychology:

1. Asynchronous e-mail frees clients from the shackles of time constraints. Clients are able to compose and send e-mails whenever they choose and are not limited to a consultant's schedule. Moreover, the process of e-mail allows clients and professionals alike to gain reflection time. Individuals may read, synthesize, and reflect upon thoughts shared through e-mail and develop responses at their own pace, without interruption. Of course, effective professionals will be expected to respond relatively quickly (24 to 72 hours).

2. E-consulting may be more cost effective than traditional consulting. Fee structures are often established per e-mail or per unit time of communication (using e-mail, chat, or video conferencing) at a reduced rate compared to face-to-face sessions.

3. E-consulting provides an increased sense of anonymity for clients that cannot be provided in face-to-face sessions. Athletes may feel more secure in disclosing their thoughts and behaviors during competition online. The stigma of using a "shrink" that may still permeate the athletic community could largely be dissolved through anonymous e-consulting. Perceived anonymity also allows clients to disengage from consultation that they believe is not helpful without consequence. With the click of the mouse, an athlete could change to a potentially more effective consultant.

4. Arguably the greatest advantage of using the Internet for sport psychology consulting is that it evaporates geographical boundaries. Currently, AAASP cannot accommodate many requests from geographical areas because they are out of range of a certified consultant. Many of these interested consumers could benefit from evolving e-consulting techniques. Additionally, athletes are a very mobile subset of the general population, traveling from competition to competition. Advances in mobile Internet technology and e-consulting would allow sessions to be conducted "on the road," without the added expense of travel for the consultant. With adequate computer hardware in place, e-consulting can be conducted virtually anywhere.

Despite the advantages, Internet research and consulting have considerable risks that must be addressed by professional organizations, as well as individual scholars and practitioners. The most fundamental concern regarding communication via the Internet centers on securing the transfer of information across the complex expanse. According to Howard et al. (2001, p. 118), information security can be reduced to three independent but complementary facets:

- *confidentiality:* keeping information hidden from all but the intended viewers
- *integrity:* keeping information intact, or at least being able to detect whether information has been altered
- *authentication:* identifying the origins of information

Just as ethically responsible professionals lock their offices and file cabinets containing physical information, professionals must also ensure that electronic data are not available for public access. Obviously, confidentiality is of the utmost priority in sport psychology research and consultation.

Even if confidentiality is maximized, assurances must be made that original data remains intact. Suppose an athlete who completed an online psychological assessment as part of tryouts for a national team must reach a standard score to be eligible. As part of the process, the athlete is provided immediate feedback that she did not pass. Although the athlete may have access to her results, she is not allowed to change her responses after they have been submitted. This example speaks to maintaining integrity of data collected.

Arguably the most difficult risk to the quality of electronic data is authentication. How do we know the data came from the source stated? Traditional face-to-face or voice-to-voice (telephone) communication affords instant visual or auditory cues that confirm, or disconfirm, the source of information. Similarly, we can recognize cues in written documents, such as letterhead and signatures, that authenticate their origins. Given that e-mail, chat, and instant messaging are mediating communication methodologies that inherently do not provide direct cues regarding the originator of communication, the authenticity of the information may be compromised.

In sum, sport psychology researchers and consultants must take steps to maximize confidentiality, integrity, and authenticity of information transmitted via the Internet. Thankfully, information technology specialists continue to enhance digital security to deal with these central issues. The current text is not focused on presenting technical aspects of information security; however, developing sport psychology professionals who are interested in utilizing advanced technology are encouraged to gain further understanding of the concerns presented.

Role of Young Professionals in Advancement

From the time students begin preparing themselves to enter the job market, they are in a unique position that challenges them to elevate their commitment and contribution to the field. The success of individuals in the field will be determined by their willingness to commit themselves to their students, clients, and colleagues through teaching, research, practice, and service. More importantly, the success of the field relies upon dedicated young professionals who are willing to present new ideas and issue new challenges. Having recently completed their formal training, young professionals have a much better sense than their more established colleagues of the relationship between training needs and the current state of training opportunities. This perspective should be used to guide the advancement of training standards in applied sport psychology. Training models today should be more advanced than the training models that were in place 15 years ago. Tomorrow's training models should be even more advanced than the models in place today. Students should be receiving better preparation, education, and training than their mentors received. With this in mind, young professionals must strive to prepare future generations of sport psychologists better than they were prepared themselves. Given the dynamic nature of the field, it is nearly inconceivable that the status quo will continue to meet the training standards needed in sport psychology indefinitely. Program development is an area in which the field must continuously strive to advance. Students and young professionals have a tremendous role to play in the advancement of the field. Many issues remain to be resolved, and new issues, such as those just noted in technology, will need to be addressed. The mobilization of young professionals into leadership roles will increase the probability of new ideas and opportunities being generated and brought to reality for applied sport psychology and for those preparing to practice sport psychology.

References

Adler, A. (1958). *What life should mean to you.* New York: Capricorn.

Alderman, R. B. (1980). Sport psychology: Past, present, and future dilemmas. In P. Klavora & K. A. W. Wipper (Eds.), *Psychological and sociological factors in sport* (pp. 3–19). Toronto: University of Toronto, Publications Division.

Alleman, J. R. (2002). Online counseling: The Internet and mental health treatment. *Psychotherapy: Theory, Research, Practice, Training, 39*, 199–209.

American Counseling Association (2004). *State licensure chart.* Retrieved April 15, 2004, from http://www.counseling.org/AM/Template.cfm?Section=SUMMARY_CHART

American Psychological Association (2003). *Summary: Sport psychology a proficiency in professional psychology.* Retrieved May 23, 2004, from http://www.apa.org/crsppp/archsportpsych.html

American Psychological Association Division 47 (2003). *Division projects.* Retrieved May 23, 2004, from http://www.psyc.unt.edu/apadiv47/about_divprojects.html

Anderson, M. B., Williams, J. M., Aldridge, T., & Taylor, J. (1997). Tracking the training and careers of graduates of advanced degree programs in sport psychology, 1989 to 1994. *The Sport Psychologist, 11,* 326–344.

Association for the Advancement of Applied Sport Psychology (1990). Certification criteria. *AAASP Newsletter, 5,* 1, 3, 8.

Association for the Advancement of Applied Sport Psychology (1996). *Ethics code of the Association for the Advancement of Applied Sport Psychology.* Retrieved December 7, 2004, from http://www.aaasponline.org/governance/committees/ethics/standards.php

Association for the Advancement of Applied Sport Psychology (2003). *Standard application form: Certified Consultant AAASP.* Retrieved December 7, 2004, from http://www.aaasponline.org/cc/pdf/standard.pdf

Brown, J. M. (1982). Are sport psychologists really psychologists? *Journal of Sport Psychology, 4,* 13–18.

Burke, K. L., Sachs, M. L., & Smisson, C. P. (2004). *Directory of graduate programs in applied sport psychology* (7th Ed.). Morgantown, WV: Fit Information Technology.

Clark, B. (2003, June 28). UO making some changes in football locker room. *The Register Guard,* D1.

Cobanoglu, C., Warde, B., & Moreo, P. J. (2001). A comparison of mail, fax and web-based survey methods. *International Journal of Market Research, 43,* 441–452.

Cook, S. W., Darley, J. G., Jacobsen, C., Kelly, G., Russell, R. W., & Sanford, N. (1958). Committee on relations with psychiatry. *American Psychologist, 13,* 761–763.

Dishman, R. K. (1983). Identity crisis in North American sport psychology: Academics in professional issues. *Journal of Sport Psychology, 5,* 123–134.

Dunlap, E. (1999). *An assessment of the nature and prevalence of sport psychology service provision in professional sports.* Unpublished master's thesis, University of North Carolina, Chapel Hill, North Carolina.

Ellis, A. (1962). *Reason and emotion in psychotherapy.* New York: Lyle Stuart.

Feltz, D. L. (1987). The future of graduate education in sport and exercise science: A sport psychology perspective. *Quest, 39,* 217–223.

Fisher, K. (September, 1982). Sport psychology comes of age in the 80s. *American Psychological Association Monitor, 1,* 8–13.

Freud, S. (1900). *New introductory lectures on psychoanalysis: New introductory lectures on psychoanalysis.* New York: Norton.

Give it a rest, Jerry. (1996, April 14). *The News and Observer,* p. 11C.

Glasser, W. (1965). *Reality therapy: A new approach to psychiatry.* New York: Harper & Row.

Gosling, S. D., Vazire, S., Srivatava, S., & John, O. P. (2004). Should we trust web-based studies? A comparative analysis of six preconceptions about Internet questionnaires. *American Psychologist, 59,* 93–104.

Gould, D., Horn, T., & Spreeman, J. (1983). Sources of stress in junior elite wrestlers. *Journal of Sport Psychology, 5,* 159–171.

Hanin, Y. L. (2000). Individual zones of optimal functioning (IZOF) model: Emotion-performance relationships in sport. In Y. L. Hanin (Ed.), *Emotions in sport* (pp. 65-89). Champaign, IL: Human Kinetics.

Harrison, R. P., & Feltz, D. L. (1979). The professionalization of sport psychology: Legal considerations. *Journal of Sport Psychology, 1,* 182–190.

Heinlen, K. T., Welfel, E. R., Richmond, E. N., & O'Donnell, M. S. (2003). The nature, scope, and ethics of psychologists' e-therapy web sites: What consumers find when surfing the web. *Psychotherapy: Theory, Research, Practice, Training, 40,* 112–124.

Howard, B., Paridaens, O., & Gramm, B. (2001, 2nd Quarter). Information security: Threats and protection mechanisms [Electronic version]. *Alcatel Telecommunications Review,* 117–121.

Howard, G. S. (1993). Sports psychology: An emerging domain for counseling psychologists. *The Counseling Psychologist, 21,* 349–351.

Joint Interim Committee for the Identification and Recognition of Specialties and Proficiencies (1995). *Principles for the recognition of proficiencies in professional psychology.* Retrieved May 23, 2004, from http://www.apa.org/crsppp/ prof-principles.html

Kraut, R., Olson, J., Banaji, M., Bruckman, A., Cohen, J., & Couper, M. (2004). Psychological research online: Report of Board of Scientific Affairs' Advisory Group on the conduct of research on the Internet. *American Psychologist, 59,* 105–117.

Kroll, W. (1979). The stress of high performance athletics. In P. Klavora & J. V. Daniel (Eds.), *Coach, athlete and the sport psychologist.* Champaign, IL: Human Kinetics.

Maheu, M. M., & Gordon, B. L. (2000). Counseling and therapy on the Internet. *Professional Psychology: Research and Practice, 31,* 484–489.

Mahoney, M. J. (1987). Thoughts on academic preparation in sports psychology. *AAASP Newsletter, 2,* 6–7.

Manhal-Baugus, M. (2001). E-therapy: Practical, ethical, and legal issues. *CyberPsychology & Behavior,* 4, 551–563.

Martens, R. (1980). From smocks to jocks: A new adventure for sport psychologists. In P. Klavora & K. A. W. Wipper (Eds.), *Psychological and sociological factors in sport* (pp. 20-26). Toronto: University of Toronto, Publications Division.

McNair, D., Lorr, M., & Droppleman, L. (1992). *Profile of Mood States manual.* San Diego: Educational and Industrial Testing Service.

Meichenbaum, D. (1973). *Cognitive behavior motivation.* New York: Plenum.

Meyers, A. W., Coleman, J. K., Whelan, J. P., & Mehlenbeck, R. S. (2001). Examining careers in sport psychology: Who is working and who is making money? *Professional Psychology: Research and Practice,* 32, 5–11.

Naglieri, J. A., Drasgow, F., Schmit, M., Handler, L., Prifitera, A., & Margolis, A. (2004). Psychological testing on the Internet: New problems, old issues. *American Psychologist,* 59, 150–162.

National Board for Certified Counselors (2004). *National Certified Counselor 2004 application packet.* Retrieved April 15, 2004, from http://www.nbcc.org/pdfs/cert/NCCApplication.pdf

Nickelson, D. W. (1998). Telehealth and the evolving health care system: Strategic opportunities for professional psychology. *Professional Psychology: Research and Practice,* 29, 527–535.

Nideffer, R., Feltz, D. L., & Salmela, J. (1982). A rebuttal to Danish and Hale: A committee report. *Journal of Sport Psychology,* 4, 3–6.

Petrie, T. A., & Watkins, C. E. (1994). Sport psychology training in counseling psychology programs: Is there room at the inn? *Counseling Psychologist,* 22, 335–341.

Perls, F., Hefferline, R. F., & Goodman, P. (1951). *Gestalt therapy.* New York: Dell.

Pew Internet & American Life Project (2003). *America's online pursuits: The changing picture of who's online and what they do.* Retrieved May 23, 2004, from http://www.pewinternet.org/reports/pdfs/PIP_Online_Pursuits_Final.pdf

Rogers, C. R. (1951). *Client-centered therapy.* Boston: Houghton-Mifflin.

Scanlan, T. K., & Passer, M. W. (1979). Sources of competitive stress in young female athletes. *Journal of Sport and Exercise Psychology,* 1, 151–159.

Silva, J. M., Cornelius, A. E., Conroy, D. E., Petersen, G. E. B., & Finch, L. M. (1996). Development and validation of the Precompetitive Stress Inventory. Unpublished manuscript.

Silva, J. M. (1989). Establishing professional standards and advancing applied sport psychology research. *Journal of Applied Sport Psychology,* 1, 160–165.

Silva, J. M., Conroy, D.E., & Zizzi S.J. (1999). Critical issues confronting the advancement of applied sport psychology. *Journal of Applied Sport Psychology,* 11, 163–197.

Singer, R. N. (1987). Thoughts on academic preparation in sports psychology. *AAASP Newsletter,* 2, 8–9.

Skinner, B. F. (1953). *Science and human behavior.* New York: Macmillan.

Suler, J. R. (2000). Psychotherapy in cyberspace: A 5-dimensional model of online and computer-mediated psychotherapy. *CyberPsychology & Behavior,* 3, 151–159.

Taylor, J. (1991). Career direction, development, and opportunities in applied sport psychology. *Sport Psychologist,* 5, 266–280.

US Bureau of the Census (1995). *Statistical Abstracts of the United States: 1995* (115th Edition). Washington, DC: US Department of Commerce.

US Bureau of Labor Statistics (1996). *Occupational Outlook Handbook* (January 1996). Washington DC: US Department of Labor.

Voight, M., & Callaghan, J. (2001). The use of sport psychology services at NCAA Division I universities from 1998–1999. *The Sport Psychologist,* 15, 91–102.

Waite, B. T., & Pettit, M. E. (1993). Work experiences of graduates from doctoral programs in sport psychology. *Journal of Applied Sport-Psychology,* 5, 234–250.

Weinberg, R. S., & Gould, D. (1999). *Foundations of sport and exercise psychology* (2nd ed.). Champaign, IL: Human Kinetics.

Williams, J. M., & Scherzer, C. B. (2003). Tracking the training and careers of graduates of advanced degree programs in sport psychology, 1994 to 1999. *Journal of Applied Sport Psychology,* 15, 335–353.

CHAPTER 3

Initiating Counselor
Development

This chapter examines the interpersonal context of applied sport psychology as well as theoretical foundations for interventions that are necessary for initiating counselor development. The unique professional relationship that can develop when working with healthy individuals who want to enhance their performances is discussed. As an interpersonal process, readers are challenged to self-reflect on their anxieties about, and motives for, practicing sport psychology. The chapter then expands on the philosophy of the science-practice model and interdisciplinary training by detailing aspects of sport, psychology, and specifically sport psychology that should be learned by the aspiring professional. Knowledgeable clinicians can also enhance their consultation process by developing certain desirable qualities that are reviewed in this chapter. Concerns regarding to whom the developing sport psychology consultant is obligated (e.g., team, coach, or individual athlete) are discussed, along with many of the unique challenges related to maintaining client confidentiality in the sport setting. The chapter provides information to assist the developing clinician make decisions regarding information sharing, time commitments, and compensation for services. Readers will also learn client characteristics to be aware of that may require referrals to other helping professionals with relevant competence. The chapter concludes with a brief discussion of theoretical approaches used in sport psychology consultation including behavioral and cognitive-behavioral as well as less commonly used approaches.

Counseling and the Intervention Process

Some coaches and athletes hold a common misconception: athletes who work with sport psychologists are "head cases" or "mentally weak." Our experience has been that most of the athletes we have worked with are psychologically healthy individuals. Many of these athletes possess a desire to improve performance or overcome a specific psychological issue related to inconsistent or sub-par performance. If an athlete is experiencing serious mental health matters that may involve pathology, a referral to a licensed clinical psychologist is recommended. Participation in a stressful environment, such as sport, is not a positive or desirable situation for a person experiencing pathology or a significant mental health crisis. The well-being of the person should always take priority over an emphasis on performance.

Sport psychology is concerned with maximizing individual potential in the athletic arena. Although a difficult goal for any performer, enhanced performance can occur through the development and promotion of adaptive behavior in practice and competition. To accomplish this goal, a sport psychologist must be prepared to apply a body of knowledge drawn from sport psychology, psychology, counseling, and other related disciplines. Using this information, the clinician initiates a process of influence or intervention designed to enhance player performance. Through the intervention process, counselors and clients alike gain insight into the motives influencing many behaviors. When properly conducted, intervention is a process of self-exploration and self-disclosure for the client. The sport psychologist must be prepared to guide this exploration and assist the client in processing whatever information is generated during sessions. Depending on the quality of the counseling relationship and the nature of the performance concern, the intervention process can lead to sensitive subject matters. Consequently, the sport psychology counseling relationship has the potential to be an intense professional relationship, one that the practicing professional needs to be properly prepared to manage.

Counselor Concerns

The possibility of experiencing a little anxiety prior to a counseling session is not isolated only to the client. Before entering any counseling relationship, sport psychology counselors must be aware of their own psychological strengths, weaknesses, and personal needs. Sport psychology counselors should not enter into helping relationships if they are uncertain as to why they are seeking such relationships, or if there is some concern regarding their own motive for practicing sport psychology. An effective way to develop an awareness of one's own needs is through supervised practice. Experienced supervisors can assist trainees in developing an awareness of their needs and motivations for entering into a helping relationship with athletes. Individuals with unmet personal needs must be made aware of these needs before they enter into a counseling relationship where the possibility for transference and counter-transference exists.

Although supervision is critical for graduate students interested in practicing sport psychology, it is equally important that supervised experiences are available to all professionals who lack specific counseling experiences with athletes and coaches. Even experienced practicing sport psychology consultants should occasionally seek out fellow professionals with whom they can discuss cases and intervention strategies. Supervision by an experienced sport psychology clinician will polish one's counseling skills and enhance the likelihood of identifying when personal needs are being inappropriately transferred into a professional relationship. Supervision is a fundamental and necessary experience in the growth and development process for all counselors in training. Through this experience many positive qualities can be developed and enhanced in the counselor-in-training. The counselor-in-training is constantly developing knowledge and skill with the aid of experienced guidance. With increased interaction with athletes during actual intervention, counselor concerns often diminish significantly. Below are some fundamental questions all sport psychology counselors in training should address.

Why Do I Want to Practice Sport Psychology: What Are My Motives?

Understanding personal motives for engaging in sport psychology practice is extremely important. Specifically, such motives can influence how and why one enters a professional consulting relationship. How an individual works with an athlete, coach, parent, or team during professional interactions, as well as how professional relationships are developed, maintained, and disengaged, are all influenced by the individual's motives to practice. Why do you want to practice sport psychology? Some individuals are interested in working with professional teams or Olympic teams. It often takes many years of quality practice to develop a professional clientele that includes Olympic athletes, Olympic teams, or professional athletes and teams. Young or inexperienced professionals often must provide free services so that they can gain greater experience and, hopefully, gain the confidence of athletes, coaches, and athletic administrators. Some individuals who are interested in practicing sport psychology experienced injury or loss as an athlete themselves, and they believe they can assist athletes in similar situations. Sport psychology is a helping-based profession. If a person is truly motivated by the need to help others in the specific context of sport, they will find themselves well prepared, psychologically and emotionally, to manage some of the unique difficulties that characterize the practice of sport psychology.

For example, university professors interested in providing consulting services to athletic teams at their school may find that this work is not valued by their department as a formal part of their assigned duties. Consulting with the athletic department may not be viewed as relevant or formally considered for tenure and promotion decisions. The university professor may also be expected to provide services pro bono to university teams and national teams. Providing some service pro bono is often a necessity for inexperienced practicing psychologists and counselors. Unfortunately, since most individual athletes and athletic administrators do not know where to look for certified sport psychology consultants (Dunlap, 1999), word-of-mouth recommendation remains a major method of referral in sport psychology. The development of a client base is somewhat a function of successful experiences with clients. These clients may provide teammates with information on how to contact you for service provision. Many students and professionals exit the profession of sport psychology just as quickly as they entered because they did not fully examine and explore their personal motives for practicing sport psychology, nor did they understand the unique aspects of gaining entrance to practice for pay in the world of sport.

If you desire to be a competent and successful practicing sport psychology counselor, there are several hurdles you must be aware of and willing to jump. Knowing this information and reflecting upon these realities before making a commitment to the field could prevent career change. Perspective is one of the most powerful helping tools a professional can offer during the consulting process. A fundamental knowledge of sport psychology, a sound perspective about oneself, and an understanding of the role of potential contributor to the personal development of athletes will provide the counselor with a solid foundation to practice.

What Should I Know About Sport Psychology?

It is hard to imagine that professionals at any level-novice or established-would not strive to be as knowledgeable as possible in their chosen field. Yet, sport psychology is constantly besieged by gurus who claim instant knowledge and practice skills in a field they have never studied or in which they have not received supervised training or practice experience. While Gardner (1991) has suggested that sport psychology is simply another social setting for which the principles of psychology can be generalized, this logic is rarely used in any other branch of psychology (Silva, 1989; Silva, Conroy, and Zizzi, 1999). Specialized training and supervised internship experiences are required for child psychologists, family and marriage counselors, and counselors specializing in eating disorders or substance abuse. Sub-disciplines exist in such professions as medicine and law that require years of specialized training and supervised clinical work. Is sport psychology somehow different? Is the practice of sport psychology not worthy of the same systematic approach to professional development and training?

Psychology would be a powerful field, indeed, if there were some simple set of principles that could generalize to various settings and complex interpersonal situations resulting in effective intervention and meaningful behavior change. It seems prudent for a fledging profession, such as sport psychology, to produce generations of practitioners who have a scientific base for practice, are knowledgeable of the nuances in the sport culture, and have supervised practical experiences in the sport. The sport psychology practitioner must possess a working knowledge of both theory and research in sport psychology. Knowing information from a textbook is not the same as applying that knowledge on the spot during a counseling session with an athlete. There is little time for reflection during a session, and a trained clinician must pick up essential content that is provided by an athlete in a stream of consciousness. This information must be digested and understood instantaneously by clinicians so they can provide smooth transitions to appropriate follow-up questions or comments. Sport psychology counselors must know the body of knowledge at a very high level of proficiency before they can attempt to practice the application of this information.

What Should I Know About Sport?

This very important question has several perspectives attached to its answer. The specific knowledge the clinician possesses about a specific sport or the sport culture, in general, could influence his or her own confidence as a sport psychology counselor. Equally important is the possession (or lack) of sport-specific knowledge that could influence the athlete or coach's perception of competence in you, as a sport psychology counselor. At the very least, a working knowledge of the sport is required. If you are going to work with volleyball, for example, you should have knowledge of that sport. If you are not familiar with the sport, you should do the following before you consult:

1. Learn the rules of the sport-buy a rule book.
2. Observe the sport several times with an expert (a previous player, coach, or knowledgeable recreational player) who can answer any questions you may have.
3. If at all possible, participate recreationally in the sport yourself.
4. Develop an appreciation of the physical, psychological, and emotional challenges the sport provides to participants.

Most athletes and coaches expect you to be familiar with their sport and to have some understanding and respect for what is required physically, psychologically, technically, and tactically for success. Although athletes may find it amusing to educate the "old Doc" on the basics of their sport, this amusement evaporates quickly when athletes realize they are spending significant amounts of their session time explaining fundamental aspects of their sport to you. It would be understandable if athletes were to become concerned with your fundamental lack of knowledge of their sport and the nature of athletic experiences in that sport. "You just do not understand where I am coming from" is a common cry often heard by parents who are disconnected from the culture of their children. It would be easy for athletes to believe that your lack of immersion in their culture will limit your ability to understand and relate to their complex competitive issues. The individual interested in practicing sport psychology should take pleasure in learning about the competitive sport environment. Knowledge of the sport will facilitate a smoother session and a deeper and broader grasp of what an athlete is communicating to you. The more you know about a sport, the better. **All counseling is a process of influence. In that regard, sport psychology counseling is no different from counseling in other specializations.** If you gain the confidence and respect of the athlete you are working with through a command of both sport and psychology, your ability to influence the athlete will be enhanced.

What Should I Know About Psychology?

The past decade has witnessed a change in the preparation of undergraduate students interested in continuing their graduate education in sport psychology. During the 1960s and 1970s most students attending graduate school in sport psychology received their undergraduate training in traditional physical education departments. The likelihood of such a student receiving considerable course work in psychology was very low since physical education departments of the 1960s and 1970s were primarily oriented toward teacher preparation. The decade of the 1970s marked the beginning of specialized course work in the exercise and sport sciences. The move toward specialization in the exercise and sport sciences resulted in higher levels of training in specializations including exercise physiology, motor learning, biomechanics, and sport psychology. This new model in the exercise and sport sciences created a greater opportunity for sport psychology students to be exposed to various educational experiences in the discipline of psychology. This progression led undergraduate students who were interested in sport psychology to major in psychology or counseling or to double major in exercise and sport science and psychology/counseling. Most students currently applying to graduate programs in sport psychology have broad exposure to both psychology and the exercise sciences, as well as specific exposure to sport psychology. Students interested in sport psychology should be well grounded in social psychology, counseling psychology, adolescent psychology, psychology of learning, biopsychology, health psychology, psychopathology, ethical issues in psychology, and psychometrics.

Training in psychology at the graduate level has traditionally presented some obstacles for the student interested in sport psychology. The perception of physical education departments as a "jock" major still exists in the minds of professionals in some academic majors. The rigor of an exercise and sport science major has been well established for twenty years. The lag time in communicating this change across campus has been considerable but appears to be ending. The most effective way to continue to blaze a trail into graduate courses in psychology is through positive communication between professors of sport psychology and colleagues in the psychology and counseling departments. The continued exposure of psychology professors to sport psychology students in the classroom and the participation of psychology/counseling professors on sport psychology thesis and dissertation committees enhance the understanding of sport psychology research and practice. The relationship between sport psychology and psychology/counseling should evolve to the point where the graduate course work, research, and practical experiences are jointly planned by sport psychology and psychology/counseling faculty.

Each generation of sport psychology professionals should be better prepared to teach, research, and practice sport psychology. Sport psychology professors and sport psychology graduate students must work together with psychology and counseling professors to create the exposure and educational environment necessary for the properly trained professional of tomorrow. Through progressive educational and practical experiences, future sport psychology counselors will possess the knowledge and hands-on experience needed for a quality practice with athletes.

Desirable Clinician Qualities

The intervention process can be facilitated through the development of various clinician qualities. Consulting with an athlete is a very personal experience, and the development and enhancement of human qualities can be a great asset. This is particularly true when working through personally sensitive material that has affected the athlete's sense of well being. Important qualities that can facilitate the intervention process and nurture the relationship between the athlete and the sport psychology counselor reflect a wide array of interpersonal skills. Major interpersonal qualities include the following:

Be a caring person—show empathy. Show the athlete that your first priority is his or her well-being. Remember you are working with a fellow human being who happens to be an athlete. It is extremely difficult for many athletes to completely separate the athletic self from other aspects of their identity. Basic empathy is communicating your understanding of the athlete's point of view with respect to thoughts, feelings, and behaviors (Ivey & Ivey, 2003). Focusing on the client's point of view is useful in establishing and developing rapport and helping to clarify the presenting issues. Eventually, the empathic consultant creates an intervention to help alleviate the concern.

Be patient and invest in the athlete. Patience is essential when working with any client. An athlete may be hesitant to reveal important information to the sport psychology counselor. The sport psychology counselor must know when to talk and when to remain silent and must be patient, staying with the discussion, particularly when the athlete tries to be evasive. Exercising a little patience and allowing the client clinician relationship to develop is often rewarded with more meaningful disclosure by the client. Observing practices and competitions, in a non-obtrusive manner, demonstrates that you are working with the athletes and shows that you are invested in their improvement. When athletes understand that you are invested in their development, they work with you more effectively, and both parties achieve the possibility for greater success.

Be honest and expect honesty. This perspective should be established in the first session of any intervention. Honesty should be the standard operating procedure for each session. This is not to say that the sport psychology counselor must reveal personal material at each session; however, personal experiences can be used as an indirect platform to foster teachable moments. Without a base of honesty no intervention can be successful, because the course of action initiated by the sport psychology counselor is predicated on accurate athlete information.

Build trust. When working in almost any field, especially counseling, building trust lends credibility to the relationship. A sport psychology counselor must develop trust not only with the athletes, but also with related professionals, such as the athletic trainer, athletic administrators, and strength coaches. If the athletes trust the sport psychology counselor, then they will believe that the counselor cares about them and is working for them. Much like the relationship between a coach and an athlete, once the line of trust is broken between an athlete and the sport psychology counselor, it is very difficult to get back the athlete's trust. A sport psychology counselor should not underestimate the power of trust in the intervention process.

Be emotionally stable. Relating to the athlete's concerns and situation is important; however, the athlete must sense that you are stable and not overwhelmed by the issues brought forth in the intervention sessions. Be prepared for anything and do not let anything an athlete says surprise you. Supervised experiences are extremely important in preparing a sport psychology counselor for the intensity and diversity of issues that can be shared by an athlete during sessions.

Project confidence, but be human. The sport psychology counselor must formulate a course of action based on the information provided by the athlete. There will be times when the sport psychology counselor will make a mistake or be off in his or her formulation of the concern. It is more important to get it right than to be right. You are the expert, but if you make an obvious mistake, take responsibility for it; if something is not working, reformulate. Athletes and coaches are often turned off by consultants who present themselves as professionals who seem to know it all and have all the right answers. Learn how to use your expertise to work for and with, rather than against, the athlete or coach.

Have a good work rate. Be sure that at the end of each session, some notable progress has been made. Athletes are looking for improvement-do not consistently waste their time because you lack direction or are unfamiliar with their specific sport. Diligently prepare in advance for each session, especially when you are an inexperienced sport psychology counselor. Although it is important to be sociable with the athlete, the session should always have substance and be of significance for the athlete. All athletes want to sense that they are making progress and that their time in session is well spent.

Be cooperative. There are times when the athlete may need to change a session or miss a session for a good reason. Cooperating with the athlete will often be rewarded by the athlete cooperating with you in a future session. Remember, you are developing a two-way relationship with the athlete. Being cooperative is often viewed as a sign of respect by an athlete or coach. A simple cooperative gesture can enhance the quality of the relationship since there may be a perception of inequity of status between a coach/athlete and a sport psychology consultant.

Have a sense of humor. It is amazing how much more information you can receive from athletes when they are relaxed and they appreciate your sense of humor. If you want the athlete to loosen up, sometimes you need to loosen up yourself. People have a tendency to speak more freely when they are relaxed and trusting. A little humor often goes a long way in creating a comfortable working relationship.

Maintain listening skills. If you cannot listen to an athlete, you are missing your most valuable source of information. The sport psychology counselor should interrupt the athlete as little as possible; do not talk over an athlete. When athletes are on a roll, let them go! Do not interfere with their train of thought, unless it is absolutely necessary. Sport psychology counselors need the athletes' information before they can formulate a course of intervention, and the art of listening is more complex than one might think. To fully understand the concern put forth by the athlete, the professional must listen to what the athlete is saying, which includes implied messages. A good listener will understand the overt as well as the subtle messages. Corey (2005) suggests that listening includes the art of active listening; in other words, actually hearing the real message the athlete is trying to send. It is only when active listening is employed that the sport psychology counselor can step into the athlete's shoes and develop a better understanding of his or her concerns.

Apply communication skills. Some of the best communication you may have with an athlete can be the by-product of a question you ask. Most clinicians have no trouble communicating their information to an athlete, but communication is two-way interaction! Communication received from an athlete is often the crucial information around which a course of action is planned. Communication is often facilitated by the use of appropriate eye contact with the client. Typically, eye contact assures the client that the consultant is carefully listening to his or her concerns, but sport psychology counselors should be sensitive to the fact that some athlete's cultural background may discourage direct eye contact.

Promote breadth of thinking. Help the athlete see the big picture. It is so easy for an athlete to get bogged down with the difficulties of the moment. This is especially true if the athlete has not previously dealt with athletic failure or setback in a significant and meaningful manner. Help the athlete see the bigger picture, such as the opportunity to earn more playing time, to gain a starting position later in the season, or to see how this year's hard work could pay off next season. Breadth of thinking can facilitate motivation and sustain athlete effort when immediate performance results may be a low probability.

Offer a sense of the future. Project a realistic level of optimism when working with an athlete. If athletes think you do not see any hope for change in the future, why should they keep coming back to speak with you? Stay positive, facilitate change, and project change as a viable future option for the athletes and their specific situations.

As sport psychology counselors gain more experience and success working with athletes, they will feel greater confidence in their ability to assist an athlete, and to influence that individual in a positive and meaningful manner. The development of counselor competence includes being familiar with the dynamics of the athlete's sport and the particular position an athlete may play on a team. The dynamics of the sport environment are unique and, as discussed in chapter two, characteristics unique to sport necessitate specialized training and familiarity with sport and the subculture around various sports. When sport psychology counselors feel comfortable with their counseling skills, their working knowledge of sport psychology, and their understanding of the specific performance demands of athletes' sports and positions, several major counselor concerns will diminish in frequency and intensity. The sport psychology counselors will spend less time monitoring their own competence and behavior and will be able to focus more effectively on the athletes' concerns in the sessions.

Client Concerns and Client Welfare

Entering into a professional relationship with a sport psychology counselor is often new ground for an athlete, a coach, or a team. Each party may have a number of questions that relate to the nature of the interaction and the potential role of each party in the intervention process. There are several logistical models of intervention that vary significantly in their perspective and process. For example, a sport psychology counselor may be working with an athlete without the knowledge of the coach. A concerned parent, or the athlete himself or herself, may have contacted the sport psychology counselor and requested services. The coach may be seen as the issue or the reason for conflict. Another model exists when a sport psychology counselor is hired (paid) by a professional organization to work with a team. Who is the client now? Is the management privy to conversations between the sport psychology counselor and the athlete because the organization has hired the consultant? Another common possibility is a coach using athletic department money for a sport psychology counselor to work with a college team in a group setting and with select individual athletes. Does the collegiate coach have a right to expect feedback about the team and about specific individuals when the coach is in consultation with the sport psychology counselor? Many sport psychology counselors work with Olympic National Governing Bodies (NGBs), providing both team and individual athlete services. This setting creates a situation where not only the coach but also the Chair of the National Team may seek information about the nature of the sport psychology counselor's interactions with athletes. All of these situations create a potential controversy regarding the very cornerstone of successful sport psychology intervention-client confidentiality.

Client Confidentiality

Client confidentiality can become complicated quickly in the field of sport psychology. Often you are not simply in a client-counselor relationship, since a coach may know of the interaction or a parent may be involved in the situation.

> *An athlete comes to speak with you, but the coach is the one who requested that you speak with the player. The coach wants to know everything that goes on between you and the athlete, and the coach calls your office each week to ask if the athlete has come in to see you. The coach usually leads with, "How is everything going with Carly this week?"*

How would you manage this situation? Would you tell the coach what you and the athlete discussed? Would you tell the coach that you could not reveal any information? How will your answer affect your relationship with the coach and with the athlete, and how will it affect your future ability to work with this coach and team?

Sport psychology is unique. Working with a high-visibility collegiate athletic program, an Olympic team, or a professional athlete can thrust a sport psychology counselor into a complicated vortex of variables without warning. The higher the visibility of the program or the athlete you work with, the greater probability of media involvement or curiosity. A misguided comment about a high-visibility athlete or a prominent team can spread through the media world in a matter of moments. Today, the Internet can instantly transmit information to the entire world. In the very small world of sport, a fatal misspeak with a high-profile person or program can be very costly to a professional's future career opportunities.

A sport psychology counselor who is considered part of the staff can experience both subtle and not-so-subtle pressures to be part of the management team. Are you working with and for the athlete, or with the coach or general manager? Is it possible to work for both the player and the management and not compromise trust with either? Is it appropriate to provide insight to the coach or general manager into why a player is not performing or is unhappy or in conflict with teammates?

There is no faster way to undermine the relationship between a sport psychology counselor and an athlete than by a perceived breach in trust. It is not important if a breach actually occurred. The perception of a breach in trust can change the nature of the relationship in an irreparable manner. The essence of a productive counseling relationship is mutual trust. The sport psychology counselor must believe that the athlete is telling the truth, and the athlete must trust that the counselor will protect and preserve client confidentiality. **Athletes may opt out of intervention or simply shut down in future sessions if they believe that a sport psychology counselor is speaking with a coach or management about issues brought up in session, particularly when these issues may be very sensitive, personal, or about the coach or the management.**

An athlete's parents must be informed that information shared by their son or daughter is confidential and that this information will not be shared with the parent, unless there is a life- threatening situation. If parents insist that they should be privy to the athlete's issues because they are paying for it, the sport psychology counselor should help the parents understand why the relationship could be destroyed if confidentiality is breached. A potential solution may involve engaging a parent, or both parents, in some of the sessions. This should be done only if the sport psychology counselor believes this would be in the best interest of the child athlete. Parental involvement, unless requested by the sport psychology counselor, can lead to a strained relationship between the young athlete and the sport psychology counselor. It is hard for a high-school- or college-age athlete to connect with a sport psychology counselor if the athlete believes the counselor regularly reports back to his or her parents.

Similar ground rules must be established when working with a collegiate athletic department, an Olympic team, or a professional team. The pressure from coaches and management for information about a specific athlete can be enormous when working with multi-million-dollar-salaried athletes. These athletes can be viewed in a business model as team assets or team liabilities. Rather than risk the likelihood of being fired after establishing relationships with players and teams, sport psychology counselors are wise to clearly establish their position on client confidentiality before they are hired by a professional organization. Being seen as an insider by players will not maximize a sport psychology counselor's effectiveness and will most likely minimize the opportunity for any significant interactions with players. Unfortunately, some professional teams employ consultants who feed information about players to management and become viewed as the house psychologist by the players. Players learn to play the game and tell the house psychologist only what they want that person to hear. This model illustrates the practice of sport psychology in its worst form.

The sport psychology counselor must be very careful from both an ethical and practical perspective when addressing the matter of client confidentially. Client confidentiality should be a priority when establishing the terms of engagement with an individual athlete, a team, or management. The sensitivity of client confidentiality cannot be overstated or underestimated by the sport psychology counselor.

Time Commitment

Athletes, coaches, and team management always seem to be constrained by time compression. Collegiate athletes have school work, practice schedules, travel, competition, and social and family life pushed into an academic semester. Professional athletes have competition schedules that dwarf the college season, in terms of length and travel demands. The athlete and coach are always on the go during the competitive season and value any free time they may have to relax and share with friends and family. Sport psychology can be viewed as an effective use of time or as just another thing to take up the little free time the athlete enjoys. Often the coach wants to know, "How long is this going to take?" or "How much of our time will you need?" When presented in this manner it sounds like the coach is unhappily "working in" the sport psychology program. Although psychological aspects of competition are frequently discussed by coaches, players, media, and fans, counseling is often viewed as something extra in the schedule. Just like the coach, an athlete may ask, "How long will this take?" Parents who are paying for their child's service often want to know, "How many sessions before Johnny gets better, and how much is this going to cost?"

Of course there is no magic number of sessions, and it is difficult to predict a timeline for psychological improvement. Unlike physical training, where an athlete can expect to see some tangible results in six to eight weeks, sport psychology consultation may produce results in a month, or it may require several months before notable or quantifiable results can be documented. It is a tricky proposition to predict a timeline for results before you interview the athlete and initiate the information-gathering process. So how should a sport psychology counselor manage this obvious and important question that is sure to present itself prior to a financial commitment by a parent, athlete, coach, or organization? It is perhaps best to define an initial period of time agreeable to you and the client or organization. After this period the parent, the athlete, or the team can make educated decisions concerning continuance of service.

A consultant needs to receive enough of a time commitment by the athlete or organization to allow the consulting relationship to develop and evolve. There must be an identification of issues, approaches to resolve these issues, and adjustments to the initial intervention plan. When working with an individual athlete, a consultant should consider a time frame of between 8 and 12 weeks based on a 60- to 90-minute session per meeting. This time frame will give both the sport psychology consultant and the athlete plenty of time to move well into an intervention and assess the progress made. When working with an organization, a consultant should consider a minimum of 12 months, because of the complexities that will be involved in connecting with coaches, management, team, and individual players. Even in organizations where there is support for sport psychology services, a consultant will encounter some resistance at some level of the organization. It may be a star player saying, "Anyone who needs sport psychology is weak-minded." It may be a coach or management person "going along with it" but working behind the scenes to make sure the consulting does not go too far. It will take time to integrate a sport psychology program into any organization, and a significant amount of time is needed to permit a fair and reasonable evaluation of the fit between the sport psychology counselor and the players, coaches, and the organization. In most cases, one year will be enough time to determine whether continuation between the two parties is desirable.

When the macro concerns about time commitment have been addressed, the sport psychology counselor must focus on the more tangible micro aspects of time commitment and scheduling. Since most teams work from daily, weekly, monthly, and seasonal schedules, setting a schedule can actually be fairly simple with athletes and athletic teams. The athletes know when their free time is during the season and during the off-season (scheduled off-season mini-camps for pro teams are often set well in advance), and coaches have the days and weeks scheduled to the hour and minute during the season. Fitting into the athlete's schedule, in a predictable and consistent manner, fits into the flow of the week and the flow of the season. Of course there will be instances when flexibility is needed and rescheduling necessary; however, establishing a day and time, and making it routine, gives the athlete structure. The last thing a busy professional or collegiate athlete needs is to keep track of the constantly changing day and time of appointments with the sport psychology consultant. The same analogy can be made for meeting with the coaches and management if these meetings are part of your program. Schedule and lock in a day and time that generally fits their schedule. Sport psychology then becomes part of the routine for the athlete, the coach, and the organization. An organized and professional schedule, established at the very beginning of the commitment process, will be to the benefit of all parties.

Compensation for Services

How much do I charge for a consultation service? How many times have graduate students and young professionals asked this question at AAASP conferences over the past twenty years? How much one should charge for services is often uncharted territory in sport psychology. There is little published information that provides guidance in this area; however, several common sense principles can help guide professionals when they are addressing the issue of compensation for services. First, it is important to remember your expertise is worth something. Many young professionals are concerned about charging for their services. If you are a trained professional, you should be compensated for your knowledge, specialized training, education, and time investment. If you are retooling or you are still in the process of receiving formal educational experiences or supervised practicum, perhaps compensation is not justified. In these situations, working with a team or an athlete (particularly if you will be interacting with or being supervised by an experienced AAASP-certified sport psychology professional) is worth something to you! Experience level, breadth of experience, specialized expertise in a sport, and expertise with a specialty position (place kicker, baseball pitcher) are all factors that can impact per-hour compensation. Taking the considerations noted above as guidance, a sport psychology service provider's compensation could range from $50 per hour (novice) to over $300 per hour (experienced and AAASP-certified). Compensation for legal services follows a similar sliding scale, with novice lawyers who have passed the bar receiving compensation in the $100 to $150 per hour range, and experienced lawyers receiving compensation from $300 to over $500 per hour (Ross, 2006).

The sport psychology professional should be aware of other factors that affect the issue of compensation for services rendered. Is the per-hour fee specifically for contact time in the office or will clients be charged for consulting time on the phone and on the Internet? If clients are to be charged for telecommunication contact, will the charges be at the same rate as the office contact charge? When working with a minor or an athlete who is not directly paying for the services rendered, compensation matters should not be discussed directly with the client. The matter is between the sport psychology professional and the parent or the entity that is providing the compensation. Often, when a young athlete or even a collegiate-age athlete becomes aware that parents or the team's budget is paying for their individual services, an awkward pressure can be placed on the athlete. Young athletes may feel pressure not to waste their parents' money and they may experience more performance pressure. College athletes may feel that they are receiving special treatment that other team members are not receiving, and they will be cheating the team and their teammates if they do not make dramatic improvements in performance. It is often best not to involve the athlete who is not directly providing the compensation in the discussion of or the delivery of payment for service.

These are important considerations for both the client and the sport psychology counselor. All contractual agreements should be clearly discussed and written out and signed by both parties before formal contact meetings or interactions via telephone or Internet are initiated. Addressing compensation and the schedule of compensation should be managed professionally, providing the client a period of time to reflect on the arrangements before deciding to start a consulting relationship. After compensation has been addressed and resolved, the client and the sport psychology counselor can initiate consultation and maintain full focus on the intervention process.

Compensation on a per-hour basis is a common practice in many professions; however, it is not the only compensation model available to a practicing sport psychology professional. Often, sport psychology counselors may have an opportunity to work with a part of a team or an entire team or to work with a professional athlete on an annual basis. Work with a small group (e.g., quarterbacks on a professional football team), an intact team (e.g., a professional baseball team), or an athlete over an annual period (e.g., a professional basketball player who wants consultation access for the full calendar year) can be contracted. When a contract price is negotiated, the sport psychology counselor must take into consideration many factors that could result in direct personal costs and significant consumption of the professional's time. For example, are travel, lodging, and meals calculated into the contracted cost? If the team or athlete contracts for on-site services, the consultant will be required to travel to the location of competitions and may be on-site for two days or possibly a week or more for golf and tennis events. Often this is dedicated time, and the sport psychology counselor may not be able to engage in many other personal or professional activities. This dedicated time often translates to 24 hours a day of service, since other personal and professional activities are not feasible while on-site. Significant amounts of time can be committed when on-site services are contracted between an athlete or team and a sport psychology counselor. The sport psychology counselor must carefully plan contracted services, particularly when they involve extensive travel and on-site service. There is no doubt that contracted services can be extremely beneficial to both parties. The sport psychology counselor has ample opportunity to directly observe the athlete or team in live competition, and the players or team have access to the sport psychology counselor at the competition venue. This type of service is often very appealing and exciting because you are there; however, the time commitment and potential for ancillary expenses must be calculated on a case-by-case basis. If contracted compensation is not carefully calculated, a sport psychology counselor may have a small number of clients contracted to a time commitment that exceeds a fair rate of compensation.

The Referral Process

Given that licensure as a sport psychologist does not exist in the field of sport psychology today, the practicing consultant may be faced with important referral decisions. When athletes' concerns seem to cross over from a performance enhancement concern to a clinical concern, consultants must appreciate and understand their competencies, as well as limitations. This understanding enhances the ability to determine when a referral is the appropriate action for a sport psychology counselor to take. All helping professionals should be familiar with appropriate ethical guidelines and be conscious about not practicing outside of their areas of expertise and training. Those practicing in the field of sport psychology should be familiar with AAASP and APA ethical guidelines, in particular.

Professionals will inevitably be faced with ethical dilemmas throughout their careers. Some of these dilemmas will revolve around the issue of the referral process. This is particularly true if a consultant is not a licensed counselor or licensed psychologist. An athlete may initially seek performance enhancement assistance but, after a couple of sessions, the athlete may present potential signs of a clinical concern.

You are working with an athlete who came to you on his own. In the initial intake sessions he clearly indicated he needed help dealing with his fear of failing and his fear of performing poorly. Now that a few sessions have been completed, the athlete feels more comfortable with you. He indicates that his fear of things is not only keeping him from performing his best on the field but it is growing. He mentions having fears about leaving his dorm room most days. He does not want to interact with friends or teammates, and he mentions that recently he has felt no desire to come into contact with the outside world.

How would you approach this situation? What ethical considerations would you have to consider? Would you refer the athlete to another professional? Would you address the problem yourself? What types of cues should a sport psychology counselor look for that may indicate the need for referral? Some common cues are provided below:

- The athlete constantly returns to a personal or family issue during sessions focused on performance enhancement. This may signal family problems, relationship/spouse concerns, or significant parental conflict.

- On several occasions toward the end of a session, the athlete indicates that there is something he or she wants to speak with you about next session but never brings up the issue. This may signal a possible lifestyle concern, an eating disorder, or concerns with interpersonal relations.

- The athlete constantly asks you if he or she is okay, crazy, normal, or really different from other athletes you have worked with. The athlete has poor grooming habits throughout the time spent with you. This may signal self-esteem concerns, inadequacy concerns, or concerns about his or her own well-being.

- The athlete repeatedly indicates that things are hopeless and cannot be changed. The athlete cries very easily and often during sessions. He or she has either not slept and/or eaten much, or has slept and/or eaten a great deal in the past few weeks. These concerns may signal the existence or the onset of depression.

- The athlete doubts everything he or she does, as well as everything the consultant recommends. The athlete constantly wants to know what time it is, and wants to know if he or she is "curable." This may signal possible anxiety concerns.

- The athlete speaks openly and coolly about hurting himself or herself or hurting others. This could reflect possible suicidal or hostile impulses toward self and others.

- The athlete indicates that he or she has given away personal items or no longer has any attachment to tangible and material possessions. This is a fairly common sign of the potential of suicidal thinking.

- The athlete "gets religion" or has a sudden and dramatic change in personal values or religious beliefs. This may suggest a significant lifestyle change, rejection of some form, or possible drug use.

- The athlete consistently describes himself or herself as being different from teammates-no one understands the athlete, and he or she is very confused about identity. This could be a preliminary indication of concerns about sexuality.

- The athlete routinely jokes about or downplays the use of alcohol, creatine, and/or performance-enhancing drugs and seems to have a preoccupation with substances. Such statements may reflect possible substance abuse or the consideration of using illegal substances.

- The athlete has noticeable mood swings (possible bipolar disorder concerns).

- There is a family history of a mental health disorder.

It is essential that the sport psychology counselor not trained to intervene in these matters refer the athlete. It is a very important matter for both the well-being of the athlete and the well-being of the client-counselor relationship. Any referral matter, unless it is deemed an emergency, should be discussed with the athlete. Sometimes just discussing the matter with the athlete will open a watershed of information and validate the need for a referral.

The referral should be done in the most considerate manner possible. If the athlete and the sport psychology counselor have developed a professional relationship, and the athlete does not want to see another mental health professional, a bridge must be built. If the athlete is resistant or wants the sport psychology counselor to address an issue he or she is not trained to address, a link must be formed between the athlete and the new mental health care professional. It may be necessary to go to the first meeting with the athlete, or have the new professional join you and the athlete for a session at your office.

After the referral relationship has been established, the sport psychology counselor and the mental health care professional should discuss whether it is in the best interests of the athlete to continue meeting with the sport psychology counselor, or whether the situation is best managed if the athlete suspends meetings with the sport psychology counselor. This can be a sensitive matter if the athlete has a very positive relationship with the sport psychology counselor and believes in the counselor's ability to assist him or her with personal as well as athletic situations. If the athlete is unstable, the professionals must work in concert to make sure the athlete does not feel abandoned or betrayed by someone the athlete trusted and had confidence in as a helping professional.

A referral list should be compiled by the sport psychology counselor. This list should contain contact information on various mental health care professionals with various specializations. The list should be made up of professionals with whom athletes have experienced positive interactions when referred in the past.

Theory-Based Intervention

A final area of discussion, relating to initiating counselor development, is the general theoretical orientation a counselor takes when working with an athlete or a team. There is no standard theoretical approach to intervention in general, athlete intervention, or intervention in the sport environment. The approaches reviewed in this text are commonly used in both sport and non-sport settings. Each approach to intervention has advantages and limitations, and it is necessary for the counselor to recognize how the advantages and limitations of an approach match up with his or her personal counseling skills and professional perspective on behavior change.

Behavioral Theory of Intervention

Behavioral interventions focus solely on understanding and influencing external actions. Behavioral interventions are grounded in several theoretical assumptions:

1. Human behavior is the result of learning (i.e., conditioning). Thus, maladaptive behavior, defined in sport as behavior that is counterproductive to optimal performance and function, results from previous experiences, not intrapsychic conflict or acute psychological trauma.

2. Adaptive behaviors can be strengthened while maladaptive behaviors are weakened by using learning principles.

3. Behavior is limited conceptually to specific situations and is uniquely defined by antecedents and consequences. For instance, an athlete may execute fluidly in most competitive situations but may hesitate in critical competitive situations. Importantly, behavioral consultation involves attending specifically to behavioral boundaries and defining how the athlete does and does not act in specific situations. Consultation from a behavioral perspective avoids applying broad labels to clients (e.g., "choker" in the previous example).

4. Given the specificity of the behavioral approach, behavioral counseling entails establishing precise goals for the intervention. Moreover, goal setting requires collaboration between consultant and athlete to ensure empowerment of the athlete.

5. Behavioral interventions are specifically customized for each athlete and focus on behavior in the present.

Behavioral interventions are unique in their emphasis on the specificity of goals. Consultants using behavioral interventions focus on changing a specifically targeted behavior. Of primary importance to the consultant is assessment of the problem. Behavioral problems must be clearly and accurately defined in order to precisely establish the target behavior, as well as its antecedents and consequences. If an athlete presents multiple problems, the consultant and athlete collaborate to determine the hierarchy of problems, prioritizing the sequence of problems to be addressed.

Several interventions applicable in sport psychology consultation can be categorized under the general heading of behavioral theory, including goal-setting (Locke, Shaw, Saari, & Latham, 1981; Weinberg & Weigand, 1993), covert modeling (Cautela, 1976; Cautela & Kearney, 1993), progressive relaxation training (Jacobson, 1939), and systematic desensitization (Wolpe, 1958; 1990). Each of these specific interventions can be used with athletes to systematically replace maladaptive behaviors with adaptive behaviors; however, these interventions, conceptualized from a behavioral perspective, fail to address internal processes of the client.

Cognitive-Behavioral Theory of Intervention

Working with cognitive behavior therapy (CBT) allows clients to understand how their behaviors, emotions, thoughts, and physiology are interrelated (Meichenbaum, 1977). As a result, change in any one of the four areas can facilitate change in the remaining three. CBT begins by addressing one's thoughts and looking for cognitive distortions, which may create and maintain maladaptive emotional and/or behavioral responses in an individual. Cognitive distortions are mistakes that individuals make when processing information about situations or events. These maladaptive thought processes often reflect inaccurate, or at least ineffective, reasoning. When clients have recognized that their thoughts are creating or maintaining emotions, they may begin to realize that these emotions lead to suboptimal behavioral and physiological responses for sport performance.

A cornerstone to rational emotive behavior therapy (REBT), a specific cognitive therapy, is the A-B-C theory of personality (Meichenbaum, 1977). In the REBT model, A represents the activating event or adversity that stimulates maladaptive thinking; B represents the athlete's belief system, through which all experiences are filtered, whether rational or irrational; and C represents the emotional, cognitive, or behavioral consequence that results from the interaction between A and B. Within the CBT model, the A-B-C's can be conceptualized as the situation or event (activation), automatic thoughts (belief system), and reactions of the individual (consequences). REBT, like CBT, is based on the assumption that individuals' thoughts, emotions, and behaviors are fully integrated, as opposed to separate functions (Ellis & MacLaren, 1998).

The *activating event* or *adversity (A)* **may be either external or internal to the individual.** It is often the existence of a fact, an event, or the behavior or attitude of the individual (Corey, 2005). Though it may appear that the individual's A can only be a confirmable event or situation in the past or the present, it may also be an imagined event regarding the past or the future. For example, a football quarterback's activating event could be imagining the difficulties presented in an upcoming game against a very strong opponent. He may see the situation as threatening, with many obstacles that will make it difficult to perform well. His personal tasks, and those of his team, may seem insurmountable and his thought process might lead him to have an irrational belief about the game. ("It doesn't matter how well I perform, my team cannot win.") The underlying belief system (B) could easily create anxiety, doubt, and a loss of confidence. These consequences (C) could increase the possibility of a poor performance by the quarterback that contributes to a poor offensive team performance.

Within the CBT and REBT models, the *belief system* consists of core beliefs and intermediate beliefs that can be either rational or irrational in nature. The beliefs are often so ingrained in the individual that the thoughts are automatic and do not require much conscious awareness or intentional processing. Individuals may not be always aware of these thoughts, and thus may not realize how what they are thinking affects how they feel about the situation and how they will react. These beliefs are evaluative cognitions or constructed views of the self, the world around them, or their future. CBT operates under the premise that cognitive schemas are the structures that contain individuals' fundamental beliefs and assumptions. Schemas develop early in life from personal experience, are reinforced by further learning experience, and influence the formation of beliefs, values, and attitudes (Corsini & Wedding, 2005). When individuals maintain beliefs that are flexible, they allow for adaptive cognitive processing. Individuals able to evaluate the activating event (A) according to flexible belief systems (B) process the information with balanced thinking. Dysfunctional behavior often occurs when the beliefs are rigid (Corey, 2005). When belief systems are rigid, individuals perceive the activating event (A) from an irrational or inflexible standpoint or belief (B), and then process the information according to unbalanced thinking (C).

The emotional and behavioral consequence (C) or reaction of an individual can be either healthy or unhealthy (Corey, 2005). Oftentimes, an individual may interpret a highly charged emotional consequence (C) that follows a significant activating event (A), as in fact having been caused by the activating event itself. However, one of the main purposes of CBT is to demonstrate to individuals that B has a substantial impact on C. In other words, the emotional consequences (C) that individuals experience can often be attributed to their beliefs (B) about activating events (A), rather than activating events themselves. In general, individuals tend to perceive situations as the direct cause of consequences or reactions. The short amount of time during which individuals have their thoughts before an action occurs is exactly the moment that CBT consultants attempt to uncover. It is important to understand how athletes think, as well as what beliefs may be having an impact on those thoughts and the eventual behavior or performance response.

There are three different levels of beliefs: (a) automatic thoughts, (b) intermediate beliefs/assumptions, and (c) core beliefs (Corey, 2005).

The level of belief that is closest to the surface is that of automatic thought. An automatic thought is defined as a personal notion or idea that is triggered by particular stimuli that leads to an emotional response (Corsini & Wedding, 2005). As one's emotions change, so too do one's thoughts, yet these thoughts enter and exit the mind almost instantly and often go unnoticed. To identify automatic thoughts, individuals must notice what goes through their minds when there is a strong feeling or strong reaction to something. This requires individuals to make conscious efforts to recognize their thoughts. In order to do this, individuals need to be vigilant. The most direct way for individuals to be able to identify their thoughts is through noticing when they are experiencing emotions related to specific events, adversity, or situations. Emotions can be translated into thoughts if individuals take the time to become aware of what they were thinking at the time that an emotion took place. The generic CBT counselor will give individuals assistance with uncovering their thoughts; the REBT counselor seeks to challenge the validity of individuals' beliefs.

When automatic thoughts are examined, errors in reasoning are often uncovered. These errors may lead individuals to experience dysfunctional cognitive processing of information, which is nonadaptive (Corsini & Wedding, 2005). Beck (1995) outlined six systematic errors in reasoning called **cognitive distortions** that are evident during psychological distress, including (a) arbitrary inference, (b) selective abstraction, (c) overgeneralization, (d) magnification/minimization, (e) personalization, and (f) dichotomous thinking. Blaming, catastrophizing, labeling and mislabeling, and the fallacy of fairness are additional cognitive distortions that can be exhibited in sport. These major systematic errors in reasoning are briefly discussed below.

Arbitrary inference. This cognitive distortion refers to drawing a specific conclusion without supporting evidence or even in the face of contradictory evidence. Arbitrary inferences may be present in one of two forms: mind reading or negative prediction. In mind reading, individuals think they know what another person is thinking about them. For example, an athlete may conclude that her coach no longer values her because her coach has significantly reduced her playing time. Indeed, the coach may have other reasons for limiting her playing time, such as resting her for the playoffs or allowing others opportunity to develop and contribute. Individuals who believe something bad will happen without any supporting evidence engage in negative prediction. A tennis player may predict that he may perform poorly in an upcoming match on grass, even though he has performed quite well on grass before and is fully prepared for the upcoming match. In either case, inferences are made without proper attention to and/or considerable distortion of available evidence.

Selective abstraction. Individuals who characterize a situation on the basis of a detail taken out of context and/or ignoring other information engage in selective abstraction. For example, a volleyball player who has had several kills, and even a couple of aces, may focus and dwell solely on a missed serve. The athlete has selected one event out of a series of events in order to draw negative conclusions.

Overgeneralization. Abstracting a general rule from one or a few isolated incidents and applying this rule too broadly and to unrelated situations is referred to as overgeneralization. For example, a basketball player may conclude that she is a second-half-player because she has had a few games where she performed extremely well after halftime.

Magnification and minimization. When something is perceived as far more or less significant than it actually is, magnification or minimization occurs. Often mistakes or negative events are magnified while success or positive events are minimized. An example of magnification is a sprinter who pulls a hamstring during warm-ups for a track meet early in the season and thinks, "I won't be able to compete in the 100 today. This injury will probably ruin my season and prevent me from qualifying for the conference championship." On the other hand, the sprinter who uses minimization may think, "Although I got off the block well, had good speed, and won my event, my performance is not good enough. I should have done better. I should be much further along than I am."

Personalization. Personalization refers to attributing external events to oneself without evidence supporting a causal connection. This is a common cognitive distortion for athletes who are not successful when the game is on the line. For example, a place kicker who misses a field goal with his team trailing by one point as time expires may take too much responsibility for the loss. He may not sufficiently consider the deficiencies of the defense and the offense during the game. He missed the game winner-it is his fault the team lost. Another example is when an athlete who is injured thinks she caused her team to lose because she was unable to compete.

Blaming. In complete opposition to personalization, blaming refers to individuals who do not take enough responsibility for their own behavior, attributing the fault to myriad external sources. Common examples include blaming failure on the referees, coach, teammates, or weather, when in fact these entities had little impact on the actual experience of failure.

Dichotomous thinking. Individuals who categorize events into one of two extremes, as either a complete success or total failure, demonstrate dichotomous thinking. Athletes who engage in this all-or-nothing thinking can also demonstrate perfectionist thinking. A hockey goalie who thinks he should save every shot in a game exhibits dichotomous thinking. He needs to be perfect when he plays, allowing no goals-one goal allowed is one too many.

Catastrophizing. In this cognitive distortion, individuals over-exaggerate a single negative event. For instance, a soccer player who thinks, "If I don't hit this penalty shot and we lose the match, I will probably be benched for the rest of the season," demonstrates catastrophizing.

Labeling and mislabeling. Individuals may self-label based on specific events rather than considering them as isolated incidents. In this cognitive distortion, self-worth is often perceived as contingent upon achievement; therefore, athletes who make a few mistakes may inappropriately label themselves as losers or worthless. They may be quick to label others or place them in a category without having a factual data base to do so. Young athletes and athletes who over-emphasize the athletic aspect of their identity are particularly prone to this distortion.

Fallacy of fairness. Individuals may inappropriately equate fairness with having their own desires met. For example, a team handball player may think, "It is not fair that I only get into the game on defense. I never get to play on the offensive end of the court." This athlete blurs the boundaries between a beneficial act for the team versus an ideal experience for him or her as an individual.

These cognitive distortions are based on the conditioned belief systems of an individual. Conditioned beliefs become automatic thoughts. These automatic thoughts are developed in response to specific situations and are responsible for the emotions and behaviors that individuals experience after they have interpreted the situation. Emotions, behavior, and physiological variables can all interact and influence the response. For example, an individual could cringe (emotion), slam a locker (behavioral), feel butterflies in his or her stomach (physiological), or have some combination of the three in response to a coach's unexpected pre-game announcement that the individual will be starting in the nationally televised tournament game tonight.

Using the CBT model, the first step toward helping athletes change their beliefs is to assist athletes with becoming aware of their thoughts. Often athletes are not aware of specifically what they are thinking and of how the thoughts may affect their performances. Likewise, athletes may have thoughts about their performances that stem from their core beliefs. The goal of CBT is to teach athletes to identify, evaluate, and modify their thoughts in order to change how they view the world. Ultimately, CBT consultants desire to challenge cognitive distortions held by athletes, allowing them to approach competition with cognitions that are effective and adaptive for their sport. By removing distorted and dysfunctional thinking, athletes have a better opportunity to fully manifest their abilities in actual game performance.

Similar to the CBT model, the REBT model requires sport psychology counselors to assist athletes in identifying and changing irrational beliefs to rational beliefs. A more rational perspective and belief system provides the opportunity to improve emotional and behavioral functioning. Athletes can better focus on game-related tasks instead of defeating themselves with beliefs that lead to impaired sport performance (Ellis & MacLaren, 1998).

Theories of Intervention Less Commonly Practiced in Sport Psychology

There are a few theories of intervention used in mainstream psychology that may have potential within the realm of sport psychology: (a) existential (May, 1969), (b) person-centered, and (c) interpersonal theories (Benjamin, 1974; Kiesler, 1996; Sullivan, 1953).

In existential counseling, clients are encouraged to be the authors of their own lives through the development of self-knowledge. By understanding perceptions of four central concerns (death, freedom, isolation, and meaninglessness), clients may discover optimal coping strategies for dealing with the reality of basic existence. Although it is not commonly used in sport psychology, Ravizza (2002) has suggested that this theory may be a promising and productive approach for some professionals.

Person-centered counseling works under the central assumption that client growth will occur when the counselor communicates authentic, unconditional positive regard for the client. Through the use of active, empathic listening, counselors empower clients to voice their emotions freely, allowing for personal growth. A person-centered approach may be useful for some sport psychology consultation given the natural evaluative dynamic between athlete and coach. Given that athletes are constantly judged by coaches, person-centered counselors can serve as impartial and non-judgmental sounding boards for athletes to release many of their feelings that they otherwise may not with coaches or teammates.

Interpersonal theorists define personality as "the relatively enduring pattern of recurrent interpersonal situations which characterize human life" (Sullivan, 1953, pp. 110–111). From this perspective, patterns of affect, behavior, and cognition are developed through experiences of relating to other people. Thus, it is important to develop an understanding of clients' perceptions of how people relate to them, how they relate to others, and how they treat themselves (Benjamin, 1974). Critical to understanding clients' distress is gaining awareness of their history of interaction patterns between themselves and important figures in their lives such as a mother or a father. Additionally, it is important to understand the interpersonal process between the athlete and an important figure in his or her sport (i.e., coach, teammate) that may be catalyzing acute distress and subsequent performance decrement. For example, it may be discovered that an athlete who is very anxious and self-blaming in competition has been exposed to an extremely controlling and hostile coach at some point in his or her career. It is crucial to understand the interpersonal experience of the athlete and work with him or her to alter self communications that may be overly hostile and/or rigid. The maladapted response patterns are replaced with more affiliative and interpersonal responses. Recent work by Conroy & Benjamin (2001) has supported the application of contemporary interpersonal theory in the sport and athletic setting.

The Goal of Your Practice Is to Help

There is obviously opportunity for experimentation with various theoretical perspectives that relate to behavior change in the sport environment. The ability to experiment under the direct supervision of a professional who has experience with various approaches is an important aspect of applied training in sport psychology. While cognitive approaches to behavior change are popular in competitive sport environments, each emerging professional should be exposed to several intervention strategies. The selection of a theory and a specific approach to intervention should be developed with consideration of the following factors:

1. Examine the research and applied data in and out of sport that supports, or is critical of, the theory.

2. Select a theoretical orientation that fits your perspective on behavior formation and behavior change.

3. Select a theoretical orientation that you feel comfortable using and seems to fit with your personal strengths as a counselor.

4. Remain open to other theoretical orientations and new perspectives as they develop.

5. Remain flexible and consider developing your own style, which may be an eclectic blend of two of more orientations.

Perhaps of greatest importance is the ability to remember that, as a sport psychology counselor, the goal is to help individuals learn to help themselves. [gl]If our ability to facilitate reflection, the identification of concerns, or ultimate behavior and performance change becomes compromised or diminishes in effectiveness, we should not hesitate to look for alternate theories or additional sources of information that may improve our performance in counsel.

References

Beck, J. S. (1995). *Cognitive therapy: Basics and beyond.* New York: Guilford.

Benjamin, L. S. (1974). Structural analysis of social behavior. *Psychological Review,* 81, 392–425.

Cautela, J. R. (1976). The present status of covert modeling. *Journal of Behavior Therapy and Experimental Psychiatry,* 6, 323–326.

Cautela, J. R., & Kearney, A. J. (1993). *Covert conditioning casebook.* Pacific Grove, CA: Brooks/Cole.

Conroy, D. E., & Benjamin, L. S. (2001). Psychodynamics in sport performance enhancement consultation: Application of an interpersonal theory. *Sport Psychologist,* 15, 103–117.

Corey, G. (2005). *Theory and practice of counseling and psychotherapy* (7th ed.). Belmont, CA: Brooks/Cole.

Corsini, R.J., & Wedding, D. (2005). *Current psychotherapies* (7th ed.). Belmont, CA: Brooks/Cole.

Dunlap, E. (1999). An assessment of the nature and prevalence of sport psychology service provision in professional sports. Unpublished master's thesis, The University of North Carolina at Chapel Hill, Chapel Hill, NC.

Ellis, A., & MacLaren, C. (1998). *Rational emotive behavior therapy: A therapist's guide.* Atascadero, CA: Impact.

Gardner, F.L., (1991). Professionalization of sport psychology: A reply to Silva. *The Sport Psychologist,* 5, 55–60.

Ivey, A.E., & Ivey, M.B. (2003). *Intentional interviewing and counseling: Facilitating client development in a multicultural society.* Pacific Grove, CA: Brooks/Cole.

Jacobson, E. (1939). Variation of blood pressure with skeletal muscle tension and relaxation. *Annual of Internal Medicine,* 2, 152.

Kiesler, D. J. (1996). *Contemporary interpersonal theory and research: Personality, psychopathology, and psychotherapy.* Oxford, England: John Wiley & Sons.

Locke, E. A., Shaw, K. N., Saari, L. M., & Latham, G. P. (1981). Goals setting and task performance. *Psychological Bulletin,* 90, 125–152.

May, R. (1969). *Existential psychology.* New York: Random House.

Meichenbaum, D. (1977). *Cognitive-behavior modification: An integrative approach.* New York: Plenum Press.

Ravizza, K. H. (2002). A philosophical construct: A framework for performance enhancement. *International Journal of Sport Psychology,* 33, 4–18.

Ross, A. L. (2006). Personal communication with John Silva. Charlotte, NC.

Silva, J. M. (1989). Toward the professionalization of sport psychology. *The Sport Psychologist,* 3, 265–273.

Silva, J. M., Conroy, D. E., & Zizzi, S. J. (1999). Critical issues confronting the advancement of applied sport psychology. *Journal of Applied Sport Psychology,* 11, 163–197.

Sullivan, H. S. (1953). *The interpersonal theory of psychiatry.* New York: W. W. Norton & Company.

Weinberg, R., & Weigand, D. (1993). Goal setting in sport and exercise: A reaction to Locke. *Journal of Sport and Exercise Psychology,* 15, 88–96.

Wolpe, J. (1958). *Psychotherapy by reciprocal inhibition.* Stanford, CA: Stanford University Press.

Wolpe, J. (1990). *The practice of behavior therapy* (4th ed.). New York: Pergamon.

CHAPTER 4

Educational and Training Experiences Fundamental to the Practice of Sport Psychology

To this point, the current text has set the stage for training in applied sport psychology. The authors now focus on particular experiences, skills, and knowledge that are fundamental to obtain in the development of competence to practice sport psychology. Traditional classroom experiences can be fruitful for students to have a safe environment to gain knowledge, ask questions, and solve problems without placing clients at risk. The authors' philosophy of client growth hinges on helping athletes to engage in self-exploration and disclosure; therefore, the chapter details several skills necessary for building a strong client-consultant relationship. The skills that developing professionals can learn include trust building and active listening, as well as using empathy, acceptance, and openness. Readers will learn how to begin an intervention with new clients, use these skills to foster self-discovery and independence in their athletes, and ultimately transition out of consultation, allowing clients to disengage from consultation. Consultants-in-training are provided information on how to gain information from clients through two general techniques: interviewing and psychological assessment. With these skills and tools in hand, developing consultants can benefit from the latter half of the chapter, which provides a specific model for sequencing practical experiences. Readers will learn how to pre-plan a session, role-play a session, and engage in systematic supervised practica. Additionally, consultants-in-training will appreciate the logical ordering of experiences that allows them to progressively move from a team consultation approach, through consultation with a supervisor as a safety net, to independent practice.

The fundamental preparation for the practice of sport psychology comes from formal and informal educational and training experiences. These experiences range from classroom settings to role playing, to supervised experiences, to informal discussions with peers, athletes, and supervisors. Each experience plays a developmental role in the process of becoming a confident and competent sport psychology counselor. Although the classroom is the most traditional setting, creative teaching and active dialogue can provide a solid foundation for the application of information to be used when consulting. A diverse and rewarding classroom experience will not only enhance the knowledge base of the counselor-in-training, but it can also enhance confidence and create a feeling of excitement. A sound education and proper training experience allow the new counselor to look forward to counseling on his or her own with an athlete.

Classroom Experiences

A key component to the provision of quality services in any profession is the formal classroom experience provided to the student or retooling professional. Although life experience plays an important role in the knowledge base of any professional, great personal growth and advancement in preparation can be actualized in a classroom setting. This growth potential is particularly true when the counselor-in-training receives exposure from experienced and trained professionals. It is important for sport psychology graduate programs to have a critical mass of faculty who possess broad perspectives and a practical, hands-on consulting history with athletes at all levels of competitive sport. The knowledge gained in the classroom provides a structure within which professionals-in-training can base their practice. It also provides the opportunity for questions, dialogue, and role-playing opportunities in a stimulating yet "safe" setting. The classroom should be a dynamic setting where the professional-in-training is challenged intellectually and practically. The classroom setting should be an environment where the professional-in-training challenges, explores, and finds out first-hand how theory may or may not translate into practice! It should provide a guided context for the development and refinement of the consulting skills needed to conduct an effective practice.

For the education and training of a person who desires to practice sport psychology, the curriculum should include learning opportunities that require the organization of material (e.g., pre-planning an individual session or setting up a workshop for coaches or a team), the application of material (e.g., role playing an intake interview with an athlete, or role playing a team meeting to address interpersonal conflict in a team), and the evaluation of the intervention (e.g., self evaluation, peer evaluation, evaluation by the client athlete). Professionals in preparation must learn how to work independently, yet they must be receptive to feedback from peers and supervising professors who can enhance their development.

Moving from absorbing information to mastering the application of information is an important goal in the classroom setting. Many athletes know what they need to do but cannot bring themselves to do it during competition. Knowing and doing are clearly different skills, particularly under stressful conditions. Many aspiring sport psychologists are very "book smart" but have difficulty translating that knowledge into a working platform. Applying information in an effective manner under real time with a real athlete can be very challenging and stressful for a novice practitioner. Honing one's skills in an educational environment where mistakes can be identified and corrected is an important part of a professional's development. The classroom setting provides knowledge, rapid feedback and the opportunity to apply knowledge. Most importantly, however, it provides a "second chance." Mistakes made in the classroom setting can be identified and student clinicians have an opportunity to "see" their mistake through the eyes of an experienced peer or supervising professional.

One day the student clinician will leave the classroom and the supervised environment to begin his or her own practice. The knowledge base provided by formal course experiences and supervised counseling experiences will enhance the clinician's ability to think quickly and correctly while an athlete is speaking. The second-chance experiences provided in the classroom setting will prepare the clinician for both the expected and the unexpected content shared in a consulting dynamic. The value of formal course work specifically in sport psychology and the opportunity for classroom experiences with a veteran sport psychology practitioner should not be underestimated. Well-structured classroom experiences will provide for an easier transition to less-structured practice environments such as direct and indirect supervised consulting with athletes. The formal and informal classroom experiences will offer many opportunities to develop and fine tune counselor skills that are fundamental to the successful practice of sport psychology.

Developing Sport Psychology Counselor Skills

Much like an athlete develops physical and mental skills, a counselor must develop professional skills that facilitate the counseling process and effective intervention with an athlete. Some counselors will find dominant aspects of their personality allow them to interact easily with an athlete during a session. Other counselors may feel slightly inhibited or timid when they initiate dialogue with an athlete. Whatever the starting point for the counselor-in-training, developing skills that foster positive and open environments is an essential element in the educational and training process. It is rare to find individuals interested in the counseling field who cannot improve upon their skills. The counselor-in-training is often eager to improve and perform at a higher level. In this regard, supervising sport psychology counselors-in-training is very similar to working with athletes-they are very motivated to learn and will work hard to improve. There are some fundamental skills that all counselors should continually develop and refine. These skills will set the stage for successful intervention and a positive relationship with an athlete during sessions.

The Ability to Build and Enhance a Counseling Relationship

Perhaps the first skill the counselor-in-training should develop is the ability to build and enhance a counseling relationship with an athlete. If the counselor does not have a positive and trusting relationship with the athlete, there is little chance for a successful intervention. It is very important to be as natural as possible when interacting with an athlete. If counselors are not relaxed and comfortable, how can athletes be expected to trust the counselors' ability to assist them with stressful situations? Be professional, but be as natural and "regular" as you can be.

Most athletes are not looking for someone who thinks he or she knows everything and will "fix" the problem in just a few sessions. Most athletes have much to say, and it is the job of the competent counselor to assist athletes in such a manner that they feel comfortable speaking about difficult or sensitive information. The athlete needs to take advantage of the opportunity to speak freely to an objective third party who will maintain confidentiality. Trust between athlete and counselor is developed slowly but can be lost in an instant if insensitivity to the athlete or his or her particular situation is demonstrated. A client should never be laughed at or ridiculed in any manner because doing so can fracture a fragile and developing relationship. It is important to remember that counseling is based on the effectiveness of your influence. The more trust and rapport you build with the athlete, the greater likelihood the athlete may be open to your influence. Supporting the athlete and making it clear that you are there for him or her starts the building process. Without this foundation, the effectiveness of any counselor will be compromised. The first few sessions will set the tone and the dynamic of your relationship with your client. These sessions will provide you with a platform from which you can make great strides or they can place you in a situation where the dynamic between you and the athlete is not a positive connect.

The foundation for a positive relationship with an athlete begins with the initial interaction. Strong fundamental counseling skills allow the counselor to advance beyond basic interaction and into a meaningful dialogue designed to move the intervention toward exploration, discovery, and change. These skills include the ability to listen and demonstrate empathy, acceptance, and openness when the athlete is disclosing information about his or her personal or athletic situation.

Basic Relationship-building Suggestions

1. Always greet the athlete with a smile. No matter what has transpired before the session and no matter how difficult your day has been, greet the athlete with a genuine smile and a handshake.
2. Ask athletes about their day, their classes, whether they went to the big game last night. Place the focus of the conversation on the athlete, not on you.
3. Engage in at least three to five minutes of "small talk" that is not heavy or in any way related to the athletes or their concerns—make it interesting and pleasant conversation. This may be the best five-minute investment you could make to build the relationship.
4. Be upbeat and use some humor in the first few minutes of the small talk. Make it easy for the athletes to sit down and feel relaxed. You want the athletes to feel conversational and not as if they are walking into a doctor's office for an examination!
5. Find an easy—not rehearsed—segue into the session. If you are good at this, the athlete (and even a trained observer) may not realize that you are into the session!
6. Always reward the athlete for hard work and progress. Be optimistic-set a positive tone in the closing of the session that makes the athlete want to come back for the next.

Listening Skills

What does it mean to demonstrate listening skills? Everyone has been told at one time or another, "You need to listen better," or "You don't hear what I am saying." When these statements are made, it clearly indicates that the sender and the receiver of a message have different perceptions. On the other hand, some people are told, "You are a good listener," after they engage in dialogue with someone who believes the listener received the content and the meaning of the spoken words. To possess good listening skills, a counselor must be focused on the person speaking and the message he or she is trying to send with verbal and non-verbal language. Too often listeners are only "half listening," meaning that some of their attention is on the athlete and some of their attention is on the response they are formulating while the athlete is still speaking. This is not a good habit; not only can the significance of the communication be lost, but the athlete may pick up on the counselor's preoccupation with responding (as opposed to an active interest in understanding and then reflecting back on the information with the athlete). Speaking over the athlete is a common mistake made by many counselors. This is done by not allowing the athlete to finish his or her thought or sentence or by speaking louder than the athlete while the athlete is still formulating the sentence. The message the athlete receives in this situation is "Listen to me. I really do not need to listen to you." This shows a complete lack of empathy for the athlete's personal experience and is not conducive to facilitating greater depth of dialogue.

A counselor with good listening skills rarely interrupts athletes when they are speaking. It is the athletes' experience you are seeking-let them speak! If the counselor interrupts the athlete while he or she is speaking, it should be to request clarification or ask if the counselor understands the information correctly. Only after the athlete is clearly finished speaking and has completed his or her thought or description of an event should the counselor begin the response and dialogue. It is very effective to reflect back on the information the athlete has shared, to ask questions, and to show the athlete that you did hear what he or she said and that you are interested in learning more.

Empathy, Acceptance, and Openness

Understanding the emotional content of the statements the athlete makes demonstrates empathy by the counselor. If athletes sense you care and you can relate to their experience, they will be more likely to share deeper information with you in the intervention session. In addition to demonstrating empathy, the counselor should demonstrate acceptance and openness throughout the session. Whether the counselor agrees or disagrees with the athlete's perceptions, the perception should not be denied. Remain open and allow the athlete to continue on with the dialogue; accept the fact that the information shared is the athlete's perception. Understanding the athlete's position does not necessarily mean you agree with it. It is the ability to connect with the emotional aspect of the dialogue that permits the counselor to ask questions that stimulate the thinking of the athlete and may even challenge the position taken by the athlete during the dialogue. Premature rejection of the athlete's dialogue combined with a lack of connecting emotionally with the content will often psychologically distance the athlete from the counselor rather than make the athlete receptive to the questions asked and to the reflection requested by a counselor during a session.

A simple question counselors should always ask themselves is: "Am I more interested in what I have to say to the athlete or am I more interested in what the athlete has to say to me?" Your actions during the session will provide the actual answer.

Facilitate the Process: Self-Exploration and Athlete Disclosure

As the counselor continues to develop dialogue with the athlete it is important to communicate that intervention is a *process* that involves a cooperative spirit. This process orientation is essential to develop and is facilitated by the ability of the counselor to ask meaningful questions that require the athlete to reflect on the psychological underpinnings of the issues they bring up in the session. Athletes should not be in a rush for results and should not come to the sessions believing that they can be taught a set of "mental skills" that will result in all their concerns fading away. *A process orientation fosters self-exploration and athlete disclosure, which, in turn, provides a platform from which athletes can develop a better understanding of the relationship between their thought process, their behavior, and their athletic performance.* With no understanding of the way their thought process relates to the function or dysfunction of their behavior, the likelihood of meaningful and long-lasting behavior change is diminished.

Understanding of and insight into the relationship between the athlete's thought process and subsequent athletic performance are key elements in the process of meaningful behavior change. The counselor must develop skills such as patience and the ability to ask meaningful and timely questions in order to facilitate athlete self-exploration and athlete disclosure. The counselor must skillfully and in a well-timed manner maneuver through material that may be very difficult for an athlete to speak about and confront in the open, perhaps for the first time. Yet it is these very situations that create the opportunity for "breakthroughs" where the athlete knows he or she has revealed a concern or issue in a manner unlike ever before. Not only has the athlete achieved disclosure but now "sees" and understands how this issue has inhibited or in some way limited him or her from the possibility of performing at a higher level. The process of self-exploration and disclosure is well worth the time investment. Once the process reaches a breakthrough point, it will be evident to the counselor that the athlete now believes he or she can approach the concern (e.g., anxiety about mistakes, fear of the competition, their coach's hostile attitude, an interpersonal problem with a teammate) with a constructive psychological game plan-a game plan that can be initially put together in concert with the counselor (restructuring in CBM) and tested out in the real world of athletic competition.

At this point it is essential that the athlete understand that testing out is also a process and it may require some fine tuning. The psychological commitment made by the athlete is to work toward change and enhanced performance. The athlete will project more optimism and this must be reinforced because the first attempt to use the "plan" may bring marginal results in the eyes of the athlete. However, meaningful change often takes time and repeated attempts. Persistence and resilience must be fostered in the athlete; meaningful change often takes place more slowly than desired. The psychological commitment is to the process that is now in place, and that process may be refined.

To move an athlete to the point of psychological commitment requires considerable counselor skill. *Just as athletes must demonstrate persistence and resilience, counselors must remain patient, optimistic, and focused not on success or failure but on their ability to continue to work with athletes to achieve the goals of enhanced well-being and enhanced athletic performance.*

Fostering Athlete Independence

The process of meaningful behavior change and performance enhancement requires many counselor skills, as noted above. While bonding with the athlete and building a positive professional relationship are very important to this process, the counselor must also possess the skills that foster athlete independence. It is often personally rewarding to see an athlete move through the intervention process and use the information and material gained through the interaction with the counselor. While this healthy process is developing, it is crucial that the counselor continue to ask questions and assist the athlete in developing the ability to "figure things out on their own." The process orientation previously discussed should be designed to stimulate the athlete's thinking and problem-solving skills. *Counselors must constantly remember that their function is to facilitate the process of change. The athlete is the agent of change and the athlete is the only entity that can sustain meaningful change.*

After significant progress has been made with an athlete and performance is at least stabilized at a desirable level (a laudable goal in and of itself), an emphasis should be directed on further development of adaptation and coping skills. The counselor now uses his or her skill to promote in the athlete an ability to "see" situations that have been problematic in the past or situations that could create problems in the present. Adapting to the changing competitive landscape and coping with stress, frustration, disappointment, and challenge become skills the counselor now promotes in the athlete. In the early stages of this task, the athlete frequently will seek the advice of the counselor. As athletes develop confidence in their ability to problem solve successfully in previously problematic areas, they will gain confidence in their own management skills. Eventually, the counselor and the athlete seek the ultimate goal of facilitating the self- administration of sport psychology information by the athlete.

Transition and Disengagement

When the athlete consistently problem solves, makes adjustments that the counselor would have suggested, and manages difficult situations successfully with little or no participation by the counselor, success has been attained on both sides. Do not be disappointed by the athlete's less frequent visits. When you have been successful with athletes they will "need" you less. In positive counseling relationships, the athletes know that the counselor is always there if they need to talk with someone, share a triumph, or relate a disappointment. Perhaps one of the most important skills a counselor working with athletes can develop is the ability to foster independence and self-management skills. Counselors must learn how to balance their hard-earned professional relationships with athletes with the skill of disengaging the athletes from the formal consulting relationship. Obviously this is a delicate process and should be presented in very positive terms to the athlete and introduced over a period of time (usually weeks). Once an athlete is self-sustaining and management skills are consistently demonstrated over a period of time, the counselor should reinforce this pattern by slowly disengaging from regular meetings. This can be done by changing the meeting schedule to once every two weeks, once a month, or an as-needed basis. Although disengagement means less frequent formal interaction with the athlete, the counselor should remain a stable factor in the athlete's life-always accessible and part of the athlete's support system.

Interview Skills

The fundamental counselor skills discussed above can be viewed in a manner similar to tactical skills in a sporting event. A good game plan or fundamental "big picture" understanding provides a guide or general road map. This helps the counselor understand which skills will foster the development of interaction at various stages of the intervention. These fundamental skills not only provide direction to the counselor, but they also increase the professionalism of the counseling environment. As with sport itself, sport counseling requires that good tactics be combined with good technique and execution. The interview, perhaps the first formal exposure the client receives to the counseling experience, is an essential first step in the intervention process and can set the tone for comfortable future disclosure by the athlete. Following the interview, many consultants find that standardized assessments provide an effective way to gather valuable information that will aid in developing the direction of the intervention.

Objectives of the Interview

The objectives of the interview are fairly clear cut: **develop an informational base that includes important information from the athlete's past and present, as well as a glimpse into future expectations and aspirations.** To achieve these objectives, the counselor and the client will engage in a dialogue in the form of questions and answers. Most of the questions naturally come from the counselor and the answers are provided by the athlete. While the sessions may appear straightforward, conducting an interview requires a high level of skill on the counselor's part.

Help the athlete relax. The counselor must be sure the athlete is at ease with the interview and the presentation of the interview; otherwise, the athlete may simply provide superficial information to the counselor. The very first bonds of trust are established or broken during the ice-breaking and initial interview sessions. The counselor must ease the athlete into the interview and make sure the athlete understands that the counselor needs his or her unique perspective; it is the athlete's view that is most important in the interview. It is often helpful for the counselor to initiate the dialogue and information sharing by providing some information first. The counselor might say: "You are going to be sharing some information about yourself for most of the session, so it is only fair that I start out by sharing a little information about me with you." The counselor should be careful to provide a very brief biographical sketch that takes no more than three to five minutes of the session. It is common to include information such as where the counselor grew up, extracurricular high school activities, college attended, extracurricular college activities, graduate schools attended, length of time practicing with athletes and teams.

Connect with the athlete. It is helpful to connect with the athlete on a personal level to help build a relaxed and trustful environment. If you know that you have common interests- fishing, rooting for the Red Sox, or enjoying dogs, for example-share some light moments discussing them. These brief comments can go a long way in connecting with the athlete as a person, and they can relax both the counselor and the athlete.

Be as natural as possible. It is important for the counselor not to appear mechanical or programmed in the first few sessions. The counselor wants the dialogue to flow naturally as in a conversation between two friends. Do not be in a rush to get the athlete to talk. Forcing a pace on a client, especially in the first few sessions, often creates a stiff environment. The pace of the counselor should place athletes at ease, not make them feel as if they are being interrogated. Counselors must stay relaxed during interview sessions so they can listen and digest information and move the sessions at a reasonable pace.

Transition smoothly and ask good follow-up questions. After you have established a rapport with the athlete, it is fairly easy to transition into the questions you would like to ask during the interview phase. Most interviews last from one to two hours; however, there is no magic time limit on the interview phase of intervention. It is important to keep the dialogue conversational and not interrogational. It is also extremely important to ask good follow-up questions to incomplete or avoidance responses that the athlete provides during the interview. The counselor's main goal is to acquire useful, honest, and meaningful information from dialogue during the interview. This is an important early goal of the intervention process and it should not be strictly bound by time constraints. This body of information or client data provides the counselor with a deeper understanding of the athlete's perspective in a number of important areas that may have a bearing on sport performance or interpersonal dynamics in the sport setting.

Take accurate and concise interview notes. No matter how experienced counselors are, it is important that they take concise and accurate notes during the interview and during all sessions. It is a developed skill to listen, write accurate notes, stay in the flow of the dialogue, and prepare the appropriate follow-up questions. Interview notes can be reviewed during a session and serve as a cue for an area the counselor wishes to revisit later in the session. Interview notes also provide documentation of the session that can be reflected upon post- session. This reflection provides an opportunity to determine whether subject matter was addressed appropriately, whether reoccurring themes appear, and whether certain topics should be revisited in the next session or at an appropriate time in the future. Good interview session notes help guide the counselor in deciding the initial direction of intervention. The counselor will be able to identify the central issues or the presenting problem, which will help in determining the direction of the first few intervention sessions.

Types of Interviews

The two common interviews used in counseling are (a) the structured interview and (b) the unstructured interview. Although the approach of these interviews may differ, the overall goal of each remains as stated above: to acquire useful, honest, and meaningful information from the athlete that may have a bearing on sport performance or interpersonal dynamics in the sport setting. Both types of interview can be effective in achieving this goal, and a counselor-in-training should experiment with each type, under direct supervision of an experienced supervisor.

The structured interview is often more manageable for a counselor-in-training or novice counselor. The counselor comes into the interview session with a set of prepared questions that cover a number of important areas in the athlete's life. It is often helpful to start with general questions and gradually transition to specific questions. The athlete may also be less defensive and more inclined toward disclosure if the sport psychology consultant moves conversation from the past to the present. Starting out an interview with very specific questions about issues that are highly sensitive is unnatural and can make the athlete a little uncomfortable. Investing a few minutes in small talk and asking a few general "get to know each other" questions can effectively create a more open environment for dialogue and the exchange of information.

The structured interview is based on a working set of questions, but the sport psychology counselor will also need to use sound follow-up questions and allow the dialogue to flow. The sport psychology counselor should keep the pace of the session moving without rushing the client through his or her responses. The questions and answers should flow as dialogue rather than a series of stop-and-go questions and answers. The type of questions addressed in a structured interview should be based on information gathered prior to the first meeting from the athlete, the coach, or a parent (if the parent is requesting the intervention).

The counselor can certainly add to this sample or add questions "on the fly" as a live session unfolds. It is the objective of the structured interview to start the flow of information from the athlete to the sport psychology counselor. It is common for a counselor to supplement the initial questions in the structured interview with those that are generated from the dialogue during the session. Although it is called

---

Common questions in a structured interview would include the following:

• Information about the athlete's family history
• Past and current relationships with parents and family members
• The role of significant others in the athletic development of the client
• A brief review of the athlete's competitive history and significant accomplishments
• A review of the athlete's youth, high school, and collegiate experiences
• The athlete's current perception of his or her role and position on the team
• The athlete's current perception of his or her relationship with teammates
• The athlete's current perception of his or her relationship with head coach and any appropriate position coaches
• The athlete's perception of his or her psychological strengths
• The athlete's perception of his or her psychological weaknesses
• A self-assessment by the athlete regarding what he or she needs to work on from a psychological perspective
• A self-assessment by the athlete regarding why he or she has not made significant progress in the self-identified "work areas" to date
• Any other personal or athletic issues that the athlete would like to address

---

a structured interview, the counselor must remain flexible in order to achieve the primary goal, which is to receive useful information from the athlete that addresses concerns, frustrations, and issues that remain unresolved. With practice and experience, the counselor will develop the ability to multi-task during the interview. Taking good notes, staying engaged with the dialogue and with the flow of conversation, and staying lucid with material that requires follow-up are skills that develop and improve with experience.

The unstructured interview is actually fairly similar to the structured interview in that the goals and objectives are to acquire important information from the athlete. The major difference is that the unstructured interview is much more open and the counselor allows the athlete much more liberty to speak about whatever issues or concerns arise. The counselor, while far less active and directive in the unstructured interview, must still guide the athlete with questions that may provide useful information for the intervention.

Because of the free-flowing nature of the unstructured interview, the counselor can be placed in a situation where the information provided seems to digress from meaningful issues. An athlete who is not fully ready for disclosure may also circumvent relevant issues and concerns in the less structured environment. An advantage of the unstructured interview is that it can produce a less formal, less intense setting for the exchange of information. The athlete is far less likely to be led into an answer or feel he or she needs to say the right thing in response to fairly specific questions. Eventually the athlete may disclose information and disclose it in a manner that has great personal relevance. The unstructured interview can take a considerable amount of time, and if not carried out in a skillful manner it can be punctuated with long periods of silence or awkward attempts to stimulate the athlete to address important issues.

Counselors should experiment with both types of interview techniques and should be comfortable in using both during a session. The type of interview technique used by the counselor should not be viewed in "one or the other" terms. In reality, the counselor often moves along a continuum from more structure to less structure during the course of an interview. Frequently, a well-worded question is very effective and sometimes silence or a long pause is effective in helping the athlete relate personal information. Perhaps one of the most important aspects of the counselor's approach is the ability to read the athlete and understand which would be more helpful-a question or a little silence.

Transitioning Out of the Interview

When the counselor believes that a significant amount of useful information has been provided by the athlete, it is time to transition out of the interview mode and into the next stage of the intervention process. The information provided by the athlete (client data) will be extremely useful in helping the counselor start to create a "big picture" or intervention plan with the athlete. Considering the rich information presented during the course of an interview, sorting it all out can be a difficult task. The counselor must assess which concerns are central and in immediate need of attention, and which concerns or issues may be related or linked to each other psychologically.

During the course of the interview, there are moments in which it is impossible not to do "instant intervention." When a particularly intense concern is brought forth and the athlete wants to address the matter, it is often wise to do so. When this situation occurs during the interview phase of the intervention, the issue should be addressed at least in a manner that brings some type of insight or sense of better understanding to the athlete. The counselor should most certainly note this concern in writing and determine how it may factor in to the overall intervention plan. The interview cannot be done in a vacuum and with disregard for questions the athlete may have for the counselor. The counselor may find that it is during the interview that the athlete first takes initiative in seeking assistance. This opportunity for relationship building and role function should not be missed because of an insistence on sticking with the interview plan. *The counselor who remembers to stay flexible and recognizes "pearls" when the athlete throws them out will be more likely to connect with the athlete.*

Pre-planning the interview can play a role in the ability to effectively transition out of the interview. In the sample of a structured interview presented above, the last four questions are designed to start the transition out of the interview and into assessment. In the final stages, athletes are asked to provide what they perceive to be their psychological strengths and weaknesses, as well as a self-assessment that addresses what they need to work on from a psychological perspective. Athletes are also asked to self-assess why they have not made significant progress in the self-identified "work areas" to date. These extremely thought- provoking questions offer invaluable insight into the psychology of the athlete. Ending the interview with such substantial material also sets up a seamless movement from the interview phase and into assessment. The counselor can transition easily from the strengths and weaknesses dialogue to the administration of standardized psychological measures that may have relevance to performance.

Psychological Assessment

Psychological assessment of the athlete is integral to the intervention process. It is difficult to understand how sport psychology counselors could argue against the use of assessment once they have actually used it in their practice. Assessment provides the important second element in the triangulation of information. The interview provides a source of subjective information, the assessment provides a source of objective information, and the actual observation of the athlete in competition provides an in vivo behavioral source of information. When all three sources converge, the information is not only powerful for the counselor, but powerful for the athlete as well. The issue for the contemporary sport psychology counselor should not be a question of whether or not to use assessment. *The issue should be a matter of choosing which standardized assessments benefit the interaction and education of the athlete being counseled.* It is counterproductive for experts to admonish sport psychology practitioners for using standardized assessment measures in their practice. This is particularly noteworthy when the "experts" are not individuals who frequently consult with athletes or teams. Assessment can provide very useful information to both the counselor and the athlete, and it can assist the counselor in determining issues that merit serious attention. The counselor should experiment with various standardized assessment inventories and find the tool that works best in attaining the educational and behavioral goals of the intervention.

Assessment is used in every aspect of sports preparation and performance and should play a role in any good intervention program. Psychological assessment can be a valuable asset to an athlete's development when measures are selected carefully and used properly.

To interpret scores appropriately on objective psychological assessments, sport psychology professionals must critically consider the psychometric properties of the measures they wish to employ. The evaluation of psychometric properties allows the consultant to select tools that will help educate athletes on the principles of sport psychology.

In the evaluation of appropriate sport psychology assessments, some fundamental concepts to consider relate to validity (Does the test measure what it is purported to measure?) and reliability (Is the test consistent over time?). The sport psychology consultant must be aware of these aspects of the test. A brief review of these important psychometric considerations is provided below.

Construct validity

Validity is the most important psychometric property of scores generated by a psychological assessment tool (i.e., self-report questionnaire, behavioral observation coding, etc.). Construct validity addresses whether or not scores generated from a measure accurately reflect the construct intended to be measured. According to Messick's (1989) unified concept of validity, construct validity is an "integrative evaluative judgment on the degree to which evidence and theoretical rationales support the *adequacy* and *appropriateness* of *inferences* and *actions* based on test scores" (p. 13). Construct validity is a property of the meaning of test scores in test interpretation and use, and not a property of the measure itself. Therefore, it is inappropriate to regard a psychological measure as valid because validity addresses properties of scores on a particular instrument. To explicitly appraise the adequacy, appropriateness, and meaning of test scores, Messick (1995) differentiated six aspects of validity: (1) content, (2) substantive, (3) structural, (4) generalizability, (5) external, and (6) consequential.

Content aspect. The first aspect of construct validity is content validity, which establishes a clear definition of the construct and the boundaries of the domain to be measured. Content validity is more readily established if a clear and concise theoretical foundation for the boundaries and structure of the domain are developed and articulated. Items written to assess a proposed domain should adhere to both the boundaries of the domain and the structure offered by underlying theory. Items that meet these criteria are content-relevant; however, items that fail to meet these criteria introduce construct-irrelevant variance. Increased variability in scores that are irrelevant to the central construct of interest can contaminate true scores and mislead interpretations based on them. An acceptable strategy to avoid this problem and to establish content-relevance of items is to have a panel of expert judges rate the degree to which items fit the particular domain of interest (Dunn, Bouffard, & Rogers, 1999; Hambleton, 1980). Content-representativeness, the second aspect of content validity, concerns the degree to which assessment items cover the content of interest. Just as scholars are charged with drawing a representative sample from a population to ensure valid inferences, assessment tools must contain a representative sample of the universe of items relevant to the domain. Cook and Campbell (1979) identified two problems associated with content-representativeness: construct under-representation and surplus construct irrelevancy. In the first, a measure does not sufficiently cover the expanse of possible domain-relevant alternatives. Regarding the latter problem, although relevant, too many items may introduce construct irrelevant variance into scores on the domain. To avoid content under- or over- representation, researchers should draw from existing theory, clearly define the breadth of a domain of interest, and develop assessment that adequately spans this breadth. A third aspect of content validity, face validity, concerns the technical quality of assessment items. Items that are face valid appear on the surface to tap the intended domain. Use of face validity to evaluate quality of items may occur in the creation phase of assessment design; however, in later phases of assessment evaluation, establishment of content-relevance and representativeness takes precedence.

Substantive aspect. Responses on a scale that demonstrate evidence of consistencies expected, based on substantive theories or models of domain processes, have achieved substantive validity. A technique for establishing substantive validity is to compare or contrast the psychological processes of two samples. For instance, the fear of success construct was historically assumed to reflect achievement processes prevalent in women but not in men because of gender-role socialization differences (Horner, 1968, 1972; Metzler & Conroy, 2006). Not surprisingly, measurement of this construct highlighted gender differences in support of the substantive validity of the instrument being used (Horner, 1972; Zuckerman, 1976). Stronger evidence for substantive validity can be garnered through experimental studies that manipulate critical variables theorized to be integral to the psychological process. For example, individuals who score highly on a fear of success measure should feel more distressed or particularly anxious when faced with success than when faced with failure.

Structural aspect. Scores on a measure must demonstrate evidence of internal structure that is consistent with that of the construct domain as defined by the underlying theory (Loevinger, 1957). For instance, Smith, Smoll, and Schutz (1990) conceptualized sport anxiety as a multidimensional construct comprised of attentional, cognitive, and somatic aspects. Scores on 21 items written to tap these aspects of sport anxiety revealed three factors, subsequently labeled concentration disruption, worry, and somatic anxiety. Structural fidelity of scores is compromised when items designed to measure an aspect of a construct do not co-vary with conceptually similar items. In early stages of measurement development, researchers employ a technique called exploratory factor analysis as a data-driven method to reveal the structure of scores and the items that co-vary. Alternately, confirmatory factor analysis, using a data analytical technique called structural equation modeling, allows researchers to evaluate the structure of scores based on a priori theory.

Generalizability aspect. How far scholars can extend interpretations of scores on objective psychological assessments is a question of generalizability. This aspect directly affects consultants in practice because a measure that has demonstrated evidence for validity in one population may not necessarily reveal the same evidence in an alternate population. In other words, score properties may differ across populations, groups, situations, and tasks. For example, responses stimulated by a questionnaire regarding group cohesion administered to corporate management teams may differ in structure from those generated by collegiate football teams. Consequently, interpretations of these scores may also differ considerably. In discussing generalizability, it is important to consider the theoretical foundation of an objective instrument. Some instruments used in sport psychology assess individual differences and thus are fundamentally oriented toward processes in operation at a personality level. Given this foundation, these instruments need not be criticized for not specifically targeting an athletic sample in validation studies. When evaluating an instrument, consultants are highly encouraged to determine its generalizability within the context of the underlying theory in order to establish its utility for the intended client.

External aspect. The main reason we use objective assessment is to monitor a particular variable that is theorized to relate to other variables. In sport psychology, we are ultimately interested in the optimal performance, development, and/or experience of athletes; therefore, we are interested in psychological predictors of processes and phenomenon directly or indirectly related to these aims. Scores on a particular instrument should predict theoretically relevant criteria and should not predict irrelevant criteria. To describe these two respective principles, Campbell and Fiske (1959) originated the terms *convergent validity* and *discriminant validity*. Bivariate correlations are often used to provide evidence for convergent and discriminant validity with significant correlations indicating an amount of shared variance between two scores. Scores on measures designed to assess similar constructs should converge by demonstrating significant positive correlations (i.e., significant shared variance). Scores on measures theoretically independent of one another should be discriminated from one another by demonstrating non-significant associations (i.e., little shared variance). It is also important to note the method used to obtain scores on a construct. For example, scores for mental toughness generated from multiple methods (athlete's self-report vs. coach's report vs. behavioral observation) may vary in part due to variations in the method of assessment. Although we would expect these scores to correlate highly (i.e., converge), the resulting bivariate correlations may be attenuated by method variance-error in score due to the method of assessment. Similarly, when theoretically divergent constructs are measured using the same method, they may actually exhibit a relationship because part of the score contains variance due to the method of assessment.

Consequential aspect. An aspect of validity that is often overlooked in both mainstream and sport psychological research and application is evidence focused on the effect score interpretation may have on the client and/or other groups (e.g., coaches, teammates, schools, and society in general). For instance, if a psychological test is administered and scores are used (whether intended or not) for personnel selection in sport (e.g., draft ordering, college recruitment, etc.), the administrator must consider test bias and fairness. More frequently, sport psychology consultants may be confronted with the conundrum of reporting results to individual clients for educational purposes and then having these results leaked to teammates and coaches. Imagine assessing fear of failure within a team to assist with creation and implementation of individualized interventions. Now imagine that the head coach demands individual results and, hoping to avoid "choking" and losing to a rival opponent, promptly benches athletes who score high on the instrument. Obviously, score interpretation in this case could have severe consequences to those who respond to the measure; therefore, consequential validity (i.e., valid use of the measure) is a paramount consideration in objective assessment.

Reliability

Scores on an instrument that demonstrate validity must also be reliable. Of course, no measurement procedure is without error. In the hard sciences, practitioners do their best to minimize human error that may affect scores produced by physically calibrating equipment. Similarly, in psychological assessment, we must ensure the consistency of any instrument used to guide consultation. Stated directly, there are three central questions:

1. If multiple items exist on a measure, are these items tapping the same construct (i.e., internal consistency)?

2. Do alternate forms of an instrument produce scores that are similar (i.e., equivalence)?

3. How stable are scores over time (i.e., temporal stability)?

Internal consistency. Cronbach's (1951) alpha is used as evidence for homogeneity of item content for multi-indicator assessments. Lower values of Cronbach's alpha (i.e., $< .70$) are indicative of increased variability of item content, likely attributable to measurement error. It is important to note that Cronbach's alpha is affected by both inter-item correlations and test length. In general, the longer the test, the greater the alpha. The relationship between scale length and alpha is negatively accelerating, indicating a point of diminishing returns (addition of a 6th item has more impact than the 20th item). Nothing is gained by adding items to measures that are highly content saturated (e.g., high inter-item correlations), as opposed to those that are content diluted (e.g., low inter-item correlations). Additionally, dimensionality cannot be assessed using alpha. Although low alpha may point toward the existence of multiple latent factors (e.g., more than one form of anxiety), only factor analysis procedures can provide evidence for the structure of scores on an instrument.

Equivalence. Oftentimes in measurement, we are interested in developing alternate or parallel forms that measure the same psychological construct. Sport psychology consultants may want to minimize memorization of and robotic responses to these items particularly if multiple assessments are planned. More frequently, sport practitioners want to avoid belaboring athletes and coaches with cumbersome assessment tools that draw time away from physical preparation; therefore, they often develop abbreviated versions as parallel forms of assessment. Short form measures contain a smaller number of items and are assumed to produce scores that provide equivalent interpretation to their long form counterparts. Evidence that supports the reliability of parallel forms is conveyed with a Pearson correlation. Importantly, alternate forms, including short forms, should be subject to rigorous psychometric procedures to confirm the aspects of validity discussed above.

Temporal stability. Measurement developers customarily assess test-retest reliability (correlation coefficients) between two administrations of an instrument to evaluate the reproducibility of scores over time; however, collapsing all sources of variability into a single coefficient may be misleading (Conroy, Metzler, & Hofer, 2003; Schutz, 1998). Advanced statistical methods, such as structural equation modeling (SEM) techniques, may offer a more precise approach to evaluate temporal stability of scores. Indeed, SEM affords opportunity to examine three distinct aspects of temporal score stability: (a) structural stability, (b) differential stability, and (c) latent mean stability.

Structural stability refers to consistency in measurement properties over time. If a measure consists of multiple items purported to be indicators of a single psychological construct, each of these items contributes to the variance in this construct. Typically, we assume that each item contributes equally; therefore, we assign equal weights (e.g., 1) to each item and sum to produce a single score representing the general construct of interest. In reality, it is likely that each item contributes differently to the general construct and thus should be weighted uniquely. Assessment of structural stability using SEM allows measurement developers to test whether or not these item weights (known as factor loadings) are invariant over time. If evidence for invariant weights over time is not achieved, then it is possible that changes in scores are due to measurement error (Hofer, 1999).

Differential stability is analogous to test-retest reliability; however, rather than a correlation between calculated scale scores, it is represented by a correlation of individual latent scores in an SEM framework assessed at two separate occasions. Differential stability is a relative measure of temporal stability; that is, it is a measure of the extent to which individuals maintain the same relative position in the group over time (Schutz, 1998, p. 396). In other words, if we assess confidence for 100 athletes on two separate occasions, we would obtain evidence for high differential stability as long as those athletes who reported the highest confidence at time 1 also reported the highest confidence at time 2. Differential stability cannot provide evidence for changes in absolute scores of individuals over time. Using our example, all athletes in our sample could decline in confidence from time 1 to time 2 while maintaining their relative rank ordering (highest remain high, lowest remain low, etc).

To address the limitations of differential stability, measurement developers should provide evidence of a third aspect of temporal stability—**mean stability.** Using SEM, and specifically latent growth curve modeling (McArdle, 1988), researchers are able to retain information about individual score trajectories over time. This allows them to evaluate mean stability or change at the group or population level, as well as individual differences in variation in rate of change over time. Importantly, mean stability cannot be assessed before ensuring structural stability. Without evidence for structural and mean stability, any substantive changes observed in clients (e.g., reduced fear of failure) cannot be attributed solely to intervention (e.g., cognitive-behavioral consultation) because change may be due to measurement properties.

Unfortunately, sport psychology measurement development traditionally has failed to demonstrate rigorous psychometric evaluation; however, as technology and education advances, the field will evolve. As interpreters of scores, sport psychology consultants must be aware of both the evidence and lack thereof in respect to the validity and reliability of scores. In summary, it is the responsibility of the sport psychology practitioner to take great care in selecting psychological measures to employ in consultation.

Assessing Psychological Characteristics of the Athlete

A sport psychology consultant can gain greater insight into an athlete's make-up through the use of carefully selected standardized assessments. Assessment can provide new sources of information as well as an opportunity to validate information gained in the interview or through direct observation. For example, an athlete may state in the interview that one of his or her psychological strengths is emotional control under pressure. This may be an accurate perception or it may be the athlete attempting to manage the situation by distorting actual behavior in competition. While sport psychology counselors would like to believe that athletes are being very honest in interviews, there is no way of knowing if this is the case. Athletes, like many people in an interview setting, may try to present themselves in a positive manner that is inconsistent with the way they actually behave. Some athletes may consciously manage the impressions they make on the sport psychology counselor; others may not be fully aware of or are in denial of their real-life actions.

Results from a standardized test that measure this psychological variable can provide a second source of information. If information gained in the interview is at variance with information provided from the assessment tools used, the counselor must try to resolve this discrepancy. Does the athlete have emotional control as noted in the interview or was the athlete saying something he or she knew the sport psychology counselor would like to hear? Does the athlete want to appear good, or does the athlete want to overcome obstacles that may prevent him or her from being good? When interview and assessment information is at variance, actual observation of the athlete in competition becomes an important third source of information. If the athlete is not a starter or a regular player on the team, it may be necessary to observe practices in as unobtrusive a manner as possible. Observing practice or competition without being noticed increases the likelihood of observing unbiased behavior. The mere presence of the sport psychology counselor may bias the behavior of the athlete, the coach, and the nature of the practice environment in general.

If the athlete behavior is observed over a period of time, in different situations, and as unobtrusively as possible, it can be an excellent indicator of an athlete's behavioral tendencies, which, in turn, is essential to developing a meaningful intervention. When an athlete cannot or will not acknowledge a particular problem, facilitating change in that area will obviously be made difficult. The counselor must remember that maintaining the athlete's cooperation is integral to the process. An athlete who recognizes the need for improvement in a psychological area and is motivated to see it through will benefit from sport psychology intervention.

Psychological assessment can play a contributing role in the identification of psychological responses that may assist or debilitate performance. The specific assessment(s) to be used should hold sound psychometric properties as discussed previously. It should also be presented to the athlete as an educational opportunity. The information gained from this experience is a part of the self-discovery process as well as the performance enhancement process. Some of the assessments that are selected should measure enduring characteristics, relative tendencies, or traits. Many applied scientists from criminology to business understand that the human being is complex but that behavioral tendencies do exist, can be identified, and can affect the nature of performance. Many fields use standardized psychological assessments as a tool in the evaluation of performance potential. Professional teams regularly administer psychological tests to athletes at NFL combines. If a team has an opportunity to draft one of two players of fairly equal skill and physical ability, the "psychology" of the athlete can be a determining factor in the draft decision. Would it be valuable information to the coach or general manager if he or she knew that one potential draft pick had psychological characteristics such as emotional control, self-discipline, and a high work rate and that the other scored poorly on these characteristics? Would the coach or general manager consider this information as a part of the decision-making process?

Although important, research and development of sport-specific tests that accurately measure tendencies deemed contributory to athletic success are neglected by many sport psychology researchers. Assessment is being used on a regular basis in professional sports, and applied sport psychology researchers could assist in the development and validation of sound measures that will evaluate those qualities coaches deem important for success. Assessment is an area that has tremendous educational potential. Those outside of mainstream sport psychology recognize this potential and work on a regular basis with professional sport teams and athletes providing selection guidance and educational information to players, general managers, and coaches. By becoming involved in this area, sport psychology can participate in a more formal manner and influence the validity of assessment and the ethical use of assessment tools.

Assessing behavioral tendencies can contribute to an athlete's self-understanding and may provide information to the counselor for the triangulation process. It is also helpful to assess an athlete's pre-competitive state of affect. Coaches and athletes know that the hours spent in training can be negated if athletes cannot manage their frame of mind in the hours just before competition and while in the heat of actual competition. How many times have talented athletes self-destructed the morning of an event or "lost their nerve" during the final pre-match warm-up. Coaches are constantly addressing the importance of making good decisions during a contest, and everyone has witnessed teams coming out mistake-riddled at the start of a big game. Having good psychological management over pre-competitive affect can make a significant difference in performance.

Assessing affect provides another piece of information that can be educational to both the counselor and the athlete. Few coaches seem to be interested in a good practice player who becomes anxious and confused and who loses competitive vigor right before competition. How difficult would it be to play interactive sports such as soccer, basketball, or football with an anxious and confused mindset? Would a coach want a center midfielder, point guard, or quarterback unable to think quickly and make sharp and correct decisions because he or she was hampered by anxiety, confusion, and a loss of competitive will? Assessing affect during the pre-competitive period provides valuable information that may be combined with other assessments, including that of the athlete in actual competition. *The combination of interview information, assessment information, and actual observation of competitive behavior provides a fairly powerful mosaic of the psychology of an athlete.* The educational and informational value provided by the combination of these three sources should not be underestimated, particularly by individuals who have not used assessment in their practice.

Assessment as Feedback

Every counselor should experiment with various assessment tools to determine the value of each instrument to his or her own practice. When working within a team setting, it may be helpful to consult with the head coach. Experienced college and professional coaches often have very specific ideas of what they expect from a player, psychologically speaking. Confidentiality of the athlete should always be protected; however, coaches can offer insight regarding qualities they would like to see developed to a high level in their players. A player may be an outstanding talent yet thinks nothing of showing up two minutes late for practice or a meeting. If that player's coach is very high on discipline, "the talent" may be running stadiums or sitting on the bench. The coach may see the tardy behavior akin to selfishness and a lack of precision. This lack of discipline can be devastating to a team in a close game against a talented opponent. A good coach knows that in these evenly matched competitions, little differences in precision and timing make big differences in the outcome. *Knowing the perspective of the coach can guide the counselor in the selection of valid instruments that may measure the psychological constructs noted by the coach.*

Although some sport psychologists may argue the value of assessment tools for selection purposes (they are widely used in NFL combines and other sport selection venues) the educational aspect of assessment can be a valuable experience for any athlete. How well do you think you know yourself? Is your impression of yourself the same as your colleague's or spouse's description of you? How well athletes know themselves can be very valuable to the intervention process. If athletes know their psychological strengths, they are better positioned to reinforce them; similarly, if they know their weaknesses, they are better able to address them. When athletes are unaware of their psychological strengths, their resources to call upon in times of competitive difficulty are limited. If psychological strengths are weak, there is an obvious need to develop them. If athletes distort psychological weaknesses or deny they exist, there is little opportunity for successful intervention.

When psychological assessment is used, it is very educational to have athletes plot out on blank assessment profile sheets their subjective perception of their scores. The athlete's score on the assessment and his or her subjective profile are both representations from the same person. This psychological exercise provides some insight into how well athletes know themselves. Given the psychometrics of specific assessments, the counselor can often determine when the two assessments are congruent and when they are incongruent. When there is incongruence, the counselor and athlete attempt to resolve these responses. This dialogue is frequently very insightful, as real competitive situations are often discussed by the athlete. The counselor may also weigh this dialogue against the interview material and the behavioral observations. *The feedback provided by assessment can be rich with information and insight.* When feedback is provided in a confidential, supportive, trusting, and educational environment, athletes often respond very favorably. They are often excited to get to work on implementing the actual interventions that may help them improve the psychological weaknesses that were identified. Prior to the interview and the assessment feedback, psychological weakness was an abstraction that neither the athlete nor the coach could ever really get a handle on. Now, the athlete believes it is possible to improve upon his or her approach to competition and performance.

transition from assessment to intervention implementation is fairly easy following assessment feedback. As noted earlier, many athletes are excited to have discussed and placed understandable labels on psychological responses or feelings that have hampered them in the past. It is important to help the athlete understand at this point that the commitment is to the process itself, and as such, there are no guarantees. You can do many things right and lose; you can pitch a one-hitter in a baseball game and lose. The commitment is to a standard of preparing for competition and responding when in competition. This standard has the potential to increase the athlete's enjoyment of competition and enhance the likelihood of performing close to his or her ability level on a consistent basis. At this point, the major dilemma for the counselor is to determine which issues are affecting the athlete most significantly. This determination will at the very least define the initial point of departure for the intervention process.

Putting Counselor Skills into Practice

As professionals in preparation move through a sequence of classroom experiences, they will begin to piece together a picture of how the consulting process is structured and how it unfolds for the athlete and the clinician. *It is very important to emphasize to the professional-in-preparation the unique aspects of both people participating in the counseling experience.* It is important for clinicians to have structure-to recognize their counseling history with the client, where they are now, and where they may be going. Without this structure, the clinician can flounder and be without direction for several sessions. It is not uncommon to hear novice clinicians-in-training say, "I don't know where to go now," or "I don't know what to do next," during the actual ebb and flow of a supervised counseling session with an athlete. Time is often an issue when working with an athletic population. An open-ended, unstructured approach may take more time than the athlete, coach, or an organization can risk spending. When working with a collegiate, professional, or Olympic athlete, performance and results are the standard by which a clinician (rightfully or wrongfully) is often evaluated. At high levels of competition, an investment in a sport psychology consultant is considered an investment in performance enhancement. When athletes can see progress and can see the structures they are working within, there is often a motivation to continue. An athlete who invests time and effort but sees little or no tangible improvement has no practical reason to continue the interaction.

Develop a Program, Not a Package

The term *structure* or *program* indicates that there is a big picture or general plan guiding the clinician. The structure should be logical and orderly, yet provide the flexibility needed to address issues as they come up. This is particularly important

Sample Intervention Program, or a Structured Approach to Intervention

- Ice breaking and ground rules
- Informal dialogue leading to initial and mutual background exchange
- Explanation of need for interview (information collection) with athlete
- Structured intake interview
- Education of athlete on the use and value of psychological assessment
- Administration and review of psychological assessments
- Convergence on presenting issues based on interview, assessment, and observation
- Counselor identification and selection of issue(s) to be addressed
- Initiation of Cognitive Behavior Modification (CBM) Intervention Program
- Movement through CBM stages
- Relationship of issues identified in CBM to athlete preparation and performance
- Establishment of practice and game objectives
- Development of sport-specific preparatory routines
- Enhancement of psychological responses to specific issues identified in CBM
- Development of personal goals
- Development of relaxation skills
- Development of rehearsal skills in conjunction with relaxation
- Development of Performance Feedback Sheets
- Development of ability to self-adjust to performance obstacles
- Enhancement of client independence
- Initiation of movement toward program closure
- Written formal feedback from the client
- Progressive disengagement from client-clinician relationship

when working with an athlete during the season. A new issue can come up every week when an athlete is in season and playing contests once or more between meetings. A program or structure is not bound by specific time limits, but the logical progression provides a framework, an order, and a direction for both the clinician and the athlete. A structure provides a "unit plan" without a sense of being bound or locked down to a predetermined path.

Sport psychology clinicians should develop their own "signature" program based on their training, individual consulting experiences, and consulting goals when working with athletes. During direct and indirect supervised consulting experiences, clinicians-in-preparation work with the supervisor to establish and refine their programs. As experience is gained, the programs will continually be refined and improved as clinicians learn more about themselves as counselors and facilitators of meaningful behavior change in the sport environment.

Athlete Performance Enhancement "Packages"

As important as structure and a programmatic approach may be to a practicing professional, it is easy to over-structure and go from a program to a package. Packages have become popular in psychology as noted by the multitude of self-help tapes, videos, CDs and infomercials promising immediate and dramatic results. Self-help is a laudable goal, and the attractiveness of self-improvement in all aspects of life has resulted in the creation of a multi-million dollar industry. Thus, it has become relatively easy to market a packaged-cookbook approach to performance enhancement in any field, including sport performance. Advertising giants know sales can be enhanced if they attach a celebrity or well-known athlete to a self-help package.

Slick marketing and celebrity may sell a product, but what promotes its success are science and substance. *A package approach to sport psychology does not take into consideration individual differences or specific psychological concerns an athlete may be experiencing.* The assumption that a package approach covers most of the important psychological areas that an athlete should attend to seems naïve at best. It is not surprising that this type of cookbook approach has rarely been documented in the literature. Human behavior is complex, has stable as well as transient characteristics, and is extremely difficult to change. After it has been changed, new behavior patterns are difficult to maintain over time. The high failure rate of popular diets provides an appreciation of how difficult it is to achieve and then maintain changed behavior over time.

Packaged approaches can fail to achieve or sustain meaningful behavior change because thoughts and behaviors reinforcing the maintenance of the undesirable behavior or habit are never specifically identified and addressed. While packaged approaches may look attractive and provide the appearance that they work (testimonials are common), the broad stroke approach may miss many of the concerns particular to an athlete's situation. The sport psychology consultant must think of himself or herself as a professional, not a technician. A packaged approach requires no particular expertise in understanding the psychological dynamics of a situation. A technician may be able to teach relaxation in the packaged approach but may not be able to determine or resolve the stress or conflicts that may continue to generate anxiousness and the need for relaxation and stress management.

By developing an ability to interview, assess, and then intervene with an established intervention approach, the professional can aid the athlete in identifying and reducing the cause of the anxiety. The athlete becomes a more dynamic, informed, and participating member of the consulting process. This investment creates a process that provides a better opportunity for self-identification and self-application both on and off the field of play. The athlete develops an ability to adapt by being actively involved in the intervention process. Practicing a set of psychological skills is often a superficial exercise. It does not provide an athlete with "why" information. Why information is an understanding of why an undesired response exists and why it has persisted and resisted change. Knowing what psychological variables initiate and sustain undesired athlete behavior is an important first step in a meaningful attempt to change.

Some professionals have advocated a "psychological skills" approach with athletes (e.g., Gould & Udry, 1994), and others (Chartrand, Jowdy, & Danish 1992) have advocated teaching coaches how to be "sport psychologists." Most coaches do use psychology on a daily basis in conducting practices and interacting with athletes. Most, however, do not have the training or the time to initiate systematic approaches to behavior change. Coaches trying to "practice" sport psychology in a meaningful manner often experience other potential obstacles, such as conflicts of interest and dual-role relationships with the athlete. How many athletes would be willing to tell the coach (the person who controls their playing time) that they are not confident, are highly anxious or losing motivation to practice, or think they deserve more playing time? There are many real-life situations players share with a sport psychologist that they would be very reluctant to share with their coach. Most importantly, packaged approaches and psychological skills approaches grossly underestimate the difficult challenge confronting both the athlete and the clinician when attempting to make meaningful changes in behavior and athletic performance. Effective counseling skills take time to develop and require planning, practice, and feedback from experienced observers. Placing a coach in the role of a counselor with the athlete can harm the player, the coach, and their relationship.

Coaches have recognized the value of professional decisions offered by physicians, athletic trainers, and strength trainers in areas related to injury and conditioning. A sport psychology consultant has the capacity to addresses complex issues confronting an athlete. A positive service can be provided to coaches and athletes when these issues are addressed by an individual with expertise, objectivity, and professional training in sport psychology. Properly supervised experiences for professionals in training are where these abilities and practice skills are developed and honed.

Pre-planning a session

The thought and organization involved in pre-planning a session for an athlete is one of the foundational growth experiences for a counselor in preparation. Some counselors in preparation have little or no hands-on experience conducting an

---

Samples of pre-plan assignments

Pre-Plan Assignment One: Design your "program" or "unit plan" for 20 one-hour sessions with an athlete.

Pre-Plan Assignment Two: Design a structured intake interview to be conducted with a women's varsity lacrosse player.

---

intervention session. Providing an opportunity for guided discovery in planning a sequence of intervention sessions can be one of the more valuable learning experiences possible at this stage of professional development. Supervisors should work with novice counselors to establish the general framework or program as noted earlier in this chapter; however, they should provide the counselor-in-preparation the opportunity to pre-plan the session. This process, while initially tougher for the counselor-in-training, fosters the type of creative and applied thinking necessary to be a successful counselor.

The pre-plan should be e-mailed to the supervisor at least two days prior to the scheduled meeting with the athlete so that comments and constructive feedback can be provided to the novice counselor and, if necessary, enhancements can be made. The pre-plan serves as a general guide for the counselors. It frames what was accomplished in the previous sessions and provides direction and objectives for the current session.

Sometimes sessions go relatively smoothly and a sound pre-plan is followed fairly well. Sometimes the athlete comes into the session with a "bomb"! A bomb is an issue that may not have come up before, but now the athlete is ready to let it drop. A bomb can also be an issue that was just generated from a recent game, practice, or interaction with the coach or a teammate. Usually, the counselor has no way of planning for a bomb. When a bomb is dropped, you will know it! The athlete will speak freely, often emotionally, and with urgency. The athlete will want the particular matter of concern addressed right now and the intensity will be obvious. In these situations a counselor can not force a pre-plan on the athlete. The pre-plan may now be a bomb! By addressing an unanticipated and stressful issue, you show the athlete that his or her well-being and concerns really are your focus. It is a great opportunity for the counselor to demonstrate good listening skills, empathy, and flexibility.

These situations reveal much to the athlete about the sport psychologist, and they surely reveal much to the sport psychologist about the athlete. You may have to work hard in the intervention setting to get the pure response the athlete provides when sharing a bomb. These are the situations that will bond your relationship and build trust between you and the athlete. Forcing your pre-plan on an athlete in such a situation could easily be perceived by the athlete as evidence that "you really do not understand me" or that "you have your own agenda or set plan for me."

Sample Session Pre-plan Submitted by a Counselor-in-Training

I. Small talk / Icebreakers.

II. Discuss weekend competition and have athlete review from his or her logbook if necessary.
   A. Walk us through last weekend from the night before the race to race time.
   B. Tell us about your pre-race for the 400 hurdles (prelims).
   C. Did the 110 hurdle race have any positive or negative affect on the 400 race?
   D. How did the race objectives you developed work in the 400 competition?
      1. Were you ready to go as you approached the starting line? Were you clear-minded at the beginning when in the blocks? What was your final pre-race routine? When did you go on automatic?
      2. Did you get out fast? Attack each hurdle? Did you run through each hurdle?
      3. Let's discuss your psychological approach at the end of the race. How did you come off the last hurdle? How was your push to the finish? Did your place in the race have an impact on how you finished the race?
   E. Were you satisfied with your performance?
      1. What are the positives from Saturday that you want to use again next week?
      2. What are some specific psychological preparation and perform-ance issues you can continue to improve upon?
      3. Did you have fun and enjoy the competition?

III. Work with "Eddie" and have him understand how to set up perform-ance windows.
   A. 110 hurdles
   B. 100 meters
   C. 400 hurdles

IV. Transition to psychological objectives for the next race and move toward closure and end of the session.

V. Closure.

VI. Ask Eddie to express what he has learned in today's session and what he is going to take out of the office with him and implement in this weekend's competition.

VII. End on a positive-have him leave the office feeling good and looking forward to returning next week!

counselor must demonstrate that he or she is interested in the athlete's unique
sses and challenges. In fact, it is common to find that the bomb ends up fitting
into the larger intervention picture that unfolds as the counselor begins to better
understand the client's psychological composition and challenges.

Common Pre-Plan Mistakes by Novice Counselors

Counselors-in-training learn a great deal from attempts to conceptualize and
organize an intervention session through a pre-plan. While in training, novice
counselors will learn from positive experiences and mistakes; both will help the
counselors be more prepared and professional when they consult under supervision and eventually on their own. Common mistakes made by counselors-in-training when producing pre-plans include the following:

1. A lack of conceptual organization

What influences the order of the content the counselor-in-training wishes to cover
in each session? What influences the order of the content the counselor-in-training wishes to cover from session one to session two to session twenty?

For example, do you want to introduce assessment or relaxation training in session one? Probably not! What is the rationale behind the order of the pre-plan the
counselor-in-training presents? This must be articulated by the counselor-in-
training.

2. A technique-oriented or "psychological skills"-oriented approach

A pre-plan should be characterized by the use of counselor questions rather than
constant counselor direction or skills training. "How to" skills have their use but a
counselor needs to facilitate an athlete's ability to verbalize his or her concerns in
an open and honest manner. Athlete-specific disclosure often results in the sharing of concerns the athlete has been suppressing, denying, or has been unsuccess-
ful in resolving to date. The use of psychological skills as a "mental trainer" cannot
be used in a vacuum. If underlying concerns that initiate and/or reinforce
unwanted behavior or poor performance are not addressed, the superficial use of
psychological skills may result in superficial enhancement of athletic performance.

3. Judging how much time each segment in the unit may take

This is a very difficult aspect even for the experienced professional. It is difficult
to estimate "error time." It is not unusual for counselors-in-training to grossly
underestimate the amount of time it takes for a high-quality intervention to
unfold and develop. Always think in terms of "flex time"! This thinking allows you
to move on when sessions go very smoothly and make adaptations when the work
is good but slow.

4. Failing to recognize how to move toward closure in closed ended time periods

If you have one hour to meet with the athlete, you should pre-plan moving toward a stopping point at least 10 minutes before the end of the session. Pre-plan to avoid bringing up new or sensitive information toward the end of a session. If sensitive information has been opened but not effectively addressed or closed, and if you and the athlete both have free time on the back end of a session, ask the athlete if he or she would like to stay for a few minutes and continue the dialogue.

5. Organizing when and how psychological assessment should be integrated into an intervention unit

Some sport psychologists have criticized psychological assessment without any history of actually utilizing assessment tools themselves! Assessment can play a significant role as part of a well-organized intervention program. Knowing when to use assessments and how to use them to complement your interview and direct observations provides the opportunity for triangulation. Triangulation is the degree of convergence found in information from three different sources; interview, assessment, and observation.

6. Forgetting to build into the pre-plan appropriate time to review performances and provide performance feedback

Reviewing a past performance (e.g., last week's game) is important; however, this review and dialogue can take a considerable amount of time. A game experience is often loaded with rich material for both the athlete and the counselor. Reviewing a performance can often lead to new psychological issues being brought up by the athlete. This may result in the counselor covering much less new material than originally planned or addressing a significant issue that took place during the competition. The novice counselor should not feel "time crunched." If real-game content is being offered and is addressed by the athlete and the counselor, the opportunity for quality intervention is being presented. The counselor should be aware of how the game events may be related to issues that are already being addressed or how they may be psychologically connected to issues that have been previously identified.

Role Playing a Session

The counselor-in-training should receive a solid foundation of information and applied knowledge from classroom experiences. Once the counselor-in-training has planned and received structured feedback for an intervention unit and for individual session pre-plans, he or she is ready to role play a session. All role-play sessions should be filmed and the "actor" should receive verbal and written feedback on his or her performance from the supervisor and a class peer. Role playing serves a very important function in the education and training sequence for a counselor-in-training. It places novice counselors in leadership positions and in a position where they must absorb and determine the relevance of information, as well as determine how this information can affect the athlete and his or her performance. Perhaps most important, the novice counselor must do all of this processing in real time. Role playing creates a performance pressure prior to actually working with an athlete. It is a simulation that should be made as close to the "real thing" as possible!

Counselors-in-training should prepare for the role-playing session just as they would for an actual intervention session. They should be required to pass in a pre-plan and should be provided feedback on it. They should come to the supervisor's office dressed professionally and ready to run the session. Counselors-in-training often report "butterflies" and nervousness before role playing. Learning effective management of these emotions will have a positive impact on the sessions; a confident, assured counselor is ready and able to assist athletes in their quest for enhanced performance.

The session should be started on time and the content of the session should be role played by the experienced supervisor. This is important because the experienced supervisor knows how a session *could* go. This knowledge can allow the supervisor to provide a much more realistic role-playing experience for the counselor-in-training than a fellow student or even a senior graduate student with training in athlete intervention. The office should be set up exactly as if the counselor were working with the athlete in a supervised session.

Counselors-in-training should have an opportunity to play the role of the lead counselor at least twice prior to engaging in a supervised consulting experience with an athlete.

Examples of sessions that are helpful to role play include:

1. The first session with an athlete
2. The interview session
3. The assessment and assessment feedback sessions
4. The resistant athlete and the "shy" athlete
5. A session after an athlete has a bad real-game performance
6. Setting up a goal sheet with an athlete
7. Setting up and reviewing a performance feedback sheet
8. Athlete drops a "bomb" during session
9. Relaxation training, mental rehearsal
10. Closure meeting-athlete's last scheduled meeting

While this list is certainly not exhaustive it gives the reader an idea of some of the major areas that should be role played. If logistics constrain how much time

A Suggested Office Set Up

- Have all seating arranged at right angles. The athlete should sit in the middle position so he or she can turn to either side and make eye contact with the counselor-in-training or the supervisor.
- Have a video camera set up so that it is focused on the athlete and the counselor-in-training.
- Have the peer observer(s) seat(s) slightly back and away from the triad of the athlete, counselor-in-training, and the supervisor. Arrange this seating to avoid a close and direct line of eye contact between the peer observer(s) and the athlete.
- Have a small clock in the office that is visible to the counselor-in-training and the supervisor. It can be positioned discreetly on a table, desk, or bookcase.
- It is often helpful to have some reading material on a table in front of the athlete that is from the athlete's school or university or from the local professional team.
- Have your door open when you greet the athlete. Have a sign already posted on the door saying, "Session in Progress—Please Do Not Disturb" or "Meeting in Progress—Please Do Not Disturb."
- Have a box of facial tissue off to the side but reachable by the athlete. (Occasionally this may also be of use to the counselor-in-training!)

these experiences can be allocated, it is important to role play the high probability events noted in the ten suggested cases above.

It is also important to have all members of a class observe the role-playing exercise so they can benefit from the success and mistakes of their classmate's experience. Each student should have a student peer yoked with them for the role-playing experience. The yoked student peer not only observes the exercise but submits a written feedback narrative to the supervising professor and the student performing the role play. Peer feedback speeds the learning process for all the participants; it offers another valuable source of feedback by a peer who observes the session with a defined and constructively critical eye. Peers often describe the experience as a virtual experience—it is as if the peer is doing the role play—and the learning curve is sped up considerably.

Another great benefit of role playing is that it can facilitate the building of confidence in a counselor-in-training. Experienced counselors must remember how threatening the first few counseling experiences can be for a novice counselor. The anxiety of a new situation combined with age differences of only two to three years between the counselor-in-training and the athlete sometimes can create self-doubt and stress. The counselors-in-training are placed in a setting that may seem extremely unstructured to them even if they are conducting a pre-planned session. The counselor-in-training knows that when dialogue with the athlete starts, the athlete could go in any direction! The role playing requires the counselor-in-training to think quickly, manage the flow of the conversation, work in real time, and maintain control of the session. These are all formidable challenges, particularly since we have not even mentioned that counselors-in-training are trying to process the psychological significance of what the athletes are saying to them!

Much like rookie athletes, counselors-in-training are consciously working on three different processing levels: (a) Do I know the play? (b) Can I run the play? (c) Can I make the play? Eventually, as a function of positive training experiences, less conscious attention will be allocated to the simultaneous attention to all three of the concerns. Some concerns, (e.g., Do I know the play?) may even become diminished to the point where they are not a stress on the system. Role-playing experiences and observations assist the novice counselor in learning to focus on the material being offered by the athlete and how it should be addressed rather than focusing on their own feelings of concern or inexperience. While the supervisor needs to provide realistic role-playing experiences, he or she must also provide constructive and supportive feedback that enhances efficacy in the novice counselor. This feedback is essential to the learning and growth process for a counselor-in-training.

Supervised Practica

Counselors-in-training should move through an educational and training sequence that culminates in supervised practica. Counselors-in-training have received significant classroom experiences that provide a knowledge base in the disciplines of sport psychology, counseling, and psychology. They have engaged in repeated pre-planning experiences and role-playing sessions, and have observed live sessions conducted by an experienced sport psychology counselor. It is time for the counselor-in-training to "go live" and experience being an active counselor in a supervised session. Much like a team in the latter stages of a pre-season training camp, the counselor-in-training should now feel ready to "start the season." Although there may still be some feelings of doubt and anxiety, the counselor-in-training now has an opportunity to test out his or her aptitude for counseling athletes in a real-life setting. For many, this will be a very rewarding experience; for some, it will demonstrate how much more work they have before them; and for others, it may cause them to rethink sport psychology consulting as a career path.

It is important for counselors-in-training to have an experienced sport psychology counselor as a mentor during these important and personal developmental experiences. The sequence of the supervised experience is important to counselors-in-training as is the feedback they receive from the supervisor and the athlete. Supervised practica should be presented in a logical progression from a highly supervised to an indirectly supervised environment. The educational goal is to facilitate the development of counselors in training to a level of competence that allows them to feel comfortable consulting independently with an athlete. The supervised experience should also facilitate the development of confidence beyond what can be gained from classroom experiences. The educational and training experiences of a supervised practicum should highlight the recognition that counselors-in-training can play a beneficial role in enhancing the well-being and athletic performance of their clients.

Recognizing Individual Differences

The supervised setting provides an extremely rich environment for the continuation and progression of professional development through hands-on experiences. The counselor-in-training will move closer to independent practice through the supervised experience. Thrusting a student into an independent consulting experience too quickly can result in a bad experience for both the athlete and the counselor-in-training. *A progression from more structured supervised experiences to less structured experiences is a very individually defined process.* Not all counselors-in-training will move toward independent consulting at the same rate. Supervisors need to keep individual differences in mind; however, at the same time, they must also guard against novice counselors becoming dependent on the security afforded to them in the highly supervised environment. Some counselors-in-training may express hesitation or doubt when the supervisor believes that they are competent and ready for a less-structured environment. Some anxiety on the part of a novice counselor should be expected but should not prevent the accrual of more responsibility in conducting the intervention. A proper progression is an important responsibility of the supervisor and can be pivotal in the confidence-building process.

On the other hand, it is also possible to encounter a counselor-in-training who is very comfortable with the interactional aspects of working with an athlete but is still lacking in counseling and intervention expertise. This counselor may show great enthusiasm and social interaction skills yet have difficulty providing substance and depth to the intervention process. Although everything moves along fine at a superficial level, significant and meaningful progress may not be achieved with the athlete. The counselor-in-training may think that the ease with which he or she interacts with the athlete is a justification for the opportunity to work more independently from the supervisor. Again, the skill of an experienced supervisor will be crucial in providing feedback that maintains the counselor's interpersonal skills or enthusiasm while sharpening his or her application of sport psychology and intervention principles.

A Progression of Supervised Experiences

By following a progression, the supervisor will have ample opportunity to evaluate the counselor-in-training from his or her direct experiences with an athlete and from peer feedback. Placing a counselor alternately in the roles of "actor" and "observer" not only dramatically speeds up the learning curve, but it also promotes empathy. As in many professions, "it always looks easier than it is." Learning from doing and learning from watching provide parallel yet distinct experiences that develop an appreciation of what it takes to be a quality counselor.

The progression recommended for the supervised experience is broken into a four-step progression detailed below. It is important to reemphasize that all counselors-in-training have considerable experience at each step in the progression. Some counselors-in-training will move more quickly than others. The speed of the progression should be the decision of the experienced supervisor. It is easy for counselors-in-training to overestimate their consulting abilities based on two or three early positive experiences or question their ability based on one or two significant mistakes. Following the progression recommended below provides both the counselor-in-training and the supervisor with ample opportunity to evaluate progress in counseling skill.

First Supervised Experience: The Team Approach

After role playing has been successfully executed, the first supervised experience presented is the "team approach." In this supervised experience, the counselor-in-training, the athlete, and the experienced supervisor are presented to the athlete as a "team." In this early stage the majority of the interaction will be between the experienced supervisor and the athlete; however, the counselor-in-training pre-plans, observes, and is integrated into the dialogue of each session.

If the novice counselor is too passive, the supervisor skillfully engages him or her in the interaction with a leading question. If counselors are very active and keep up with the flow of the sessions, their involvement is reinforced. All sessions are videotaped and the counselor-in-training provides a brief verbal self-analysis afterward. He or she will also immediately receive verbal feedback from a designated peer and from the supervisor. The counselor-in-training submits the self-analysis to the supervisor, while the peer observer will write up an evaluation of the counselor-in-training during the session and will electronically submit it to both the counselor and the supervisor. This exchange of information has been a great learning tool for all parties. The likelihood of distortion by the counselor-in-training is dramatically reduced by the two sources of feedback and the video. A healthy respect for the challenge of enhancing one's skill as a counselor is developed and appreciated.

Perhaps the most significant aspect of this process is that it teaches peer counselors to provide insightful feedback without being abrasive to one another. This interpersonal counseling skill will be important when peer observers soon find themselves in the role of the actor, and when all the counselors-in-training find themselves taking on more responsibilities in the intervention process.

The team approach should be followed for approximately a 15-week time frame. This interval should provide enough time for the supervisor and the counselor-in-training to make significant progress with an athlete and cover many of the stages in a structured program of intervention. As the team moves deeper into the 15-week block, the counselor-in-training should take over more and more of the dialogue in the session. This natural progression should be fostered by the supervisor and will create a smooth transition into the next phase in the supervised sequence.

Second Supervised Experience: I Have You Covered

After an extensive period of observing and working with an experienced sport psychology supervisor, the counselor-in-training is now ready to take on more responsibility. Progressing from the "team approach" to an environment where the counselor-in-training now has the lead is a natural extension. The sessions are still presented to the athlete as a team approach with all three participants working together; however, in this segment, the supervisor will play the supportive role and the counselor-in-training will lead the session from beginning to end. The supervisor will make sure the sessions are effective and rewarding for both the athlete and the counselor-in-training. If the counselor gets in a bind, cannot answer or effectively address an issue, or just gets in over his or her head, the supervisor is there to offer guidance. One method of redirecting a problematic sessions is to ask questions directly to the counselor-in-training that may help get him or her back on the track with the athlete. Supervisors must show some maturity of their own and should not jump in and take over if a session encounters a few rough spots. If the counselor-in-training does not get back into the flow after a few guiding or leading questions, then the supervisor should pick up the dialogue with the athlete to maintain the integrity and success of the session. The counselor-in-training may ease back in and take over the session at any time.

The skills of the supervisor are vital in these situations. Mistakes or missed opportunities by the counselor-in-training should not be dealt with punitively. A session should not be taken over by the supervisor as "punishment" for mistakes or an inability to deal with complicated athlete issues. It is important to remember what is was like to be a novice counselor and also to remember that counselors-in-training are often trying very hard to perform and address issues that may overextend their limited experience base. Just as athletes will find that practice isn't the same as game time, counselors-in-training find that supervised consulting is markedly different from a live session-especially when that session seems to be moving very fast and they are not! An effective supervisor will understand that there are two very equally important goals in the sessions where they are providing "cover": (a) the athlete must be provided with a meaningful intervention experience, and (b) the counselor-in-training must be provided with a meaningful learning experience. The effective supervisor must work toward providing a healthy learning environment for both the athlete and the counselor-in-training.

The counselor-in-training pre-plans each session and submits the plans via e-mail to the supervisor at least two days in advance. All sessions are videotaped and

Sample Student Clinician
Post-Session Self Evaluation

The first thing I noticed on the tape was my attempt at a strong reinforcement of Eddie taking the POMS approximately 10 minutes before he ran the 110 hurdle preliminaries. I felt like I was more animated than I actually was, which means that I must continue to try to improve my animation in order to get up to the level that is appropriate. I feel more comfortable working with Eddie now, so I must think about being a little more animated in order to really achieve an improvement in this area.

I thought that a pearl came out real early when Eddie said he thought about not false starting when he approached the 110 hurdle prelims. I caught this right away and didn't let it slide. I felt that I should see if he had any past experiences false starting in the 110 hurdles. If he did not, I would ask why he thought he might do it this time. Indeed, he had not false started before in this event. My next step was to discuss how the technique in coming out of the blocks is different in the 100 meters than the 110 hurdles. The idea was to stimulate insight that the two races are different, and as such, it may be counter-productive to worry. That approach seemed to be faltering because Eddie was not following my train of thought, so I thought about discussing the concept of not focusing on the past. However, Dr. Jones jumped in and took an approach that I did not see. If an athlete is fairly confident of getting through the prelims, there is no need to blast out of the blocks and possibly false start. A "conservative" start and a strong race can get the athlete through the prelims and safely into the finals. After watching the tape I realized that this is a very fine line.

I noticed that I did rehash the false starting topic after Dr. Jones had closed it. I think I wanted to restate it to see if I understood, and as a transition to the next topic. However, on the tape it was somewhat of an awkward situation to try to go back to what had already been worked out. An alternative would be to simply connect with the information just worked on and transition into the next topic.

I then went into his objectives for the race. I realized that I let him off the hook by letting him look in his logbook. The race objectives should be automatic to him by now. If he does not know them in the office how can we expect him to be using them out on the track during his final psychological preparations? I felt that I did a good job at reworking these by doing a quick check with him. Then I used a teachable moment and suggested to him that he should get the race objectives logged in his mind so that he can go over them before getting up into the blocks and before he goes on automatic.

Dr. Jones worked this a little more by using a scenario. I learned a couple of things from this event. First, Eddie can get caught up thinking about other things and we must let him process so he is ready for anything we will say. He did not follow the scenario put forth by Dr. Jones at first. Dr. Jones put Eddie in a hypothetical race a few minutes before the start and asked him what he would be doing. Eddie responded incorrectly by saying he would panic. In retrospect, it seems as though Eddie needs time to think, and when he looks off past Dr. Jones or me in the future, we must be aware of the fact that he may be thinking, and we should let him finish before proceeding. The other thing that I learned was to emphasize the simplification aspect of the objectives. I know that is what they are for, but I forget to articulate that to Eddie.

Each session I learn a new technique from Dr. Jones. During this session, he used the window diagram to explain the relationship between intensity and tension. I thought that this technique really helped Eddie to visualize and internalize the idea that he can be intense but relaxed, which is ideal for competing.

After that I felt that I had a good transition back into how it relates to his objectives. I said, "How can you get into that square (high intensity, low tension)?" Then I took an attempt at closing it by having him restate what happens when anxious thoughts come in. I thought he had internalized it, and I was ready to move on. It always seems like I forget to tie something in, and Dr. Jones incorporated all of the principles into one closing idea. He mentioned that Eddie should use the objectives to counter anxious thoughts and then run his best race and see what happens. He also reinforced the fact that Eddie ran a clean race. This is something I knew, but failed to do. We previously acknowledged that Eddie had not run a clean race in a long time and we discussed the idea of reinforcing it.

As I discussed the 400 hurdles I felt in a bind again. Eddie had not run it in a long time (three years) but I did not want to let him get away with his approach, which was to keep up with the guy in the next lane. I wanted to see if he was going to continue to run it. Because he seemed interested, I decided not to let this approach slide, and I discussed setting up objectives. As I watched the tape I realized that I lost control of this part of the session. Once Eddie starts talking, it is difficult to stop him. I think this is an aspect of my problem with keeping up the pace. I don't want to interrupt him, though.

Because he expressed interest in running the 400 hurdles, I felt that setting up objectives was a good idea. This would establish a routine for each event, as well as each race. However, I spent too much time on this. It probably could have been done in a matter of a couple of minutes. I thought that I did do a good job of holding him accountable for these objectives by asking him to articulate them as we were all writing them down.

As I was discussing the finals of the 110 hurdles, Eddie said that he "wanted to score points." Dr. Jones jumped in and asked Eddie what he was running for. When Eddie said he was running to get a good time Dr. Jones confronted him, "Are you sure?" I am not sure that I could get away with this. As we saw in Jane's session, there is a certain way they respect Dr. Jones and a certain way that they respect the student clinicians. Dr. Jones can use confrontation to get the desired effect where I probably could not.

Another teachable moment for both Eddie and me was the idea of building a foundation. It was not that I did not know what this was; however, I hadn't thought about using this perspective to encapsulate everything that we have done thus far in clinic. It was a way to tie everything together and provide closure.

Overall, I thought that I made some more improvements in trying to grasp pearls and use teachable moments. I think the two areas I can still improve upon are being animated and up-tempo in session, as well as organizing all of the big topics so that I can simplify them for him. I was circling around all of the concepts but did not have the glue to put it all together. That is my next step.

---

the counselor-in-training provides a brief verbal self-analysis of the session immediately after it is over. As in the team approach, immediate verbal feedback from the peer observer and the supervisor is provided. The counselor-in-training will write up his or her post-session self-evaluation and e-mail it to the supervisor. A sample of a post-session self evaluation provided by a counselor-in-training is presented below.

The Post-Session Peer Feedback Sheet

The reflection time a counselor-in-training puts into the post-session self-evaluation is time well invested. The counselor-in-training reflects on interactions with the supervisor and with the athlete during the session and on the progress that can be made in future sessions. The counselor-in-training is also provided with a post-session peer feedback sheet. This feedback provides a peer based evaluation of the counselor-in-training each session. The post-session peer feedback sheet will be electronically submitted to the counselor-in-training and to the supervisor within one day post session.

Counselors-in-training may check their self-evaluations against the evaluations that are submitted from their peer observers. This comparative feedback will not only reinforce elements identified in self evaluation-it can also reveal additional learning points. The peer observer learns vicariously while the counselor-in-training benefits from a second source of feedback.

This approach accomplishes several important goals that speed and promote counselor competence. First, peer observation provides the peer evaluator an opportunity to become deeply involved in another intervention experience. The listening skills of the person assigned peer feedback can increase dramatically by observing the strengths and mistakes made by the supervisee. Observing a counselor-in-training commit an error that you have made but perhaps have not fully acknowledged can be a very effective indirect method of self-realization.

In addition to improving the observation and listening skills of the person providing the peer feedback, this process provides the counselor-in-training with another source of information that may reinforce a point made verbally or in writing by the supervisor. This can be a very powerful learning tool, given that self-perception of performance in an applied setting can be grossly underestimated or overestimated by a novice counselor. The convergence of two sources of feedback on a particular issue generally increases the level of receptivity by the supervisee.

It is interesting to follow this feedback process through weeks and months of intervention. Often, as the student assigned peer feedback becomes more skilled as a clinician, their feedback tends to converge to a greater degree with the feedback provided by the experienced supervisor. It is indeed reinforcing when students with limited counseling experience enhance their listening and feedback skills to a high level of expertise in a matter of a few months.

Third Supervised Experienced: Free Falling

The counselors-in-training have now completed two very intense supervised learning experiences-the "team approach" and the "I have you covered" approach. They have pre-planned numerous sessions and have received feedback regarding their efforts from both peer and supervisor sources. They have also acted as peer observers and provided thoughtful feedback to their colleagues. At this point in their development as sport psychology counselors, they should feel ready to "free fall." This will be a very exciting experience for the counselor-in-training as he or she will now "own" the session. The supervision will go from direct to indirect, and there will no longer be the safety net provided by the experienced supervisor. The counselor-in-training will be on his or her own during the session-free falling!

If the supervisor does not think the counselor-in-training is ready to take a session entirely on his or her own, a second directly supervised experience can be provided. In this situation, counselors-in-training should be afforded more and more ownership of each session until they gradually run the session. It is important to be aware of individual differences and to recognize that not everyone will progress at the same rate. A counselor-in-training who is ahead of a colleague is not necessarily a superior counselor. Many times, counselors-in-training may be slow to initially develop their skill, comfort level, or style, yet they develop into outstanding sport psychology counselors. The goal is to move the counselor along at a pace that is deemed appropriate by the experienced supervisor. Feedback from the counselor-in-training must be balanced with the supervisor's experiences. As previously noted, counselors-in-training can over- or underestimate their ability level because of the relative lack of experience they have as actual counselors.

Moving into the "free falling" stage of supervision requires a great deal of effort. The counselor-in-training will set up the schedule of sessions with the athlete and will conduct them without direct supervision. If in a university setting, a part of the sport psychology laboratory should be set up as a consulting or clinic area to accommodate the educational needs of a counselor-in-training. The counselor will pre-plan each session and e-mail it to the supervisor at least two days in advance. All sessions are videotaped as in the earlier stages of supervision. The counselor-in-training will write up his or her session evaluation and pass it in to the supervisor. The major differences in this stage should be obvious by omission. There is no supervisor present to provide support, guidance, or perspective. There is no peer present to offer constructive feedback or a nod of support when the counselor-in-training may be struggling. It is now the counselor-in-training, the athlete, and the video camera. While thinking, *Isn't this what I thought I was ready for back in the team approach segment when everything seemed so easy?* the counselor-in-training must follow the athlete's train of thought, ask the insightful questions, and make the "right moves" at the right time during the session. Now the counselor-in-training will truly feel what it is like to be a sport psychology counselor!

Following each session, the counselor-in-training will meet with the supervisor and review the video. Based on the post-session evaluation, the counselor will have some questions and may have segments of the video cued up or edited onto another tape for review by the supervisor. Some supervisors may want to preview the tape prior to this meeting. This can be beneficial in highlighting possible variance between what the counselor-in-training wishes to review and what the supervisor picks up on the video. The supervision has clearly reached the indirect level and there is no possibility of direct intervention during a session. Now, the supervisor's main responsibility is to provide constructive reinforcement. The supervisor will be able to determine how effective the training has been to date, as well as the level of understanding, conceptualization, integration, application, and professionalism displayed by the counselor-in-training. These indirect supervisory experiences should provide the finishing touches to a well-educated and well-trained sport psychology counselor. The counselor-in-training should now feel confident in his or her ability to conduct meaningful intervention with athletes from various sports who present a variety of personal and performance related issues to the counselor.

This is the final stage that the counselor-in-training will need to report to the supervisor.

Anchors Aweigh

At the end of the supervised experience it is a good idea to provide students with one last experience where they are entirely on their own. Help them feel free to structure the consulting process as they see fit. Providing this opportunity through an internship with a collegiate or high school athletic team is a valuable experience for the counselor-in-training and can provide quality services to the participating college or high school.

This is an opportunity for personal growth as the student draws upon all that has been learned and at the same time continues to develop a singular style and approach to intervention. There are no pre-plans to turn in, no feedback (direct or indirect), no video to review with a supervisor. Although the counselors are now truly on their own, they should be assured that their supervisors will be available for interaction and dialogue. At this final stage, the confidence built during training will afford the counselors a sense of independence and ownership over their abilities.

Transitioning to Independent Practice

It is entirely normal for a novice counselor to feel apprehensive about the transition from guided discovery to independent practice. While the step to independent practice is important, it should be a logical step if the educational and training experiences reviewed in the preceding chapters are part of the preparation process.

Counseling for many professionals is a way of life, an important way in which they contribute to other people's aspirations and life experiences. Novice counselors should always remember that help is only a phone call away and that the professionals who supervised them are interested in their development and want to help them succeed. As novice counselors interact with more athletes they will begin to feel a sense of competence and any fear of making a mistake in practice will be replaced by an anticipation to work with the next set of challenges. Chapter 5 will demonstrate how all the knowledge and skills sport psychology counselors learn in their education and training can be implemented and applied in the development of a mental training program.

References

Campbell, D. T., & Fiske, D. W. (1959). Convergent and discriminant validation by the multitrait-multimethod matrix. *Psychological Bulletin,* 56, 81–105.

Chartrand, J. M., Jowdy, D. P., & Danish, S. J. (1992). The Psychological Skills Inventory for Sports: Psychometric characteristics and applied implications. *Journal of Sport and Exercise Psychology,* 14, 405–413.

Cook, T. D., & Campbell, D. T. (1979). *Quasi-experimentation: Design and analysis issues for field settings.* Chicago: Rand McNally.

Conroy, D. E., Metzler, J. N., & Hofer, S. M. (2003). Factorial invariance and latent mean stability of performance failure appraisals. *Structural Equation Modeling,* 10, 401–422.

Cronbach, L. J. (1951). Coefficient alpha and the internal structure of tests. *Psychometrika,* 16, 297–334.

Dunn, J. G. H., Bouffard, M., & Rogers, W. T. (1999). Assessing item content-relevance in sport psychology scale-construction research: Issues and recommendations. *Measurement in Physical Education and Exercise Science,* 3, 15–36.

Gould, D., & Udry, E. (1994). Psychological skills for enhancing performance: Arousal regulation strategies. *Medicine and Science in Sports and Exercise, 26,* 478–485.

Hambleton, R. K. (1980). Test score validity and standard-setting methods. In R. A. Berk (Ed.), *Criterion-reference measurement: State of the art* (pp. 80–123). Baltimore: Johns Hopkins University Press.

Hofer, S. M. (1999). Assessing personality structure using factorial invariance procedures. In I. Mervielde, I. Deary, F. DeFruyt, and F. Ostendorf (Eds.) *Personality psychology in Europe* (pp. 35–49), Vol. 7. The Netherlands: Tilburg University Press.

Horner, M. S. (1968). Sex differences in achievement motivation and performance in competitive and non-competitive situations. Unpublished doctoral dissertation, University of Michigan.

Horner, M. S. (1972). Toward an understanding of achievement-related conflicts in women. *Journal of Social Issues, 28,* 157–175.

Loevinger, J. (1957). Objective tests as instruments of psychological theory. *Psychological Reports, 3,* 635–694.

McArdle, J. J. (1988). Dynamic but structural equation modeling of repeated measures data. In J. R. Nesselroade & R. B. Cattell (Eds.), *Handbook of multivariate experimental psychology* (2nd ed., pp. 561–614). New York: Plenum.

Messick, S. (1989). Validity. In R. L. Linn (Ed.), *Educational measurement* (3rd. ed., pp. 13–103). New York: Macmillan.

Messick, S. (1995). Validity of psychological assessment: Validation of inferences from persons' responses and performances as scientific inquiry into score meaning. *American Psychologist, 50,* 741–749.

Metzler, J. N., & Conroy, D. E. (2006). *Development and validation of a hierarchical, multidimensional fear of success measure.* Manuscript submitted for publication.

Schutz, R. W. (1998). Assessing the stability of psychological traits and measures. In J. L. Duda (Ed.), *Advances in sport and exercise psychology measurement* (pp. 393–408). Morgantown, WV: Fitness Information Technology.

Smith, R. E., Smoll, F. L., & Schutz, R. W. (1990). Measurement and correlates of sport-specific cognitive and somatic trait anxiety: The Sport Anxiety Scale. *Anxiety Research, 2,* 263–280.

Zuckerman, M., & Allison, S. N. (1976). An objective measure of fear of success: Construction and validation. *Journal of Personality Assessment, 40,* 422–430.

CHAPTER 5

Developing a Mental Training Program

Earlier in the text the authors described the importance of developing a mental training program rather than a psychological skills package. In this chapter, several intervention strategies that can be weaved into a mental training program to augment individual consultation are described and overviewed. Although these techniques are discussed in general terms, several specific examples are provided to demonstrate how a consultant can individualize each for particular athletes. Developing professionals will learn about the effectiveness and rationale for using relaxation, mastery and coping rehearsals, routines, performance feedback sheets and competitive logs, stress management, and goal setting. Most importantly, after reading this chapter, readers will understand how to develop individualized protocols for each type of intervention. Appropriate selection, development, and implementation of these techniques combined with one-on-one consultation sessions can provide for development of comprehensive mental training programs for individual athletes.

Many athletes competing either at the collegiate Division I or at the professional level of competitive sport are exposed to mental training or a psychological preparation program (Dunlap, 1999). Since most elite competitors are talented, athletes and coaches understand that performance at the top levels of competition requires technical, tactical, and psychological preparation. A high level of experience has familiarized players and coaches with various game situation strategies. The most successful performer is the athlete who can handle the stress, manage the pressure, and can get the most out of his or her talent "when the lights come on" and it is time to perform. Particularly at high levels of competition where talent is more homogeneous, effective psychological preparation and psychological management skills can affect the outcome of a match or game.

Applied sport psychology research has provided encouraging evidence to support the effectiveness of intervention and mental training in respect to enhanced performance. Greenspan and Feltz (1989) and Vealey (1994) have evaluated the effectiveness of sport psychology intervention in a review of research focused on performance enhancement. They reported that educational, relaxation-based, and cognitive behavioral-based interventions were generally effective in the sport setting. There is considerable anecdotal evidence from applied sport psychologists and athletes indicating that mental training and psychological preparation can play a significant role in athlete readiness and improved performance. The areas most commonly addressed in mental training programs include relaxation training, mental rehearsal, and the establishment of athlete routines, performance feedback reports, and personal goals. The combination of these mental preparations should be individualized for each athlete and based on information gained in the interview, assessment, and intervention stages of a program. What an athlete rehearses, how routines are developed, and how specific game performance objectives are set should be extrapolated from information acquired in previous sessions. Each athlete is unique and each athlete has different needs that require specific attention in the mental preparation process. The sport psychology counselor should not use "cookie cutter" techniques with an athlete, but should tailor the preparations based on the individual's experiences and needs. Such a comprehensive mental approach to competition can help prepare the athlete for an effective transition from practice to game performance.

Relaxation training is a basic skill that can facilitate the use of psychological preparation strategies. This training should be viewed as a precursor to other preparations such as rehearsal training. An athlete trained in relaxation may find it fairly easy to move into rehearsals while in the relaxed state. In addition, the classic work of Benson (1975) suggests that relaxation can provide some control over physical and mental (thought) responses. Staying relaxed and at a desirable level of arousal allows an athlete to remain focused and composed under stressful competitive situations.

Approaches to Relaxation Training

A combination of physiological, psychological, and behavioral responses occur when an athlete experiences stress. In order to perform at peak levels, every athlete should learn to recognize particular patterns of over-activation resulting from worry and/or stress. Relaxation strategies are a key component in regulating stress responses that ultimately affect performance. When a muscle tightens, loss of automatic control and excessive contractions of muscle can prevent trained coordinated movement and interfere with performance. In particular, worry and anxiety and stress about not performing well can trigger excessive muscle tension. To avoid this, athletes first need to be taught how to recognize unwanted physical tension and then how to relax or release it. As athletes learn to train their muscles, they develop greater sensitivity to their bodily feelings and responses, resulting in an ability to remove localized tension (Williams & Harris, 2001).

According to Williams and Harris (2001), athletes should be exposed to a variety of relaxation techniques and be taught the benefits of each. The authors suggested it is more efficient to start relaxation training after a workout because it is easier to release the tension after exercise. During the training process, athletes should learn how to relax and withdraw completely from the environment. This provides a reference point for what a zero-activation level feels like, and it also enhances awareness of the integral nature of mental and physical responses. Learning to relax momentarily can help to reduce over-activation at any point during practices and competition. Excessive muscular tension and the worry stimuli are hopefully removed with momentarily relaxation. This type of relaxation can be employed before and during warm-up, and even during brief periods or lapses in play. Relaxation skills must be practiced consistently in order for them to become conditioned responses capable of being exhibited in stressful conditions.

Relaxation Options

The first category of relaxation strategies reviewed is called a muscle-to-mind technique. This technique focuses primarily on somatic tension.

The first skill set is the ability to **control and regulate deep breathing** pre-, during, or post-competition. Performance can be enhanced by amplifying the amount of oxygen in the blood, thus providing more energy for the muscles. When athletes are placed in high-pressure situations, their breathing is typically hindered because they either hold their breath or breathe quickly and shallowly from the upper chest. Simple practice exercises in which the athlete is taught to control the physical self can initiate a sense of control over breathing and emotional arousal. Breathing is one of the easiest physiological systems to control. A relaxation response can be activated by taking a deep breath and exhaling fully. Observation of athletes and other individuals in high danger, high stress situations often demonstrates that people exhibit deep breathing and exhalation after they have resolved (made the game wining shot) or avoided (someone else made the game-winning shot) the stressful encounter.

Depending on the sport, relaxation techniques can be employed in a number of circumstances on and off the field of play. Williams and Harris (2001) have reported that some sport psychology consultants choreograph specific breathing times into the performance of certain skills such as gymnastics, tennis shots, and figure-skating routines. Specific breathing strategies include complete deep breath, sighing with exhalation, rhythmic breathing, and concentration breathing (pairing breathing with a verbal or sub-vocalized cue).

Another muscle-to-mind approach is **progressive relaxation (PR).** PR includes contracting a specific muscle group, holding the contraction for several seconds, then relaxing. The technique involves progressing from one muscle group to another. With consistent practice, the athlete will become skilled at recognizing unwanted tension and releasing it, with the ultimate goal of developing automaticity. The athlete will automatically identify and release tensions that have a negative impact on the skills associated with movement. Specific PR techniques include active PR, in which the individual relaxes the whole body. Differential PR is performed with the same sequence of muscle groups as active PR; however, the difference is the amount of tension generated. Abbreviated active PR can be practiced after an athlete has mastered the PR technique, which consists of combining muscle groups in a shorter amount of time. In passive PR, athletes learn how to relax the muscles without first tensing them. Lastly, quick body scan is a specific PR technique that is useful in situations that require momentary muscle relaxation, such as just before serving, shooting a free throw, or batting. The athlete quickly scans the body from head to toe, stopping only at muscle groups where the tension level is too high (Williams & Harris, 2001).

The second category of relaxation techniques, called mind-to-muscle, focuses on efferent nerve control, or the stimulation from the brain to the muscle. These mind-to-muscle techniques include meditation and autogenic training. **Meditation** can help an athlete with achieving deeper states of relaxation, and it can also help to facilitate concentration (Williams & Harris, 2001). A specific type of meditation is transcendental meditation, where athletes assume a comfortable position, close their eyes, relax their muscles, focus on breathing, and repeat a "mantra" or key word. This technique has been linked to reduced oxygen consumption, decreased respiration, slower heart rate, and lower blood pressure (Hardy, Jones, & Gould, 1996).

Autogenic training, popular among European athletes, consists of a series of exercises intended to create two physical sensations, warmth and heaviness. In simple terms, it is a technique of autohypnosis or self-hypnosis. Attention is focused on the sensations one is trying to produce. There are six stages in the training; athletes must learn each stage before moving to the next:

1. Athletes focus their attention on the dominant arm or leg in a passive mode of behavior, which allows them to believe the arm or leg is heavy.

2. Athletes move from believing the arm or leg is heavy to believing that it is warm.

3. Athletes learn to regulate their heartbeats.

4. Athletes become more aware of their breathing rate.

5. Athletes become more aware of the visceral organs, especially the solar plexus because it is the nerve center for the inner organs.

6. Overall relaxation is achieved through vasoconstriction by having athletes place cold cloths on their foreheads.

After autogenic training has been completed successfully, it can be combined with visualization. It is important to note that autogenic training takes a relatively long time to master (Williams & Harris, 2001).

Selecting a Relaxation Protocol

There are many options and approaches to the use of a relaxation protocol. The considerations mentioned at the end of chapter 3 regarding the selection of a theoretical perspective for practice should guide the selection of a relaxation procedure. The sport psychology counselor should examine any research or applied data in and out of sport regarding a particular relaxation protocol and should select a protocol he or she feels comfortable using; the technique should fit with the counselor's personality. After becoming practiced in this protocol, the counselor should become very effective in creating a relaxed response in the athlete. Eventually, the counselor will train the athlete to self-administer the relaxation protocol. The ability to teach self-administration is very important because there will be many times when the counselor may not be available to the athlete. Even after counselors become comfortable and proficient with relaxation protocol(s), they should remain open to new perspectives as they develop.

Preparing the Athlete for a Relaxation Session

The sport psychology counselor should discuss the role of relaxation with the athlete and discuss why this is an important skill for the athlete to acquire. This preparatory work is very important and can help relieve any concerns an athlete may have about experiencing a relaxation technique. These concerns often can include:

1. fear of letting go

2. fear of losing control

3. concern about "going down and not being able to come back"

4. worries about falling asleep during the relaxation session

5. concern about "looking silly" or being watched while their eyes are closed

6. concern that "I will not be able to do it"

Sample Relaxation Protocol

Below is an example of an eclectic protocol to facilitate relaxation in an athlete. It will be obvious that this protocol incorporates aspects from several of the relaxation options reviewed earlier in this chapter. This example demonstrates work with an athlete who has just initiated relaxation training.

Setting the Stage

Welcome the athlete to the session.

Have the athlete sit comfortably on the sofa in your office.

Engage in introductory small talk.

Briefly review the past week's athletic events.

Reinforce the positive work the athlete has demonstrated.

Briefly discuss some areas that require additional attention.

Transitioning to the Protocol

Ask the athlete if he or she remembers your recent discussion concerning relaxation.

Review what the athlete remembers about the discussion concerning relaxation.

Ask the athlete to discuss why relaxation is an important skill to learn and use as part of the preparation for competition.

Reinforce the athlete for information he or she remembered correctly.

Address any incorrect presentation of the discussion and add any information that was left out by the athlete.

Ask the athlete if he or she would like to try a brief relaxation session.

Initiating the Relaxation Protocol

Go slowly and do not rush the athlete at any time.

Ask the athlete to loosen up or remove his or her shoes.

Ask whether it's okay to dim the lights to create a more subdued environment.

Instruct the athlete to lie back on the sofa in such a manner that the athlete's face will be directly in front of your line of vision (the athlete's feet will point toward where you are seated).

Ask the athlete to get comfortable; allow the athlete to position a small pillow under his or her head.

Ask the athlete to uncross his or her legs if they are crossed, and ask the athlete to place palms of hands on thighs.

Ask whether the athlete is comfortable.

Gradually talk a little more slowly and in a slightly lower tone of voice.

Slowly go over what you will be doing in the relaxation session today. (Keep the first experience brief and simple—focus on the athlete actually experiencing what it feels like to become relaxed).

Ask if there are any questions.

The Relaxation Induction

[Name], I would like you to start out by just getting real comfortable on the sofa and taking a couple of deep breaths. *[Breathe in and out with the athlete to help him or her get the rhythm and the depth of the inhalation and exhalation.]*

Good. Now I would like you to close your eyes, and continue taking some nice, slow and easy deep breaths—way in(draw in air with the athlete) and way out— good. Just let your body and mind relax now for a few minutes. [Pause.] I want you to clear your mind of everything. [Pause.] Just let any stress you have leave your mind. Let it float away like balloons drifting up into a big blue sky. Let go of any thoughts you may have, school, sports, personal. [Pause.]Just let your mind clear and be relaxed, gazing up to that clear blue sky. [Long pause.]

Good. Now I want you to stay right with me, and we are going to relax your body along with your mind. I want you to focus your attention on your forehead and your temples. [Pause.] Any muscular tension you have in this area I want you to release. [Pause.] Just let it go. [Pause.] Let the muscles around your forehead, your hairline, your eyebrows, get heavy, relaxed. Just feel the tension release as those muscles get heavy and relaxed.

Good. Now nice and slowly move to your neck. Feel free to move your neck around and release any tension you have in your neck. [Pause.] Feel the muscles in your neck relaxing as the tension just drains out of your neck and those muscles feel heavy and relaxed. [Pause.] You can feel your head sinking down deeper and deeper into the pillow and this feels very relaxing. Just let it go down into the pillow. [Pause.] Good.

Now I want you to move very slowly down your neck to your left shoulder. [Pause.] Feel the muscles from your neck to your shoulder just relax and get heavy. [Pause.] Let them go as your left shoulder and your left shoulder blade sink deeper and deeper into the sofa. Now very slowly, move down your left arm and let the muscles in your arm relax and get heavy. Let your left arm sink down into the sofa. [Pause.] Let go of any tension you have in that arm. Just let it get heavy and sink deeper and deeper into the sofa. [Pause.] Good. Now slowly move to your elbow, your forearm, and your left hand. Let your whole left arm just sink deeper and deeper into the sofa. Now your whole left side feels very relaxed, very heavy, very warm. [Pause.] Good.

Now nice and slowly move your focus to your right shoulder. [Pause.] Feel the muscles from your neck to your shoulder just relax and get heavy. [Pause.] Let them go as your right shoulder and your right shoulder blade sink deeper and deeper into the sofa. Now very slowly move down your right arm and let the muscles in your arm relax and get heavy. Let your right arm sink down into the sofa. [Pause.] Let go of any tension you have in that arm. Just let it get heavy and sink deeper and deeper into the couch. [Pause.] Good. Now slowly move to your elbow, your forearm, and your right hand. Let your whole right arm just sink deeper and deeper into the sofa. Now your whole right side feels very relaxed, very heavy, very warm. [Pause.] Good.

Now, slowly move your attention to the base of you neck. Feel the muscles in your back just relax. [Pause.] Move slowly down from the base of your neck to the area between your shoulder blades. Feel your shoulder blades sink into the sofa and the big muscles in your back just spread and relax. Move slowly down your back and feel the muscles get heavy and sink deeper and deeper into the sofa. [Pause.] Slowly move down to the small of your back until all of the muscles in your back are heavy, relaxed [pause], your whole upper body [pause], your arms, your back [pause] just totally relax and feel comfortable. [Pause.] Let it go. [Pause.] Let your arms and back feel heavy and warm [pause], very relaxed [pause]. Good.

[Pause for 10–15 seconds and allow the athlete to feel the relaxed state of the upper body.]

Good job. Now I want you to focus on your buttocks. [Pause.] Squeeze the muscles in your buttocks and then release them. [Pause.] Let your buttocks and your mid-section just sink into the sofa. [Pause.] Relax and let those muscles just sink deeper and deeper into the sofa. [Pause.] Good.

Now, nice and slowly, focus your attention on your left quad. Let those big muscles just relax. [Pause.] Let them hang. [Pause.] Hold no tension in them at all. [Pause.] Let them get heavy and relaxed. [Pause.] Nice and slowly move from your quad to your knee; relax that joint. [Pause.] Let your upper leg relax, get heavier and heavier. [Pause.] Let go of any tension. [Pause.] Just let it go and let your leg sink deeper and deeper into the sofa. [Pause.] Now slowly move to your calf. [Pause.] Relax the calf. [Pause.] Let it sink into the sofa. [Pause.] Now slowly move to your left ankle and your left foot. Let any tension in your lower leg, ankle, and foot just go. [Pause.] Let your whole left leg just feel very heavy, very warm. Let it sink deeper and deeper into the sofa. [Pause.] Good.

[Pause for 10–15 seconds and allow athlete to feel the relaxed state of the muscles in the left leg.]

Now, nice and slowly focus your attention on your right quad. Let those big muscles just relax. [Pause.] Let them hang. [Pause.] Hold no tension in them at all. [Pause.] Let them get heavy and relaxed. [Pause.] Nice and slowly move from your quad to your knee; relax that joint. [Pause.] Let your upper leg relax, get heavier and heavier. [Pause.] Let go of any tension. [Pause.] Just let it go and let your leg sink deeper and deeper into the sofa. [Pause.] Now slowly move to your calf. [Pause.] Relax the calf. [Pause.] Let it sink into the sofa. [Pause.] Now go easy to your right ankle and your right foot. Let any tension in your lower leg, ankle, and foot just go. [Pause.] Let your whole right leg just feel very heavy, very warm. Let it sink deeper and deeper into the sofa. [Pause.] Good.

[Pause for 10–15 seconds and allow athlete to feel the relaxed state of the muscles in the right leg.]

Great. Now your whole body feels relaxed. [Pause.] Just feel how peaceful and comfortable you are right now. [Pause.]

Now we are going to get even more relaxed. [Pause.] I am going to count down from seven to zero and I want you to see each number as I say it. [Pause.] See each number in your favorite color and stay right with me. [Pause.] Do not run ahead and do not fall behind. With each number you are going to feel more and more relaxed. [Pause.] You will let go of more and more tension until we get to zero and you will be fully relaxed. [Pause.] Seven, getting more and more relaxed. [Slight pause.] Six, going deeper and deeper. [Slight pause.] Five, feeling your whole body just sinking deeper and deeper into the sofa. [Slight pause.] Four, everything feels calm, quiet, very relaxed. [Slight pause, talking slightly slower and in a lower tone of voice.] Three, coming way down now, more and more relaxed. [Longer pause.] Two, you are almost there. [Longer pause.] One, letting go of any tension that is left now, deeper and deeper. [Long pause.] Zero. [Long pause.] You are totally relaxed.

At this point the athlete should be very calm and still, breathing very slowly, and showing virtually no body movement other than an occasional twitch of a muscle in the lower arm or in the leg. The sport psychology counselor should reinforce the athlete for becoming so relaxed, and then the counselor should move in a slow pace and in a subdued tone to the content of the rehearsal phase of the session (an extensive example of a rehearsal is provided later in this chapter). It is very easy to transition to the rehearsal with a connecting statement such as: "Now that you are relaxed it is easy for you to think, to see things clearly in your mind. Everything is sharp . . . Everything is in focus. You can see everything that I say."

The rehearsal session should be interspersed with returns to the relaxed state when there is a "natural break" in the rehearsal. For example, after the athlete rehearses any single event with a defined start and end point (a shot, a play, a punt), ask the athlete to take a deep breath or two and quickly scan his or her body for tension and return that body part to a relaxed state. You can ask the athlete to signal you with the index finger of the most visible hand when the mind is clear and the body is returned to a relaxed state. This process not only keeps the athlete relaxed, but it also trains the athlete in being able to return to a relaxed state when desired, a conditioned response that will be extremely helpful in competition. These relaxation pauses also break up the session into more manageable blocks or periods rather than one long mental exercise.

When the rehearsals have been completed, the sport psychology counselor can ask the athlete to visualize something on his or her own, such as "three objectives you would like to accomplish in practice this week." It is important that the athlete take the time to visualize the accomplishment of each objective. The athlete can signal with the index finger when the self-selected rehearsal is successfully completed. When the rehearsal and visualization have been completed, the sport psychology counselor should have the athlete take a deep breath and return to a relaxed state for a few (10–15) seconds. After reinforcing the athlete's self-selected and self-paced work, the sport psychology counselor should then let the athlete know that he or she will slowly be brought up from the relaxed state. At this point the athlete should once again be comfortably positioned on the sofa, mentally and physically relaxed and calm.

Return to a Normal Resting State

The athlete will be gradually returned to a normal resting state through verbal instructions provided by the sport psychology counselor. The counselor, still speaking in a lowered tone of voice, initiates the process as follows:

[Name], you did a great job today. Now we are going to count you back up to seven, and I want you to once again see each number in your favorite color as I say it. Stay right with me as you did before. Do not run ahead and do not fall behind. As we count up, I want you to become more and more aware of your surroundings, and I want you to breathe a little more rapidly with each number until we get to seven. When we get to seven, I want you to open your eyes slowly and then just stay lying down for a few seconds before you sit up.

Okay, here we go: One, let some energy come into those feet and lower legs. Two, feel more energy coming into you lower body, and your legs. *[Speak a little more loudly and a little more rapidly now with each number.]* Three, feeling stronger and stronger, feel the energy now moving into you back, your shoulders. Four, breathing a little more rapidly now. Five, feeling more energized, feel the energy coming into your arms and your hands. Six, breathing more rapidly, coming way up now, your whole body is feeling lots of energy. Seven, feeling really good now, very refreshed, lots of energy . . . Open your eyes, stretch out those arms, and legs . . . Good! Great job, [name]! [Do not allow the athlete to sit up too fast-people can get dizzy after being relaxed and prone for 15 minutes or more.] Now just stay relaxed for a moment before you sit up and answer a couple of questions for me.

[Here you can ask the athlete questions that will validate the athlete's experience.]

[Name], were you able to hear me okay? Were you able to visualize the situations we covered today? *[If there were any difficulties, have a brief discussion].* Were you able to see the blue sky? the numbers when we counted up and down? Any trouble staying with me? How relaxed do you feel you were today-with 10 being very relaxed and 1 being not relaxed at all? Okay, slowly sit up now, [name]. Do you have any questions for me?

The sport psychology counselor then closes out the session and confirms the day and time of the next session. As previously noted, it is best to keep the first relaxation experience relatively short and simple so the athlete becomes practiced at getting fully relaxed. Keep the first session focused on the physical and mental sensation of what it feels like to be relaxed. As the athlete becomes familiar and practiced with the relaxation response, more and more content can be built into the rehearsal phase of the session.

All of these concerns should be addressed by the counselor at least one session before the relaxation session. This educational approach helps prepare the athlete and also provides a second opportunity to ask any additional questions he or she may have on the day of the actual session. The athlete should also be advised to wear loose-fitting clothing; sweats and a t-shirt often work well for both male and female subjects.

Rehearsal in Sport

Many athletes find that their minds can be very active the night before and the day of competition. It is common for athletes to go over in their minds various technical aspects of their performance, their tactical responsibilities in the game, and their concerns about carrying out these responsibilities at a level deemed acceptable by the coaching staff. Sport psychology has not introduced mental rehearsal or the use of imagery to the athlete! Most athletes, for better or for worse, have been engaging in some form of mental rehearsal their entire competitive lives. It just takes the power of imagination for the mental rehearsal process to become initiated in an athlete's visual window. Feltz and Landers (1983) and Murphy (1994) have reported mental practice using imagery can have a positive impact on performance. Both also report that the combination of mental practice and physical practice is the most effect way to enhance performance.

Because it is a given that athletes will engage in repetitive mental rehearsal and imagery of some form, the question becomes, "What kind of content is beneficial?" If an athlete is going to go over and over a visual, or repeat words, phrases or thoughts, it makes sense to have this repetition focus on information that is functional and related to performance tasks or objectives. Taking some control over the thought process during the competitive week, particularly the night before and the day of competition when athletes may become anxious, can help a performer stay mentally ready and emotionally fresh. All coaches and athletes know that it is easy for the mind to get occupied and stressed as competition nears. One of the first skills an athlete should learn involves the discipline of regulating "on time" and "off time."

On Time and Off Time

Staying mentally sharp and ready to compete can be a difficult task for many athletes. This is particularly evident when an athlete has a long day and must manage several hours of dead time before reporting to the locker room for pre-game. Many National Football League (NFL) players enjoy playing on *Monday Night Football,* but many do not enjoy the long hours of waiting on Monday leading up to the 9:00 P.M. start. An important part of using rehearsal effectively is making sure the athlete has a firm understanding of the difference between on time and off time.

On time is *any* time an athlete thinks about, sub-vocalizes, or has a visual that is related to some aspect of the upcoming game. On time can be positive, relaxing, and confidence enhancing, or on time can be destructive, stress inducing, and anxiety enhancing. Whether on time has a positive impact on a player depends upon the nature of the content being mentally processed during on time. It also depends on the ability of the athlete to shut down on time for large blocks of time. It is quality, not quantity, that is most important during on time. Athletes cannot be thinking about aspects of the competition hour after hour. This constant mental pressure will make an athlete stale and emotionally spent before the competition even starts.

The mental repetitions, thought stimulation, visualizations, and sub-vocalizations will happen whether an athlete wants them to or not. The athlete and the sport psychology counselor can use this naturally occurring event as a preparation advantage. By using confidence-enhancing and task-specific rehearsals, the athlete can take some control over on time, and in turn, can focus on positive aspects of the preparation process. Rather than having the game on the athlete's mind for extended periods of random time, on time can be predetermined, managed, and defined by the athlete.

Off time is when an athlete is not thinking about *any* aspect of the upcoming game. The athlete's mind is stress free and focused on something that brings enjoyment-talking to a friend on a cell phone, playing a video game, reading a book, listening to music, or walking the dog. Off time must be clean, and the athlete must be absorbed in the off time in order for it to be beneficial. Some athletes do not have the mental discipline to be able to generate clean off time and they get caught in what we call limbo-the psychological middle ground between on time and off time.

Limbo is the state in which athletes are engaged in an off time activity like listening to music but their minds are actively visualizing aspects of the game or worrying about game issues or assignments. Athletes in limbo may think they are on off time because they have the music playing, but they are not off because their minds are occupied and involved in repetitive rehearsal or sub-vocalizations. Limbo is often non-productive because the athlete has identified a block of time for mental rest—or freedom from the stress of the game—yet the athlete is still mentally working and processing game-related information. Why can't the athlete stay on off time? More often than not, anxiety and apprehension occupy the athlete's mind and he or she cannot quiet down these thoughts to enjoy some off time. Limbo time may start out with functional thoughts, but the athlete may soon start to drift to stress-related visualizations. Not being able to have some mental down time in which the mind is resting or relatively stress-free can be very fatiguing. As part of their preparation discipline, athletes must learn to get out of limbo, use off time to rest and regenerate mental energy, and use productive on time to focus on what they want to have happen in the competition in technical, tactical, and emotional areas of performance.

Mastery Rehearsal

Rehearsal can be an effective way of assisting an athlete in using on time in a productive manner. Mastery rehearsal is performed as part of on time that is formally built into the preparation schedule of the athlete. Master rehearsal involves the athletes "seeing" themselves perform part of a skill, the whole of a skill, or even a performance as well as it can be performed technically and tactically. Mastery rehearsal is often confidence enhancing for athletes because they visualize the control of their emotions, their actual bodily movements, and the achievement of desired performance results. There are many ways mastery rehearsal can be effectively built into an athlete's preparation schedule. Mastery can be "built up" when athletes see technical elements of their performance that they believe need to be done precisely.

Sample: A punter may use mastery to rehearse for the following technical elements of a punt:

Settling in physically and mentally before the snap.

Going on automatic . . . patient for the snap.

Receiving the snap cleanly and molding the ball.

Making sure the first step is not too long and on line.

Making the appropriate drop for the type of punt (directional, hang middle, into a wind).

Hips to target.

Vertical leg swing.

Flush contact—foot on the ball.

Head down on follow through.

Leg extension—land on the plant foot.

Each individual element can be rehearsed using mastery repetition when the athlete is in a condition of relaxation. Element segments can be built up in a logical progression and rehearsed, and the entire progression resulting in an actual punt can be sequenced together.

For example, the punter may be having difficulty settling in and relaxing before the snap. This edgy mental feeling results in the punter physically jumping at the snap with a very long first step that can throw off the rest of the technical sequence of the punt. The punter can use mastery rehearsal to focus on the settling in, going on automatic, and receiving the ball with a proper first step. Mold, drop, step is another common sequence that punters master during rehearsal. Repeated conditioning or mastering of a desired response helps mentally condition the athlete for a correct response. As long as the technical sequence that has been worked out by the coach and the punter is kept in proper order, any segment can be mastered in rehearsal.

Mastery rehearsal can also be done for the whole of the activity by simulating pre-game warm-up or by simulating actual in-game performance. Some athletes allow a bad warm-up to set a negative tone for the competition; other athletes can put a bad warm-up aside and go out and have a good game. If an athlete has difficulty with the pre-game warm-up, mastery rehearsals can be worked out with sport psychology to condition a more controlled, positive response to the warm-up. The warm-up can be used as a lead-in to the competition rather than a high-pressure block of time. Mastery rehearsal can also be used to mimic the entirety of a performance in actual competition. Punters can see themselves go through their whole routine exactly as desired from sideline preparation to on-field preparation, to the actual technical sequence of hitting the punt. This can be done with either general or very specific game information as a mental backdrop.

General game information as mental backdrop would be as follows: "You are punting late in the game, very close game, from deep negative yardage, Patriots show a rush front." Specific game information would be: "You are punting late in the game, 1:05 left in regulation. The score is Carolina 21, New England 20. It is fourth and long from your own 19 yard line. This is the second consecutive three and out for the Panthers. The Patriots have scored 10 points on their last two possessions. The momentum has clearly shifted to New England. The Patriots show the same rush front that almost blocked your last long field punt."

It is important to make sure athletes are mentally rehearsing their performances in the mastery mode, which means they are seeing them self-execute a positive pre-game warm-up or a successful set up and on-field, in-game performance. The sport psychology counselor must work closely with athletes to understand their individual positional requirements and to establish physical, technical, and mental elements in their routines that are appropriate. These routines will be mentally rehearsed and then transferred to the preparation the athlete may do on the sideline or on the actual field of play.

Coping Rehearsal

While mastery rehearsal provides an athlete with a good picture of what desired or correct performance should look like, every athlete knows "perfect" performance is an abstraction rather than a reality. Have you every witnessed a "perfect game"? Even a gymnast awarded the score of 10 is not without flaw. Most coaches and athletes strive for "zero defects" but understand mistakes will happen in the course of a performance or a game. Minimizing mistakes and costly errors of either a physical or mental nature is important in any competition. This is especially the case in situations where the teams may be equally matched in talent-as in play-offs, tournament finals, or championship games. Certainly minimizing mistakes is crucial in these intense competitions where a little mistake can cost a lot. Equally important is the ability to rebound, recover, and regain a high performance level once a mistake is made. It is costly if a player "loses it" after making an untimely error at a crucial point in a game or match.

What happens to the Olympic skater who falls on his first jump or the gymnast who loses balance when mounting the balance beam to start her routine in the Olympics? Do they lose composure in front of a world-wide audience, or do they have the mental capacity to perform the rest of the routine at a high level? Mastery rehearsal sessions are an important part of the mental preparation program; however, they should be complemented with coping rehearsals. A coping rehearsal will feature the athlete making a mistake in performance that leads to an undesirable consequence. The coping aspect of the rehearsal is the emphasis on mentally moving through the miscue and not allowing the emotional impact of the mistake to escalate and translate into further physical, technical, tactical or mental errors.

Having the ability to cope and move on is an essential mental rehearsal skill that a sport psychology consultant and an athlete must work on as a team to make as realistic as possible. It is essential that the athlete rehearse past events that were not managed effectively or that have a reasonably high probability of occurring again. Some athletes show a fear of coping rehearsal or an aversion to seeing themselves perform poorly. These are often the athletes who need the coping rehearsal the most! Athletes who show anxiety in respect to coping with mistakes are often the most anxious about making them. If they fear a mistake three days beforehand, what will their mindset be like one day before competition, the day of competition, the moment that the dreaded mistake happens? It is far better to prepare to respond to a mistake that has a reasonable probability of happening than to fear it or try to block it out. Although some athletes may believe they are successful in blocking out fearful information by "pushing it to the back of my mind," the fear is still unresolved and it is present.

Every year in college football bowl games and profession football play-off games, place kickers are positioned to kick the potentially game-winning field goal in the final moments of the game. "Wide right" is more painful for the kicker to see than it is for the coaches, the defensive unit that got the ball back for the offense, or the offense that just moved the ball 40 yards in 28 seconds to set up the climactic field goal attempt. What field goal kicker wants to miss a kick? Yet time and time again, kickers miss and games are forced into overtime (triple overtime in a 2006 Bowl Game between Florida State and Pennsylvania State Universities). Place kickers miss. They miss "chip shots," they miss "makables," they miss 50-plus shots, and they miss game winners. And in many instances what must they do? After the lonely walk back to the sideline where they will be greeted with glares from 300-plus-pound teammates, direct comments from defensive backs and wide receivers, and a pat on the back from the punter/holder, they must prepare for the possibility that the game outcome may be in their hands... again! All the while this drama is played out in front of 70,000 spectators and millions watching on international television. If athletes cannot cope, their life span in high-pressure sports has a high probability of being rather short. Time and time again athletes must perform after making a mistake. The pressure is often higher after a mistake and the consequence of another mistake compounds the psychological gravity of the situation: *Is this an opportunity to succeed or is this a second chance to fail?*

Core Aspects of Coping Rehearsal

There are several variations for presenting coping rehearsal to an athlete. The most important or core aspects of coping rehearsal are as follows:

1. The athlete is rehearsing events that have a reasonably high probability of happening, and the athlete indicates concern that he or she will not manage them effectively.

2. The athlete is rehearsing events that have previously happened, and they were not managed effectively by the athlete.

3. After the mistake is made by the athlete, he or she quickly regains composure and does not allow teammates or coaches to add further disruption. (This will be accomplished through specific breathing and cognitive techniques.)

4. After the mistake is made, the athlete objectively looks at what went wrong and takes ownership for his or her part in the mistake.

5. The athlete makes a determination concerning the correction (physical, technical, mental) that needs to be made if another opportunity presents itself.

6. The athlete puts the mistake aside and returns to his or her normal game functions or, if on the sideline, normal sideline routine.

7. When the proper time arrives, the focus is on the proper preparation for the next opportunity.

8. The athlete sees himself or herself preparing for another opportunity, following the preparatory routine with discipline, and successfully executing the kick (shot, play, etc.).

Obviously, knowledge of the sport and positional demands the athlete confronts will assist the sport psychology consultant in constructing these rehearsals. Some positions allow very little in-game time to cope. The wrestler during a match, or a basketball, soccer, or ice hockey player during game action has to learn to play through mistakes because the game goes on. In some positions, such as the quarterback in football, pitcher in baseball, or server in tennis, the athlete may have some time between plays or serves to recover and refocus. In other positions, such as the punter and place kicker in football, designated hitter in baseball, or the downhill skier, athletes may have a considerable amount of time to cope with a miscue and recover (or further lose composure) before their next opportunity. Each of these positions presents a similar yet unique challenge to the athlete. The basketball player will have to cope on the fly or her game will break down and her coach will sit her on the bench. The place kicker may have more time to reorganize before his next attempt, but his errors must be minimized because he receives so few opportunities. The place kicker may be unemployed next week if he misses three "makeable" shots in a row; a basketball player might miss three "makeable" shots in a row without the same consequence. Understanding the environment within which the athlete competes and knowing how to best facilitate recovery and refocus and to maintain athlete confidence following a mistake are essential mental skills that must be conditioned to a high level.

The sport psychology counselor and the athlete should make up a "menu" of situations to be rehearsed using coping techniques. These rehearsals are built into a session that will have several component parts (see below for details on building a rehearsal session) and are conditioned through a structured mental training program so that when a likely mistake occurs no matter the time of game or the game situation-the athlete has a practiced recovery method ready to kick in. After the rehearsed and conditioned coping skills are in place, the sport psychology counselor and the athlete should use written feedback from the athlete to carefully monitor their efficacy when put to the test in real competition. Game statistics are often a very helpful piece of information, because post-mistake performance data is often retrievable online or through team websites. If the athlete is not coping well or recovering quickly, the sport psychology counselor will need to interact with the athlete to determine whether a change in the coping rehearsal is merited or whether a more significant psychological issue needs to be visited or revisited. The sport psychology counselor and the athlete should constantly be working as a team to enhance and improve athlete preparation and performance. Rehearsal and mental conditioning should be experiences that are constantly being evaluated and modified. While some core components may carry over from game to game or week to week, the mental preparation for each competition or each opponent should be drafted in consultation with the sport psychology counselor until the athlete has demonstrated the ability to prepare independently.

Building a Rehearsal Session

Learning how to put together many of the technical skills just described is an exciting experience for the sport psychology counselor-in-training. Much will be learned when the sport psychology counselor-in-training begins to construct a mental training program with an athlete who is actually involved in competition. Working on various aspects of mental preparation and then seeing the athlete placed in some of the very situations you have been working on together is an exciting experience for all members of the consulting team.

General recommendations to consider when building a rehearsal session include the following:

1. *The sessions should be built in consultation with the athlete.* This is perhaps one of the most important general principles to remember. The athletes are the ones having the real-life experiences; listen to their concerns and to the information they may often "float by you." Enhance your listening skills so you can pick up on concerns that the athlete may not be addressing directly with you at that moment but that seem to reoccur indirectly in one form or another. Sometimes an athlete mentions something the night before or the morning of competition. It can be one of those "bombs," and you may not be in a position to fully address the matter. In fact, you may do more harm than good if you open up a very sensitive matter the night before or morning of a game. However, you may be able to build those concerns into the rehearsal session and then fully address them after the game when you speak with or meet with the athlete.

2. *Have a big picture of how the rehearsal(s) fit into the athlete's overall week and preparations in other areas.* Some practice days may be very heavy work days, and the athlete may be mentally and physically fatigued. It is common for athletes under the stress of a long season to want a night or two off. If you do not consider their work week, they may not really be motivated to do mental work that night, and they may skip through it or not do it at all. Make sure the mental preparation plan is built into the athlete's schedule so it is something that is looked forward to and not an additional burden that the athlete feels obligated to complete.

3. *During the initial introduction of rehearsal, determine if it is best to have separate mastery and coping sessions.* Some athletes are comfortable with sessions that have a mix of both types of rehearsals; some find it easier

(especially at the beginning) to focus on one type of rehearsal. It is important to provide crisp and clean rehearsal sessions during the early exposure period so the athlete remains interested. It is a mistake to overload the athlete with long and intense rehearsals that can reach a point of diminishing returns. The content of the session and its relation to game time may also be a consideration. Some athletes have a desire to engage only in mastery rehearsal close to the competition. It is a good idea to foster the confidence and flexibility that comes from being able to do either form of rehearsal within a session and during a session close to competition. However, coping rehearsals should not be forced upon athletes close to the competition if they are not yet comfortable with that rehearsal at that time. It is best to work with the athlete's personal style and attention span rather than force your model of rehearsal on the athlete. *Remember your goal is to make this something the athlete will want to do.*

4. *Request athlete feedback regarding the effectiveness of the rehearsal sessions.* This is a very important general principle and it should be initiated by the sport psychology counselor. Ask questions that relate to the days rehearsals are scheduled, the time of day they are scheduled, the length of the rehearsal, the content, and the ability of the athlete to maintain concentration during the rehearsal session.

5. *Find a medium that works.* Most athletes report that it is much easier to stay focused when the sport psychology consultant leads the rehearsal session, as opposed to leading it themselves, however, if distance and travel time prevent a one-on-one meeting, a written script (e-mailed a couple of days prior to the rehearsal) can be very effective in providing a professionally structured session for the athlete to self-administer. The electronic age also offers the option of audio, which may also be e-mailed to the athlete. The audio can be modified as easily as a written script and the athlete can play it back over a computer or copy it onto a disk. Athletes should let you know which medium works best for them—because if they are not comfortable with the medium, they may not implement the rehearsal in their preparations.

Specific recommendations to consider when building a rehearsal session include the following:

1. *Use specific technical and tactical information provided by the athlete to guide the content of the rehearsal session.*

2. *Use relaxation as an entrance to a rehearsal session.*

3. *When the athlete is fully relaxed and physically and mentally quiet, slowly start the rehearsal session.*

4. *Speak in a subdued tone of voice and a little more slowly than normal.*

5. *Start with one or two "reinforcements."* These are statements that reward and reinforce some aspect of the athlete's work or performance. They can be general or specific statements that relate to issues you and the athlete have been working on. For example, "Mick, you have been doing a great job staying relaxed on the sidelines when the defense has the ball. Your management of off time and your ability to transition into your sideline routine after the offense has crossed the 50 yard line continue to improve each game." A more specific example would be, "Mick, you did a great job last week not allowing the end-of-game chaos on the sideline to interfere with your concentration and your need to get prepared to kick the game-winning field goal. You showed great composure and discipline on the sideline sticking with your preparations, and it paid off on the field when you drilled the game winner. There will be more intense situations like this as the season moves toward the play-offs. You will continue to use your sideline management skills to maintain your composure and readiness to perform under pressure." Make sure the reinforcements are real and connected to actual events in the athlete's performance. Keep the reinforcements current and do not constantly repeat the same things.

6. *Use deep breaths (one or two) to calm the athlete back down before going on to the next segment.* Train the athlete to be able to get control of his or her physical and psychological "selves."

7. *Transition to the content of the rehearsal session by placing the athlete in the setting you will be rehearsing.* For example if you are going to do a game-day rehearsal, mentally walk the athlete into that setting. "Jason, I would like you to see yourself in the locker room dressed out on game day. It is an hour and a half before kick-off and you are getting ready to go out on the field with the other specialists for your pre-game warm-up. You feel strong and relaxed today, ready to go to work and make a contribution out there. As you run out of the tunnel, it is a brisk sunny day with a little wind—it feels like a great day for football."

8. *Move to the specific rehearsals you will work on in this session, addressing them one at a time with an interval of stillness between rehearsals.* Develop the specific or general mental backdrop as described previously. Know the specifics of the athlete's routine and build these elements into the rehearsal in the same sequence they will occur in the actual performance. For example, "Tommy, the special teams coach calls for the punt team. It is fourth and long and the ball is on the -48. It is late in the fourth quarter and the Falcons have a three-point lead. You jog on to the field from the sidelines feeling strong and ready to punt. You take your position 15 yards behind the ball and take an initial read of the defensive alignment, take a deep breath, and slowly repeat your cues, *smooth and solid,* as you take your practice leg swing. You have a good line on your target for the hang middle punt and you are ready

to go on automatic. You are still as you await the snap. The snap is a little high and to your right. You adjust to the snap and mold the ball. Your first step is short and on line. You glide smoothly forward. Your drop is nose down, your hips are to the target, and your leg swing is smooth. Your contact is solid and flush. As the ball jumps off your foot, you keep your head down and your follow through is vertical and downfield. You slowly gaze up and follow the path of the punt. As you move downfield to cover the return, you are aware of the path of the blockers and the return man's likely approach. The ball is hit very well with great hang forcing the return man to make a fair catch on the 11-yard line. Great job! *[Pause.]* Now take a nice deep breath and clear your mind; relax your body once again. Get nice and still. *[Pause.]* Good.

9. *Use deep breathing and a return to a relaxed state as a return point prior to starting the next rehearsal.*

10. *Provide the athlete an opportunity to set up and go through a rehearsal on his or her own.* Let the athlete take this rehearsal on his or her own from start to finish. Have the athlete signal you when done by raising the index finger on his or her right or left hand (whichever hand is more visible to you).

11. *After two or three rehearsals (determined by the ability of the athlete), each separated by a return to the relaxed state, start your transition out of the rehearsal session.* Reinforce the athlete for the good work he or she did in the session and indicate a move to some final thoughts.

12. *The sport psychology consultant can share some final thoughts that are motivational, positive, and enhancing to the athlete.*

13. *The sport psychology consultant can then ask the athlete to think of two or three specific game objectives he or she would like to accomplish in the game today (tomorrow).* When the athlete has a clear picture of the specific objective, ask him or her to take the time to visualize the achievement of each selected objective in an actual game situation. Have the athlete signal you with his or her index finger when done. Reinforce the athlete's efforts once again.

14. *Bring the athlete back up from the relaxed state using a count up and verbal persuasion method so that he or she is fully activated.*

15. *Briefly confirm that the session went well and that the athlete was able to visualize the rehearsals and the specific game objectives he or she set.*

16. *Ask the athlete if there are any questions.*

17. *Reinforce the athlete for the hard work in the mental preparation area, and wish the athlete and the team success in the game.* Do not wish the athlete good luck (external uncontrollable attribution)!

Rehearsal sessions should be interesting, real, and captivating. They should be related to situations that recently occurred or those that tend to reoccur and could become problematic for the athlete. Mental rehearsal should be viewed as an opportunity to simulate practice and game situations from the perspective of optimal performance (mastery) and from the perspective of adjusting to challenging situation (coping). Rehearsal can be used as an effective element in the mental training program of any competitive athlete.

Establishing Individualized Routines

The idea of athletes using mental routines as part of their approach to preparation is well established in sports. It is common to hear athletes speak with media about their mental routines during the week, on game day, or even on the field of play. Golfers frequently discuss their pre-shot routines in the media, and observation of any collegiate level or above basketball game will provide interesting and sometimes comical examples of free throw pre-shot routines. Although research on performance routines may not take the form of hard scientific data (e.g., Cohn, Rotella, & Lloyd, 1990) coaches and athletes indicate a benefit from the structure and repetition offered from a routine. Experienced sport psychology consultants report similar positive experiences and have advocated the use of routines as an important aspect in the mental training program of athletes (Orlick, 1986;1990).

Routine vs. Ritual

Just what exactly is a routine and how is a routine different from a ritual? Unfortunately, these terms often are used interchangeably even though they represent dissimilar mental sets. A routine is a set of task-related behaviors or actions exhibited by an athlete that provides a sense of control, stability, and readiness.[g1] Routines are established in conjunction with the athlete and are controlled by the athlete. The replication of behavior in a routine is predictable and can reduce error or variability in preparation that can have a negative impact on subsequent performance. Although there is the element of repetition, the athlete views a routine as flexible and preparatory; helpful, but not absolutely necessary for good performance. Routines can be established for the season, for the competitive week, the pre-competitive period, during competition, on field/in game, and post competition.

A ritual is different from a routine in that a ritual is based on superstitions, and often the behaviors repeated have no task relation to performance. Ritualistic behavior may come from a strong anxiety base because the athletes feel a lack of control over what will "happen to them." This lack of control or predictability causes them to seek predictability in behaviors that they have previously paired with a successful athletic performance or a very bad athletic performance. For example, a basketball player normally averaging 10 points a game wears a sweatband on only his shooting wrist one night and scores 30 points. Following that night, he comes out every game with that wristband only on his shooting wrist. The athlete follows this ritual night after night as if it actually had something to do with the 30-point night. Then, one night after several games of scoring around his average, he scores only 2 points. Time to find another ritual! In fact, if the ritual-bound player actually did something different the night he scored the 2 points (as in not making his last warm-up shot from the field), you can be sure part of his warm-up ritual will be to not allow that to happen again! Rituals can be "on" and then "off," but when they are on they must be followed to a level of exactness.

Sports abound with these meaningless exercises in classical conditioning. A baseball player will not cross bats or step on the base lines, a football player must dress in the exact same way every game, a tennis player has a shirt that can be worn only in the finals of a major tournament. Rituals control athletes and their belief that something bad might happen if the rituals are not followed. Placing so much belief on ritualized behaviors or inanimate objects suggests a very external locus of control. The sport psychology consultant should assist the athlete dependent on ritualized behavior to move toward a more internal locus of control for performance. Improving technical, tactical, or strategic aspects of the athlete's game should in the long run result in improvement whether or not the athlete is wearing that lucky green undergarment.

Types of Routines

As previously noted, routines can be established for the season, for the competitive week, the pre-competitive period, during competition, on field/in game, and post competition.

Seasonal routines

Seasonal routines are big-picture preparations; however, they keep a player in synch and make it easy to feel organized in the preparation required to perform in high-level sports, such as Division I college programs and professional sports. Seasonal routines can be very helpful in knowing what is ahead and in providing an "I know what I am doing" feeling.

After the collegiate basketball season has started, this weekly routine repeats itself with remarkable precision. Of great importance to the athlete and the coaching staff is the management of these time slots throughout the season and, if necessary, an effective integration of additional responsibilities as the season grinds along into March. The athlete may be falling behind in course work and require tutoring, actively treating an injury that requires daily visits for rehabilitation, or trying to help out with a family situation back home. The competitive week routine for most Division I athletes is very structured and very repetitive. It is important that the sport psychology consultant work with the athlete in an appropriate manner to build in some free time or fun time for the athlete to prevent staleness and potential burn-out in the latter stages of the season.

A brief example of a seasonal routine for an NFL player could be as follows:

FEBRUARY

End of post season (Pro Bowl?).

Move back home.

Personal time—family and friends.

Take a two-week vacation.

Reconnect with personal business venture.

Have post-season meetings with support staff (personal trainer, sport psychology consultant, physician, nutritionist, tax accountant).

Initiate Phase I of personal training program.

MARCH

Meet with agent.

Start training with technical coach.

Continue Phase I of personal training program.

Play in golf tournament.

Medical physical—take care of personal health situations.

APRIL

Initiate Phase II of personal training program.

Continue training with technical coach.

Return to team facility; meet with position coach.

Confirm season housing arrangements if necessary.

Four-day mini-vacation with family.

MAY

Continue Phase II of personal training program.

Continue training with technical coach.

Return to team facility for mini-camp.

Play in golf tournament—four-day mini-vacation.

JUNE

Gear down personal business venture.

Meet with sport psychology consultant-season preparations.

Initiate Phase III of personal training program.

Continue training with technical coach.

Return to team facility for mini-camp.

One-week vacation.

JULY

Initiate Taper Phase of personal training program.

Continue training with technical coach.

Three-day mini-vacation.

Final training preparations.

Report to team facility for pre-season camp.

AUGUST

Pre-season camp continues.

Consult with sport psychology counselor during camp.

Pre-season games.

Game visit—sport psychology counselor.

Season begins.

In-season routine. The season routine would be very specific and set up on a weekly basis. The in-season routine is defined to a large extent, of course, by the team practice and travel schedules. However, the sport psychology counselor and athlete can plan their schedule of meetings, use of phone and Internet exchanges, and weekend game visits.

The competitive week. The in-season competitive week is usually very structured for professional athletes. In some professional sports such as baseball, basketball, and ice hockey, the heavy playing and travel schedule greatly limits any blocks of free time (two or more consecutive days). Athletes' free time is often limited to travel days, a day off before a home stand, or a day off before a road trip begins. The schedule in many professional sports can be extremely demanding and fatiguing because so little rest time is built into the season schedule. Sports such as golf and tennis can also be very demanding given the need for many athletes to play in "qualifiers" just to get into a tournament. College athletes in high-powered Division I programs are also under considerable in-season pressure. Although the length of a college season does not compare to the length of a professional season, the college season can present difficult challenges. The college athlete often travels several hours by bus to the opponent's venue. They may have an evening game out of state and be expected to be back in class the next morning. The college athlete also has the pressures of school work, exams, and papers to fit into their busy practice and game schedules.

A brief example of a competitive week routine for a collegiate Division I basketball player could be as follows:

SUNDAY

Morning religious service
Breakfast
Report to training room
Team meeting
Snack
Shoot-around
Team meeting
Game time
Dinner with parents
Uptown with teammates
Bed

MONDAY

Breakfast
Class
Weights
Look at game film
Lunch
Class
Report to training room
Team meeting
Practice
Dinner
Look at game film
Study
Bed

TUESDAY

Breakfast
Class
Shoot-around on own
Look at game film
Lunch
Class
Hang out with teammates
Report to training room

Light snack
Team meeting
Shoot-around
Team meeting
Game time
Post-game uptown
Bed

WEDNESDAY

Breakfast
Training room
Class
Weights
Look at game film
Lunch
Class
Report to training room
Team meeting
Practice
Dinner
Look at game film
Study
Bed

THURSDAY

Breakfast
Class
Shoot-around with coach
Look at game film
Lunch
Report to training room
Light snack
Team meeting
Depart on team bus
Team meeting
Away-game time
Return trip to campus
Bed

FRIDAY	**SATURDAY**
Breakfast	Breakfast
Class	Report to training room
Weights	Team meeting
Meet with academic advisor	Light snack
Study	Shoot-around
Look at game film	Team meeting
Lunch	Game time
Class	Dinner with parents
Report to training room	Uptown with teammates
Team meeting	Bed
Practice	
Dinner	
Look at game film	
Uptown with teammates	
Bed	

Seasonal and competitive week routines are "big picture" routines. They are important contributions to the overall mentality of organization and direction in respect to athletic and personal life. The athlete and the sport psychology consultant should address these aspects of the athlete's life and work together to create an environment that the athlete finds workable and enjoyable. If there is too much stress or something about the seasonal or competitive week that the athlete finds undesirable, it should be discussed and addressed so that frustration and anxiety are not allowed to compound. The high-level athlete will have enough stress to manage from other sources!

Pre-competitive and in-game routines. Inside of each competitive week there will be opportunity for final preparation and then the opportunity to play the game. In professional and collegiate football, that opportunity comes once a week. Football "game day" it is often anticipated and promoted with great hype and emotional anticipation. Other sports such as professional and collegiate baseball, basketball, ice hockey, and many collegiate Olympic sports may find multiple game days within a one-week span.

The pre-competitive period is operationally defined as the 24-hour interval leading up to competition (Silva & Hardy, 1984). The athlete's mental preparation is especially significant, and a routine will provide much-needed stability during this intense time.

Athletes can be in top physical shape, technically and tactically trained and ready to compete; however, if they implode mentally as competition time draws near, all that preparation and conditioning can be undermined. Having talent and being able to perform with that talent are clearly two separate matters. Athletes must find ways to stabilize their mental activities when the pressure of impending competition begins to grow. As the time to game moves from the night before to six hours, to locker room time (two-three hours), to warm-up time (one-two hours), and to pre-game introductions (five-ten minutes), an athlete's psychological management can be tested. Mentally well-trained athletes can stabilize their mental activities during these intense landmarks and actually use some of them to enhance their readiness to compete.

It is helpful for the sport psychology consultant to work with the athlete to break up the pre-competitive period into blocks of time that smoothly transition into one another. Each block of time has a routine the athlete can follow to help him or her stay calm and get ready for the competition.

An example of this block approach might be the following:

- Night-before routine
- Day-of-game routine
- Locker room pre-game
- Pre-game warm-up
- Pre-kick sideline routine
- On-field routine
- Post-kick sideline routine
- Post-competition routine

It is important to state that these routines are flexible and can be changed if the athlete is uncomfortable with some aspects. By working with sport psychology consultants, athletes can feel comfortable that they are in control of their actions and final preparations as they move toward game time and actual game play. Providing routines can be helpful to all athletes regardless of the sport or the position they may play. The sport psychology consultant should know the sport and the demands of the position the athlete plays in order to assist the athlete in developing a meaningful mental preparation program. There is no substitute for specialized training and for supervised practica as required for AAASP certification.

Sound preparatory routines can be especially helpful for specialists (quarterbacks, place kickers, relief pitchers) and individual sport athletes (tennis, divers, and skiers). The athlete is going to be mentally engaged during the pre-competitive period and during the other intervals noted above. Having a sense of mastery and a plan, knowing when to go "on," when to go "off," and how to refocus on the sideline after throwing an important interception or missing a late-game field goal can make a significant difference in subsequent performance. Achieving solid mental preparation can mean the difference between "having potential" and being a "game changer."

Everything can happen at a fast pace in high-level competition. This is true from the physical perspective as well as the mental perspective. If athletes are not well conditioned from the mental training perspective, they may find it very difficult to come up with solutions "in the moment." A routine prepares the athlete for performance and can also prepare the athlete to make adjustments when needed.

This athlete has a sideline routine that keeps him calm and on "off time" while the defense is on the field. He then starts sideline preparations when the offense has gained possession of the ball and crossed the 50-yard line. The on-field routine is repeated each time the athlete actually takes the field to kick a field goal. The routine is followed in on-field practice during the week and it is built into his rehearsals during the week, the night before and day of the game.

The athlete also has a Plan B for any in-game routine. For example, the special teams coach may be late in getting the field goal unit out on to the field and the play clock may be winding down. The head coach does not want to use a timeout in this situation as the team only has one left and there are still four minutes of play in a close game. If the athlete goes to Plan B he must be able to smoothly shift into an abbreviated on-field routine without rushing. Sometimes there is not even time for Plan B, and the place kicker must hit the field goal with no set-up cues. In our system, this is called Plan X—the worst-case plan. If there is no time for set-up and the field goal could be missed because of the chaos, the place kicker and the rest of

---

Sample On-Field Routine for an All-Pro NFL Place Kicker

On Field Pre-Kick Routine

As I take the field, take a deep breath. Clap hands. *Go for it!*

Run to the center of field, then move to where Jack is spotting the kick.

As I approach the spot, take a deep breath—*smooth.*

Narrow my focus of attention. Slow everything down.

My plant foot is pointed to the target. Tap Jack on the shoulder and take a deep breath.

Relax. Look through the middle of the goal posts.

I have my target area.

Take three steps back—deep breath. Adjust face mask.

Smooth, firm.

Two steps over, looking through the goal posts, tap left toe.

Breathe out as I roll my shoulders.

Finish: Get clear, still, totally on automatic. Nod for the snap.

the unit (long snapper, holder, personal protector, and special teams coach) often have a pre-determined strategy. For example, they will either take a delay of game penalty if the kick is of a modest distance, or they will burn the time out if the distance is long and the points are critical at that point in the contest.

The routines that the athlete develops with the sport psychology consultant are very detailed and must be generated together. The athlete must be comfortable with the routines and should try out each one prior to implementing them in season. The sport psychology consultant provides the expertise to make sure the logic and content of the routines are consistent with sport psychology knowledge.

The off-season training period, the pre-season training camp, and pre-season games are all opportunities to fine tune the mental preparation plan. Eventually a good routine becomes as comfortable as an old pair of shoes and it is as automatic as the skills that the athlete has been mastering for years. After effective routines have been established, athletes often use them for years. When this level of preparation is achieved, it becomes as important and as automatic as physical, technical, and tactical preparation.

Performance Feedback

An athlete spends a considerable amount of time preparing for the actual competitive event. Hours upon hours are spent in a practice environment for a few minutes or hours of competition. A skier may compete for less than five minutes, a gymnast's routine may last three to five minutes, and a lacrosse or ice hockey player may be in competitive play for 30-40 minutes. The preparation is intense and often meticulous because athletes must maximize the opportunities they will experience in actual competition. One bad run by the skier, a crucial mistake in the gymnast's routine, or an untimely mistake by the ice hockey player can make the difference between a medal and a sixth-place finish in high-level competition. The very small margin of error in high-level competition makes athletes eager to reflect on their performance; the use of video offers a constructive method for self-evaluation. In many team and individual sports, there are film sessions required by the coach or a technical trainer. These sessions are often very helpful in reinforcing the positive aspects of a performance and breaking out technical and tactical mistakes. The psychological aspect of preparation and performance may not always be addressed in the required film session.

Performance Feedback Sheet

Many athletes spend a considerable amount of time breaking down aspects of their own performance. In these individual film sessions it is helpful to have an individualized feedback sheet that allows athletes to evaluate technical and psychological aspects of their performance. For example, a gymnast miscues on her last element prior to her dismount. The coach identifies the technical mistake made that resulted in the poor execution and the poor transition to the dismount. The gymnast knows that during the past week she was not hitting that dismount and she was concerned about missing it in the competition. As she approached her final element, her mind drifted for a fraction of a second to the possibility of missing the impending dismount. The athlete may or may not share this "mental miscue" with her coach; she should share it with the sport psychology consultant.

The performance feedback sheet should be developed through a team approach by the athlete and the sport psychologist. Although athletes may feel that they should fill out the performance feedback (usually after a poor performance) while it is still fresh in their minds, the most appropriate time *is within 24–48 hours following competition*. The emotional aftermath is often intense, and it is best if the athlete steps away for the rest of the day and comes back to the task once the emotions have calmed a bit. This will often result in a more objective performance feedback effort by the athlete. It is productive to have a set time for athletes to complete their individual film analyses and performance feedback sheets. For an NFL player competing on a Sunday afternoon, a good time for this work is Monday morning or afternoon because Tuesday is often a day off and Wednesday begins preparation for the next opponent.

An example of a performance feedback sheet for an NFL punter is provided below. Any information that may have identified the athlete has been replaced with generic titles.

The performance feedback sheet allows athletes to look at the film and grade their performance in technical and psychological areas that they have identified as important elements in the process of producing a good performance. In the sample provided above, the punter rates the sideline pre-kick routine, on-field routine (set up), and then five specific technical elements of the punt that need to be performed correctly to increase the probability of a good punt. A comments section is provided to allow the athlete to record punt hang time, gross yardage, net yardage, ball punted to, and any additional comments of interest to the punter.

Over the course of many weeks, the athlete and the sport psychologist may see consistencies of a positive nature or consistencies of a negative nature. For example, the punter's first step may consistently be too long (this can be caused by a little anxiety that results in rushing to punt the ball, thus throwing off the mechanics that follow the crucial first step). Both the psychological and technical aspects of this consistent flaw in performance can be addressed by the appropriate support staff.

The performance feedback sheet can also assist in identifying inconsistencies in performance that need to be corrected. For example, the punter noted above may not be consistent in generating a vertical follow-through on long field punts. The

Player's Name
Year, Team Name
Punting Performance Feedback Sheet

Game # 12   December 4, 2006, Opponent 6, Player's team 24
Location: City, State
Game Conditions: 60° 12–17 mph wind
Grade Scale: 5 = Outstanding, 4 = Solid, 3 = Average, 2 = Subpar, 1 = Poor

PUNT 1   Gross/Net: 48/50, Quarter 1, TOG 12:18, Yard Line -29, Down & Distance: 4–5

4   Pre-kick routine—good, ready
3   On-field set-up/ breathing—not bad, but could be more settled
3   Hands—could be quicker
4   Drop—good considering wind
3   Steps—1st too long
4   Contact—good, good adjustment
3   Follow—through-okay, a little across

Comments: 4.35, 48/50 good solid hit in the cross wind—rush pressure up the middle.

PUNT 2   Gross/Net: 36/36, Quarter 1, TOG 10:08, Yard Line +43, Down & Distance: 4–10

4   Pre-kick routine—good, ready
3   On-field set-up/ breathing—okay, but again could be more settled
4   Hands—good and crisp
4   Drop—good, nose down and in
4   Steps—better, shorter, smoother
5   Contact—really good, flush
4   Follow-through—good, for a less than full tempo swing from a short field situation

Comments: 4.56, 36/36 (fc 7) good contact and automatic swing—no rush pressure.

PUNT 3   Gross/Net: 43/33, Quarter 2, TOG 1:30, Yard Line -36, Down & Distance: 4–10

4   Pre-kick routine—good, ready
4   On-field set-up/ breathing—controlled, more calm
3   Hands—too slow
3   Drop—short armed
3   Steps—1st too long
3   Contact—good, considering the steps and the drop. I made a good adjustment.
4   Follow-through-good downfield and vertical
Comments: 4.33, 43/33 solid hit, but wind kept it in the middle of field. Kept head down with heavy rush pressure up the middle.

PUNT 4   Gross/Net: 46/46, Quarter 3, TOG 11:59, Yard Line -46, Down & Distance: 4–5

4   Pre-kick routine—good ready
4   On-field set-up/ breathing—good calm, still can be more calm
4   Hands—good, crisp
4   Drop—good, nose down and in
4   Steps—good, smooth and shorter
5   Contact—good, flush
5   Follow-through—good vertical and downfield into a rush
Comments: 4.66, 46/46 (9) good hit, good focus under pressure of a good middle rush.

PUNT 5   Gross/Net: 54/54, Quarter 3, TOG 5:47, Yard Line -27, Down & Distance: 4–3

4   Pre-kick routine—good ready
4   On-field set-up/ breathing—calm and automatic
4   Hands—good and crisp
3   Drop—inside and short armed a little
3   Steps—1st long
3   Contact—okay a little thin, wind moved it quite a bit
3   Follow-through—across, but good adjustment
Comments: 4.57, 54/54 (19), good hit, wind pushed away from the returner. Gained 7 to 8 yards on the roll.

Player's Name
Year Team Name
Punting
Game Summary Sheet

Game # 17   Opponent Score: 0, Player's Team: 23,
Location: City, State
Game Conditions 44° 6–10 mph wind

Number of Punts	4
Game Gross	40.5
Game Net	37.5
Game Hang Time	4.02
Touch to Toe	1.27

Comments:

Pre-game: Good, week's prep was okay, not great. Rehearsals were solid and I was well rested. Felt good going into game. I was prepared for a solid performance.

Warm-up: Good, hit a lot of good balls. No hurrying, no debating or frustration. Good flow and pace. Warm-up helped me be more prepared for the game.

Sideline: Felt good on the sideline. I was calm and relaxed. I was ready to punt. No anxiety early. I had little anxiety later. I will do a better job managing that this week and weeks to come. I will not allow fear of the "not-so-probable" to distract me from my routine and my tasks.

On Field: I was good on the field early in the game. As the game went on I became less focused on my tasks and more focused on the non-productive. I was distracted by a less than ideal handle on the ball (out of my control). I then became a bit of a micromanager. I wasn't as automatic as I need to be. This can be defeated by being more disciplined in my process and routines. I will not allow fear to take away my commitment to my swing. I will hit my punt regardless of the environment around me.

Recovery on Sideline: I will do a better job with this week and weeks to come. I have done a great job of this all year and I had a bit of a hiccup last week. I will process my last rep, take what info I need to from it and move on. Period. No baggage on the next rep. I am a much stronger minded person than I was last week.

Transition to Next Punt: Not bad, but clearly I did not move on from the prior rep on the last couple of reps Sunday. Not all of the success or lack of success on the reps, though, is under my control. I will do a better job on my end of the deal. It won't always be perfect, but I can handle any situation. I will clean up my concern with coverage that is not under my control and continue to roll through this season.

psychological aspect of this technical flaw may be a concern about touch-to-toe time and the possibility of getting a punt blocked. Because of this psychological concern, the punter short legs the ball or does not come cleanly through the ball at contact. This flaw can lower the trajectory of the ball (actually contributing to a blocked punt) and result in lowered hang time. Knowing the possible relationship between psychological and technical aspects of an athlete's performance is of critical importance in enhancing skilled performance in any sport.

Performance Summary Sheet and Competitive Log

In addition to the performance feedback sheet, many athletes benefit from the use of a performance summary sheet and a competitive log or journal. Both of these tools provide athletes with an opportunity to reflect on their performance, make adjustments, and move on. Athletes consistently report that the individual film breakdown session is the best time for them to fill out these feedback instruments. This individual session is commonly completed later in the day after the breakdown session with the special teams coach, a position coach, or the athlete's own personal coach has taken place. The summary sheet can be filled out at the same time the performance feedback sheet is completed or it can be done that evening while the athlete is at home and in a better environment to reflect upon the game. The performance summary sheet provides psychological reflection on the athlete's performance and allows for an emotional release (positive or negative), a reflection, reinforcement or correction, and game closure.

A sample game summary feedback sheet for an NFL punter is provided below. Any information that may have identified the athlete has been replaced with generic titles.

The psychological nature of the game summary sheet provides athletes with an opportunity to review their preparations in previously identified important "performance segments." These performance segments should be identified and worked out cooperatively by the athlete and the sport psychology consultant. Athletes bring their knowledge pertaining to areas of preparation that are personally significant, while the sport psychology consultants bring their experience and understanding of psychological challenges of the sport or performance to the dialogue. In the punter example, six performance segments were identified:

1. Pre-game
2. Warm-up
3. Sideline prep
4. On-field prep
5. Recovery on sideline
6. Transition to next punt

Each of these performance segments has significant psychological relevance to the athlete. The pre-game in this example is broadly defined to include the preparation during the week as well as the preparation the night before and day of the competition. Warm-up is crucial for many athletes in individual sports such as tennis, skating, wrestling, diving, and for specialists in team sports such as relief pitchers, punters, place kickers, or quarterbacks. The warm-up can either facilitate the psychological transition into the actual competition or it can be a source of great anxiety. Some athletes cannot separate their warm-ups from the actual competition and believe they are doomed to a bad performance if they have a bad warm-up. Positive psychological management of the warm-up is an important task for an athlete to master.

The sideline prep and on-field prep both refer to the ability of the athletes to stay calm, focused, and on their routines. This segment can be a challenge because the sidelines are often chaotic; decisions to punt or go for a first down can be made at the last moment, and teammates and even coaches can be a distraction. On-field prep takes a high level of self-discipline as athletes must settle down and follow their routines in the face of various factors that could be psychological distractions. The athlete may be punting out of his own end zone, facing a strong rush, punting after the last punt was returned for a long gain, or punting to the leading return man in the league. It takes tremendous psychological discipline to stay on task and stay on the routine the athlete has trained with when under the pressure of real-game conditions. Of course, adding 60,000 spectators and a national television audience can provide a little extra drama!

Recovery on the sideline and transition to the next play are crucial adaptive skills that specialists such as punters, place kickers, and quarterbacks must possess. The athlete cannot agonize over a bad play no matter how crucial or game changing that bad play may appear at that moment. The athlete must be able to quickly identify and understand if something technical or psychological was done poorly. If so, the athlete must think through the correction while at the same time shedding the emotional trauma that accompanied the poor play. The punter and place kicker often have more time on the sideline to accomplish this psychological task than the quarterback. After throwing a bad pass that was almost intercepted, the quarterback may have to make this transition in the huddle before the next play! The extra time on the sideline can be beneficial if the athlete has good mental habits and discipline. If he or she does not, the extra time can contribute to more emotional trauma, either self-imposed or imposed by less than sympathetic teammates.

Transition to the next play is also a crucial psychological skill for the specialist. After shanking a punt in a late game situation, a punter is placed back out on the field for what could be the game-ending punt. With less than a minute left in a two-point game, the punter must punt from his 12-yard line into a brisk wind with the game on the line. Is this an opportunity, or an invitation for disaster? Transition plays a role in how the athlete feels while approaching the field for that punt. These are the types of situations athletes find themselves in constantly. Being physically skilled will not keep an athlete in the league; he or she must also have the psychological capacity to manage various stressful conditions and perform under these conditions. Athletes need a psychological plan that will free them to perform in all game conditions, and top athletes want to review their ability to execute this plan after each performance.

Another helpful form of feedback and psychological release is the use of a **competitive log.** The competitive log is basically a confidential journal that the athlete keeps on a regular basis. It is helpful for both the sport psychology consultant and the athlete to read the journal entries every few weeks. This provides some "big picture" perspective for the athlete. It also provides many rich insights for the sport psychology consultant concerning how the athlete is managing the season from a psychological perspective.

The athlete should be encouraged to write in the journal as frequently as possible; however, the sport psychology consultant should not try to force the athlete to write in the journal every day. This simply does not work for many athletes for many reasons. Some of the reasons are logistical; some relate to the personality of the athlete. If keeping a journal becomes a burden, it can lose significance and the athlete just writes down anything to get it over with. When athletes are really interested in writing, they may write several pages with considerable detail and reveal motivational and psychological issues they are confronting. As with any psychological preparation, the more the athlete enjoys the work the greater the benefit. All entries should be dated, and athletes should feel free to write as much or as little as they wish. The athlete should be informed that the sport psychology consultant will occasionally review the journal entries. Sometimes journal entries provide insight into areas that the athlete wants to discuss but does not want to initially bring up in face-to-face discussions. A perceptive sport psychology consultant can often pick up concerns or repeated themes in the journal that may benefit from a discussion. Some athletes are very committed to the journal, while others are slow to see the potential benefits. After they are in the habit of entering information, most athletes seem to enjoy making entries and reflecting on them as the season progresses and after the season has culminated. The competitive log should be viewed as another opportunity for disclosure and dialogue and should not be forced upon the athlete. The log often tips off a sport psychology consultant to acute and/or reoccurring stress that is present in the athlete's life. It also can provide a window to view how effectively the athlete is managing the stress.

The Role of Stress Management in a Mental Training Program

Stress Management in Sport

Many multimodal stress management programs have been developed or adapted for use in the sport setting. Most stress management techniques originally developed in clinical psychology and were later applied to various social settings, including sport (Mace & Carroll, 1989). These techniques have included Stress Inoculation Training (SIT; Meichenbaum, 1993), Smith's Cognitive-Affective Stress Management Training (SMT; Burton, 1990), COPE (Anshel, 1990), and REGULATE (Johnson, 2005).

Stress Inoculation Training was first introduced in the early 1970s for the treatment of phobias and for anger and pain management. It originated as a flexible, individually tailored, multifaceted form of cognitive-behavioral therapy, and it was soon employed with various other populations, including sport (Meichenbaum, 1993). SIT involves many components: investigating the antecedents, behaviors, and consequences of the stress reaction; utilizing reaction training; developing useful self-instructional statements that function as coping skills; and employing imagery to induce and control anxiety reactions. Within this training, athletes learn to cope with increasingly more difficult levels of stress (Ziegler, Klinzing, & Williamson, 1982). SIT encompasses three treatment phases: education, rehearsal, and application. In the education phase, individuals are provided with a treatment rationale, and they appraise their thoughts and feelings during stressful situations. An emphasis on conceptualizing stress, while including both physiological arousal and stress-inducing self-statements, is reviewed. In order to make the stressful experiences easier to manage, clients are taught how to break the events into phases. The rehearsal phase involves teaching three types of coping skills: planning and problem-solving, physical relaxation, and self-talk/cognitive restructuring. The application phase requires the client to test out and practice the coping skills under various types of stressful conditions (Burton, 1990).

Cognitive-Affective Stress Management Training is based on Lazarus's (1966) appraisal/coping framework, where emotion and behavior are determined not by the situation itself, but by the individual's interpretation of that situation.

Stress Management Training (SMT) entails five phases:

- pre-training assessment
- training rationale
- skill acquisition
- skills rehearsal
- post-training evaluation (Burton, 1990)

These phases are very similar to those incorporated in SIT; however, SMT differs from the SIT program in two distinct ways. First, the athlete not only imagines the stressor while relaxed, but also concentrates on the emotions and images by means of self-statements and relaxation responses. Additionally, in SMT, the athlete must cope with images and feelings far more difficult than those normally encountered (Ziegler et al., 1982). Both SIT and SMT emphasize the importance of coping skills being rehearsed and practiced under simulated conditions. These conditions must be as similar as possible to the actual situations in which the coping skills will be employed. This is critical in order for the coping skills to be maximally effective.

One of the first studies exploring stress management programs in sport investigated the effect of SIT and SMT on cardio-respiratory efficiency among eight male cross-country runners (Ziegler et al., 1982). The authors discovered that those athletes who had received SIT and SMT were found to consume less oxygen during a treadmill run than the control athletes, who received no training. Furthermore, it is interesting to note that the athletes did report utilizing imagery before the study; however, after employing the combination of formal imagery and relaxation, they noticed changes in their approach to running. Athletes in the SMT group reported substantial change in their approach to warm-ups, pre-contest, and "mental sets" and in their practice and race behaviors, as well as an increased level in handling "emergency stress" situations during competition. The athletes from both groups of training also reported more confidence, the ability to control stress so that the "little things" did not get in the way of performance, and an increased appreciation for positive track experiences and how they can be used in stress management.

Mace and Carroll (1989) and Mace, Carroll, and Eastman (1986) discovered that participants given SIT displayed significantly lower psychological stress levels than participants receiving no such training immediately before abseiling from the roof of a building. Holm, Beckwith, Ehde, and Tinius (1996) reviewed the literature and reported that although the studies that investigated stress management programs with athletes showed some success, many of the studies utilized small sample sizes, there were few dependent variables assessing psychological concomitants of performance, and there was a lack of control groups. Holm et al. (1996) set out to address the efficacy of using cognitive-behavioral interventions to improve collegiate athletes' stress management skills, while improving on the weaknesses of earlier studies. Sixty-two collegiate football players and a women's swim team participated in the study. The stress management program included progressive relaxation tapes and a workbook/manual that was based on SIT, which was designed to introduce various cognitive-behavioral techniques. The techniques included: progressive relaxation, recognizing and changing cognitive errors, problem solving, imagery, and time management. Results indicated that those who participated in the stress management program showed significantly fewer cognitive symptoms of stress, and there was an improvement in their stress management skills. Findings also showed that the athletes were able to refrain from or replace stress-provoking thoughts. Burton (1990) found similar results and noted that SIT is quite effective in reducing stress; however, it is somewhat less efficacious in enhancing subsequent performance.

COPE: A Model to Control Acute Stress. Anshel (1990) and Anshel and Gregory (1990) have studied the effectiveness of an educational intervention named COPE. COPE focuses on a number of psychological techniques to help athletes learn how to control acute stress. According to Anshel (1990), many stress management programs view athletes as passive recipients of stress-handling measures. Conversely, COPE focuses on the athlete's ability to consciously attend to each of a pre-planned series of purposeful thoughts and actions. COPE is based on a cognitive-behavioral premise, in which the athlete is taught to respond first from a psychological standpoint, then behaviorally in the appropriate manner, to maintain adequate mental and physiological readiness for performance. The strategies are set up in a particular sequence that enhances mastery and familiarity of its application.

COPE is an acronym that identifies four processes: **C**ontrolling emotions, **O**rganizing input into meaningful and non-meaningful categories, **P**lanning the next response, and **E**xecuting skilled performance (Anshel, 1990; Anshel & Gregory, 1990). Controlling emotions consists of the athlete engaging in two cognitive-behavioral processes after exposure to a stressful event. The athlete's first objective is to prevent emotional turmoil. This may be accomplished by relaxing and taking one or two deep inhalations and exhalations. The athlete may also turn his or her attention to self-monitor and remediate somatic processes such as heart rate or respiration in response to the stressor. The second objective is to take responsibility for and correctly perceive the cause of his or her performance. This stage begins directly after being exposed to the stressor and might last only a few seconds or up to several minutes. Length depends on the individual's own needs, the perception of stress intensity, and the task's cognitive and movement demands. The second stage consists of organizing input and may be the most difficult. The athlete must selectively filter out insignificant, meaningless, or unpleasant information from more important content that the athlete can learn from and utilize. The appraisal process begins during this stage. For example, as an athlete receives negative input from the coach, he or she will process several external cues that determine whether the subsequent input will be desirable. External cues may include performance errors, the tone of the coach's voice or emotional disposition, and the specific situation (practice or competition). Each cue predisposes the athlete to the content of the following and immediate information. The third stage includes planning the response. The athlete employs cognitive strategies that will eventually lead to appropriate responses. Avoiding self-reflection is very important during this stage, for it is not helpful to review feelings or events that induce unpleasant images. In the final stage of executing the response, the athlete performs the necessary coping skills at optimal effectiveness. During the execution phase it is important to stay away from unpleasant thoughts such as self-doubt, negative self-talk, and memories of past failures (Anshel & Gregory, 1990).

In a study assessing the effectiveness of COPE, Anshel and Gregory (1990) implemented a series of techniques with intercollegiate male baseball players (N=24) and female softball (N=15) players to help manage and overcome acute stress. Athletes were randomly assigned to three groups: (1) the experimental (COPE) treatment group, (2) a no-treatment group that met to watch sport-related videos, and (3) a no-treatment group that did not meet except to complete the dependent measure. Findings indicated that athletes who received the COPE training reduced their fear of appearing incompetent and fear of evaluations, decreased their negative affect associated with stress due to unpleasant feedback, and associated their performance more to internal than external factors (Anshel & Gregory, 1990). In a related study conducted by Anshel (1990), the results were found to be quite similar. The efficiency of coping with acute stress was assessed as a function of exposure to various intensities on performance accuracy and affect. Twelve female college tennis players participated in the study. Findings indicated that the COPE model seemed to improve performance accuracy while reducing negative affect in skilled athletes. Limitations included the absence of a control group and a small sample size. Overall, the COPE model aims to reduce athletes' proclivity toward incapacitating self-appraisals, such as low competency, decreased self-confidence, and fear of negative evaluations. The model is designed to help enhance self-esteem and self-control.

REGULATE, another stress management technique, was offered by Johnson (2005). This stress management technique incorporates important components of the coping process and establishes the importance of perceived controllability over stressful situations. The model suggests training in the following areas:

R = *Recognize Stress.* Before implementing specific coping strategies, it is important for the athlete and sport psychologist to recognize the specific sources of stress involved. It is important to examine the situational factors, such as sport type and culture, when exploring the sources of stress. The research has clearly shown that individuality does exist in regards to which events are considered more stressful than others.

E = *Enhance Challenge Appraisals.* An athlete's appraisal of an event can be categorized as harm/loss, threat, or challenge. It is important to remember that an appraisal occurs as a result of the athlete's interpretation of a particular situation; thus, when developing a stress management program, preventing stress appraisals at the start would be most advantageous. If there is no stressful appraisal, then coping can be avoided. If an appraisal is nonetheless made, then it becomes necessary to implement coping skills to foster challenge appraisals. Challenge appraisals are most effective because they represent confidence and control. As athletes encounter stressful situations, they believe they will prevail over them. Athletes who make challenge appraisals understand that stressful situations are inevitable in sport and that they must overcome in order to be successful. Furthermore, these athletes possess the necessary confidence to analyze and manage any stressful situation with a high degree of controllability.

G = *Generate Coping Strategies.* An array of stress management techniques may be learned prior to competition to enhance an athlete's confidence and sense of control and ultimately to ensure that appropriate coping strategies are utilized. Coping strategies have been categorized into approach and avoidance, and can be further categorized into behavioral and cognitive. As mentioned earlier, approach-cognitive coping alludes to an athlete's thoughts and may include such strategies as thinking about or analyzing the stressful situation and utilizing positive self-talk. Approach-behavioral coping consists of visible actions in reaction to perceived stress, such as interacting with or confronting the stressor and actively acquiring information. Pre-performance routines can also be placed into this category. Avoidance-cognitive coping strategies include psychological distancing, reinterpreting the stressor, relaxation, and rationalization. Avoidance-behavioral coping encompasses any actions that physically remove the athlete from the stressful situation.

U = *Uniqueness of Individual and Situation.* When implementing the following coping techniques, it is very important to consider individual characteristics and the situation surrounding the stressful event. For instance, if an athlete possesses good communication skills and is able to relate to others appropriately, particularly under intense circumstances, more approach coping techniques may be beneficial. During the contest, time plays an important role as well. If there is no time to address the stressor, for instance during fast-paced sports, then avoidance coping techniques would be best.

L = *Learn and Practice.* Athletes must practice these techniques on a consistent basis. When an athlete is first introduced to a coping strategy, practicing may occur on a daily basis and taper off as the skill eventually becomes internalized and more automatic. Self-confidence is built through learning how to manage stressful events and adversity. The four basic skills that tend to underlie all others include goal-setting, imagery, relaxation, and self-talk. The goal of every coping strategy is ultimately to increase confidence; thus, the athlete will tend to make more challenge appraisals and fewer threat appraisals and will perceive situations with a higher degree of controllability. Being prepared gives athletes the confidence that they have done everything possible to ensure success.

A = *Amplify Your Confidence.* Confidence plays the single most important role in sport. Confidence consists of thoughts such as "I can" and "I will achieve my goals." It is at the core of every athlete, and by strengthening it through sport experiences, he or she will reach peak performance on a more consistent basis. Athletes will display optimal motivation when they believe and feel they have the necessary capabilities to meet the psychological and physical challenges of the sport in question. When an athlete has gained enough confidence in his or her sport, it will begin to transfer to other related situations first, and then expand to other unrelated activities throughout life, resulting in a positive outlook. It is important and necessary for both physical and mental strategies to be present and incorporated in order for high self-confidence to be established and maintained.

T = *Take Control.* When athletes perceive themselves as having some potential control over unpleasant events, they tend to experience less distress. Athletes are more likely to employ challenge appraisals toward stressful events over which they perceive themselves as having a high level of control; they associate threat or harm/loss with sources of stress over which they perceive themselves as having a low level of control. Furthermore, confidence and an increased perception of ability will yield to stressful events being perceived as controllable and subsequently less stressful; therefore, utilizing the essential coping skills for managing stress will increase an athlete's perceived control.

E = *Evaluate Coping Effectiveness.* At an appropriate time, the athlete, sport psychologist, and/or coach must assess whether the athlete's coping strategies are effective, efficient, and appropriate for specific situations. For instance, an athlete misses a free-throw and a response may be "I'll get it next time" versus negative self-talk such as "I am no good at free-throws." In order to gauge the effectiveness of either a positive or negative comment, one must observe how the athlete performs in subsequent situations. For instance, a negative comment made by one athlete may leave the athlete with feelings of frustration or anger, thus hindering performance; however, the same negative comment made by another athlete may help his or her performance. An evaluation of coping effectiveness will give the athlete the opportunity to change future performance (if warranted) by implementing newly acquired strategies (Johnson, 2005). Properly designed and developed stress management strategies can play a powerful role in athletes' sense of readiness and confidence as they approach the actual game time. Managing stress can be a specific goal for athletes, and it can facilitate the reaching of other practice and performance goals.

The Role of Goal Setting in a Mental Training Program

Goal setting is an intervention used in mainstream counseling and in sport psychology consultation. Athletic competition, by definition, is laden with goals. Athletes strive to reach goals such as improving upon performance; outperforming opponents; winning a game, match, or championship; avoiding mistakes; and avoiding injury. Moreover, coaches spend substantial effort studying statistics from previous competitive seasons to establish specific goals for the forthcoming schedule (e.g., Osborne, 1999). Given the prevalence of goal setting in sport, this intervention is familiar and comfortable for athletes when used by a sport psychology consultant. Indeed, several scholars both outside (Locke & Latham, 1990) and inside sport (Burton, 1989; Burton & Naylor, 2002; Lerner & Locke, 1995; Weinberg, 1994, 2002; Weinberg & Weigand, 1993) have explored goal setting, focusing on distinguishing between effective and ineffective goal-setting strategies.

Effectiveness of Goal Setting

In their comprehensive review of literature comprised of hundreds of goal-setting studies, Locke and Latham (1990) revealed overwhelming support for the viability and effectiveness of goal setting for increasing performance. More specifically, these authors revealed that 91% of over 200 studies conducted found ambiguous "do your best" goals to be significantly inferior to specific, challenging goals. Additionally, goal difficulty predicted increased performance: challenging goals enhanced performance more than easy goals in 91% of the studies reviewed. Although the extant literature outside of sport clearly supports the effectiveness of goal setting for enhancing performance, reviews of research within sport have revealed only partial support. Weinberg's (1994) review of goal-setting effects in sport revealed several studies that demonstrated no relationship between performance and goal characteristics such as specificity, difficulty, and proximity. In contrast, Kyllo and Landers' (1995) meta-analysis of goal-setting research in sport revealed a positive effect of goal setting on athletic performance.

Lack of universal support for the effectiveness of goal setting in sport can be explained, in part, by difficulty in controlling goals set by athletes within research observation (Locke, 1991, 1994; Weinberg, 1994; Weinberg & Weigand, 1993). The use of goal setting in sport is natural given the concrete and objective nature of sport performance. Coaches and athletes alike set goals; therefore, research designs that attempt to use a control group that does not engage in guided goal setting may actually result in members' setting their own goals. Indeed, the vast majority of research participants assigned to a no-goal-setting control group reported setting their own goals (Weinberg, 1994). Obviously, the validity of any conclusions drawn from comparing an experimental "goal-setting" group against a "no-goals" control group is threatened by this fact. Any non-significant differences between these groups may be due simply to the fact that participants in control groups engage in similar goal setting as those in experimental groups. Alternatively, individuals assigned to goal setting groups may ignore or dismiss assigned goals, choosing to adhere to their own goals (Weinberg, 1994).

How Does Goal Setting Function to Affect Performance?

A few explanations have been offered to describe how goal setting operates to enhance performance. Industrial/organizational psychologists Locke & Latham (2002), as well as Locke, Shaw, Saari, & Latham (1981) suggested that goals serve to affect performance in four distinct ways:

1. Goals function to direct attention and effort toward goal-relevant behaviors and away from goal-irrelevant behaviors.

2. Goals function to energize individuals, thus increasing effort toward goals.

3. Challenging goals stimulate persistence, or prolonged effort oriented toward achieving the goals.

4. Goals indirectly affect performance by catalyzing the development of strategies to achieve goals.

Burton (1989, 1992) suggested that goals indirectly affect performance through their impact on anxiety and self-confidence. Athletes who are focused on outcome goals (e.g., success and failure) are hypothesized to experience higher levels of anxiety and lower levels of confidence-psychological states that likely disrupt performance by stimulating doubt and drawing attention internally, away from task-relevant stimuli. Goals oriented on winning and losing may focus on aspects of the event that are outside of athletes' control and thus may stimulate anxiety. In contrast, athletes who are focused on performance goals are hypothesized to experience lower levels of anxiety and higher levels of self-confidence because of their focus on aspects of the competitive environment they can control.

Goals have been categorized as subjective goals (e.g., having fun, getting fit, or trying one's best), general objective goals (e.g., winning a championship or a gold medal in the Olympics), and specific objective goals (e.g., increasing the number of steals in basketball or decreasing a pitcher's earned run average in baseball). Hardy, Jones, and Gould (1996) extended the outcome-performance goal distinction to include process goals. This type of goal identifies the procedures or tasks the athlete will employ during performance (e.g., maintaining a good lead leg technique over each hurdle). These distinctions are important to make because different situations may require different goals in order to motivate behavior.

Characteristics of "Good" Goals in Sport Environments

The sport psychology consultant who is interested in establishing goals with an athlete can use the information reviewed above to guide the goal-setting process. Goals can be utilized for all aspects of athletic preparation ranging from performance characteristics (e.g., turnovers-to-assists ratio, free throw percentage, balls-to-strikes ratio) to strength training (e.g., bench 4 sets of 5 repetitions at 75% of 1 repetition max) to nutrition (e.g., eat less than 30% fat and fewer than 2500-3000 calories a day).

Drawing from the literature both in and outside of sport, Weinberg (2002) offered ten characteristics of effective goals:

1. *Specific, clear, measurable, and focused on behavior.* Frequently, athletes will articulate vague and immeasurable goals, such as "My goal is to be a good collegiate tennis player." The sport psychology consultant can help athletes clarify and explicitly define goals focused on their behavior that can be observed objectively. For instance, a tennis player could set a goal to successfully hit in play between 60 and 70% of first serves. If a goal is not measurable, it cannot be evaluated effectively.

2. *Realistically challenging.* Goals should be set high enough to stimulate effort but not so high that they are unattainable. Sport psychology consultants should consult with the athlete and possibly the coaches to determine reasonable goal levels; however, the most efficient and objective method to determine a realistically challenging goal is to use the athletes' own data. Drawing on the previous season's data or even the past two or three most recent seasons' data will provide a reasonable lower- to mid-point for a goal window. An interval goal-setting technique as suggested by O'Block and Evans (1984) can assist the sport psychology consultant and the athlete in establishing realistically challenging goals.

3. *Short-terms.* Short-term goals must be developed to provide tangible and logical milestones that serve as immediate accomplishments, which, over time, can lead to a long-term goal. Short-term goals can include daily, weekly, and monthly goals that are written, relatively objective, and measurable. Having a weekly schedule for mental rehearsal is a short-term goal, as is setting specific performance objectives for practice and for each game. It is important for the athlete to remain accountable to these goals, checking each day/week to determine if the goals set are actually being accomplished.

4. *Long-term.* Long-term goals can provide vision, incentive, and motivation for an athlete. Long-term goals can include monthly, seasonal, annual, and career goals. Long-term goals should not be abstract, and they too should be written, relatively objective, and measurable. An example of a long-term goal would be a tennis player having a goal to improve first serves in play by 5% by the end of the month, or a baseball pitcher having a goal to improve the strike-to-ball ratio by 10% by the end of the season. Setting measurable objectives that require attention, effort, and work over a long period of time is a characteristic of a good long-term goal. It is important that athletes write

down their long-term goals and remain accountable by checking every two weeks or so to determine if progress toward them is being made. If no progress is being realized, the goal and the behaviors being used to achieve the goal should be reassessed.

5. *Documented and reflected upon.* The saying "out of sight, out of mind" is particularly relevant in goal setting. Athletes should be encouraged to write down their goals and place them in their lockers or in an alternative place of high visibility so that they remain focused on striving toward them. Goals are useless unless the athlete remains accountable to them. Review the goals, and document the progress or the failure to make progress.

6. *Established strategies for accomplishing the goals.* A goal that lacks a specific strategy for attainment is not helpful. Sport psychology consultants should help athletes identify specific behaviors that will lead to goal accomplishment, and these behaviors should be written down in a check sheet form. This will allow the athletes to evaluate their performance in component parts that lead to the overall goal. The performance feedback sheet is an example of behaviors that lead to an increased probability of desired performance.

7. *Oriented toward effort and performance leading to outcome.* Focusing on effort and performance goals means the focus remains on task-relevant aspects as well as aspects of behavior within an athlete's control. However, anyone who has worked with high-achievement athletes, especially professional athletes, knows that winning is important. Realistically, who does not want to win? Helping athletes understand that focusing on winning (the outcome) does nothing to help them identify what they need to do technically or tactically to increase the probability of winning. Understanding that effort and consistent high-level performance are the only variables they have control over in their quest for victory can help athletes "play the point" and not be unduly impacted by the score. This is helpful whether the athlete is ahead or behind!

8. *Set at multiple levels (e.g., individual, team).* Within an individual consulting relationship, a sport psychology professional should be sensitive to any existing team goals. Within these parameters, consultants can help athletes develop personal performance goals that mesh with those of the team. Consultants can use goal-setting techniques in concert with leadership development to assist athletes in actively engaging in setting goals at the team level.

9. *Frequently and systematically evaluated.* If goals are set properly using the characteristics above, they can be easily evaluated on a regular basis. Proper goals are realistically attainable; therefore, they are inherently dynamic. As athletes reduce, or fail to reduce, the distance between their actual performance status and their goal, the goal should be adjusted accordingly. Lack of progress may require a goal to be lowered before it becomes counterproduc-

tive. In contrast, substantial progress toward a goal may require a reestablishment of a higher goal. If the goals window is set properly at the outset, major adjustments are seldom needed within the course of the season (see characteristic two above).

Goals Can Fail

Goal setting is a common yet often unproductive activity for many athletes. One of the most common reason goals fail in the athletic environment is lack of ownership. If goals are set for athletes by either a coach or a sport psychology consultant, athletes may feel that they did not have a meaningful role. Without ownership, the goals are imposed upon the athletes by someone else, and they may agree with or reject them. The easiest way to avoid this pitfall is to actively engage athletes in the goal-setting process from step one. A coach or a sport psychology consultant should not "give" athletes their goals during a meeting or a session. The goal-setting process should evolve and should be an educational opportunity, much like reviewing psychological assessments is an educational process. When the consultant is ready to initiate the goal-setting process, the athlete should e-mail a copy of his or her personal goals to the counselor and bring a copy of the goal sheet to the next session. When the next session is under way, the consultant should have the athlete state what he or she thinks is a "good goal." Let the athlete identify characteristics of a good goal and use that information to build an educational opportunity. If the athlete has goals that meet the criteria of "good goals," reinforce the effort! If the athlete has many outcome and uncontrollable goals (e.g., undefeated season, national champions, win the MVP award), use this information as an educational opportunity and ask the athlete why some of these goals may not be productive or enhancing of his or her sport performance. By working together with the information the athlete brings to this session, you will have invested the athlete in the creation of a set of "good goals" that he or she feels ownership of and commitment to achieving.

Other common problems frequently encountered in the goal-setting process include:

- Setting too many goals too soon
- Setting goals that are too general or vague
- Failing to set a realistic goal window or to alter unrealistic goals
- Not setting goals for the off-season, practice, and game environments
- Underestimating the time commitment needed to implement a goal-setting program

When combined with hard work and dedication, goals can assist athletes in reducing anxiety, enhancing self-confidence, increasing performance, and enjoying the process of competition (Gould, 2001).

Developing Intervention Skills
Under Supervision

After classroom experiences, role playing, and the observation of live intervention, the sport psychology counselor-in-training is ready to consult with an athlete in directly supervised experiences. Some students may feel anxious, reporting that they are "not ready" or that they are concerned about actually engaging in a hands-on experience with an athlete. Other students may be primed and eager for an intervention experience with an athlete. Moving through a complete mental training program from the intake interview to the final closure session can be one of the most significant learning experiences in the education of a counselor-in-training. The supervision provided will help the counselor-in-training be better prepared for additional hands-on experiences, indirect supervision, and eventually independent practice. There are several important factors that should be addressed in the supervision process that affect the supervisee, the athlete, and the supervisor. The relationship between a supervisor and a supervisee is always a significant learning experience for both parties. Chapter 6 will address the various approaches to supervision and the importance of this in vivo educational experience in the development of professionally educated and trained sport psychology consultants.

References

Anshel, M.H. (1990). Toward validation of a model for coping with acute stress in sport. *International Journal of Sport Psychology,* 21(1), 58–83.

Anshel, M.H., & Gregory, L. (1990). The effectiveness of a stress training program in coping with criticism in sport: A test of the cope model. *Journal of Sport Behavior,* 13(4), 0162–7341.

Benson, H. (1975). *The relaxation response.* New York: Morrow.

Burton, D. (1989). Winning isn't everything: Examining the impact of performance goals on collegiate swimmers' cognitions and performance. *The Sport Psychologist, 3,* 105–132.

Burton, D. (1990). Multimodal stress management in sport: Current status and future directions. In J.G. Jones & L. Hardy (Eds.), *Stress and Performance in Sport* (pp. 171–201). Chichester: John Wiley.

Burton, D., & Naylor, S. (2002). The Jekyll/Hyde nature of goals: Revisiting and updating goal-setting in sport. In T. S. Horn (Ed.), *Advances in sport psychology* (2nd ed., pp. 459–499). Champaign, IL: Human Kinetics.

Cohn, P.J., Rotella, R. J., & Lloyd, J.W. (1990). Effects of a cognitive behavioral intervention on the pre-shot routine and performance in golf. *The Sport Psychologist, 4,* 33–47.

Dunlap, E. (1999). *An assessment of the nature and prevalence of sport psychology service provision in professional sports.* Unpublished master's thesis, University of North Carolina, Chapel Hill, North Carolina.

Feltz, D. L., & Landers, D. M. (1983). The effects of mental practice on motor skill learning and performance: A meta-analysis. *Journal of Sport Psychology, 5,* 25–57.

Gould, D. (2001). Goal setting for peak performance. In J.M. Williams (Ed.), *Applied Sport Psychology: Personal growth to peak performance* (4th ed., pp. 190–205). Mountain View, CA: Mayfield.

Greenspan, M. J., & Feltz, D. L. (1989). Psychological interventions with athletes in competitive situations: A review. *The Sport Psychologist, 3,* 219–236.

Hardy, L., Jones, G., & Gould, D. (1996). *Understanding psychological preparation for sport.* Chichester, West Sussex, UK: John Wiley.

Holm, J.E., Beckwith, B.E., Ehde, D.M., & Tinius, T.P. (1996). Cognitive-behavioral interventions for improving performance in competitive athletes: A controlled treatment outcome study. *International Journal of Sport Psychology, 27,* 463–475.

Johnson, J. (2005). *Use of coping strategies following stress in competitive sport: A review of the literature.* Unpublished manuscript, Argosy University/Phoenix.

Kyllo, L. B., & Landers, D. M. (1995). Goal setting in sport and exercise: A research synthesis to resolve the controversy. *Journal of Sport & Exercise Psychology, 17,* 117–137.

Lazarus, R.S. (1966). *Psychological stress and the coping process.* New York: McGraw-Hill.

Lerner, B.S., & Locke, E.A. (1995). The effects of goal setting, self-efficacy, competition, and personal traits on the performance of an endurance task. *Journal of Sport and Exercise Psychology, 17,* 138–152.

Locke, E. A. (1991). Problems with goal-setting research in sports-and their solutions. *Journal of Sport & Exercise Psychology, 13,* 311–316.

Locke, E. A. (1994). Comments on Weinberg and Weigand. *Journal of Sport & Exercise Psychology, 16,* 212–215.

Locke, E. A., & Latham, G. P. (1990). *A theory of goal setting and task performance.* Englewood Cliffs, NJ: Prentice Hall.

Locke, E. A., & Latham, G. P. (2002). Building a practically useful theory of goal setting and task motivation: A 35 year odyssey. *American Psychologist, 57,* 705–717.

Locke, E. A., Shaw, K.N., Saari, I.M., & Latham, G.P. (1981). Goal setting and task performance. *Psychological Bulletin, 90,* 125–152.

Mace, R.D., & Carroll, D. (1989). The effect of stress inoculation training on self-reported stress, observer's rating of stress, heart rate and gymnastics performance. *Journal of Sports Sciences, 7,* 257–266.

Mace, R.D., Carroll, D., & Eastman, C. (1986). Effects of stress inoculation training on self-report, behavioural and physiological reactions to abseiling. *Journal of Sports Sciences, 4,* 229–236.

Meichenbaum, D. (1993). Stress Inoculation Training: A 20-year update. In P.M. Lehrer & R.L. Woolfolk (Eds.), *Principles and Practice of Stress Management* (2nd ed., pp. 373–406). New York: Guilford Press.

Murphy, S. M. (1994). Imagery intervention in sport. *Medicine and Science in Sports and Exercise, 26,* 486–494.

O'Block, F. R., & Evans, F. H. (1984). *Goal setting as a motivational technique.* In J.M. Silva & R. S. Weinberg (Eds.), Psychological foundations of sport. Champaign, IL: Human Kinetics.

Orlick, T. (1986). *Psyching for sport. Mental training for athletes.* Champaign, IL: Leisure.

Orlick, T. (1990). *In pursuit of excellence: How to win in sport and life through mental training.* (2nd ed.). Champaign, IL: Human Kinetics.

Osborne, T. (1999). *Faith in the game: Lessons on football, work, and life.* New York: Broadway Books.

Silva, J. M. & Hardy, C. J. (1984). Precompetitive affect and athletic performance. In W.F. Straub & J. H. Williams (Eds.), *Cognitive sport psychology* (pp.79–88). Lansing, NY: Sport Science Associates.

Vealey, R.S. (1994). Current status and prominent issues in sport psychology interventions. *Medicine and Science in Sports and Exercise, 26,* 495–502.

Weinberg, R. S. (1994). Goal setting and performance in sport and exercise settings: A synthesis and critique. *Medicine and Science in Sports and Exercise, 26,* 469–477.

Weinberg, R. S. (2002). Goal setting in sport and exercise: Research to practice. In J. L. Van Raalte & B. W. Brewer (Eds.), *Exploring sport and exercise psychology* (2nd ed., pp. 25–48). Washington, DC: American Psychological Association.

Weinberg, R. S., & Weigand, D. (1993) Goal setting in sport and exercise: A reaction to Locke. *Journal of Sport & Exercise Psychology, 15,* 88–96.

Williams, J.M., & Harris, D.V. (2001). Relaxation and energizing techniques for regulation of arousal. In J.M. Williams (Ed), *Applied Sport Psychology: Personal growth to peak performance* (4th ed., pp. 229–246). Mountain View, CA: Mayfield.

Ziegler, S., Klinzing, J., & Williamson, K. (1982). The effects of two stress management training programs on cardio respiratory efficiency. *Journal of Sport Psychology, 4,* 280–289.

CHAPTER 6

The Supervision Process

The goal of this chapter is to provide developing professionals knowledge regarding supervision, in hopes that they can become effective supervisors themselves and thereby actively involve themselves in advancing the application of sport psychology by supervising the next generation of developing professionals. The objective of this chapter is to provide readers with an understanding of supervision theories and models, the supervisory relationship, documentation and evaluation, and methods of supervision. Upon reading the chapter, consultants-in-training will be able to differentiate between varying developmental models of supervision. They will understand and appreciate the parallels between supervision and consultation but will also be able to distinguish one from the other. Analogous to consultation, the supervisor-supervisee relationship must be built on trust. Apprentices can gain an understanding of the role of a supervisor as evaluator as well as advisor—a person who provides critical analysis but also support and guidance. The characteristics of the supervisee must be evaluated to ensure competence in sport psychology; therefore, this chapter provides several examples for documenting experiences obtained under supervision and evaluative tools to assess quality of skills, knowledge, and service delivery. Similarly, developing consultants will learn about quality control regarding supervisors themselves by receiving information on and examples of supervisor evaluations. Lastly, the authors identify several methods of supervision that can be used to enhance the development of professionals and transition to independence. Direct, face-to-face supervision is advocated, however, this chapter presents alternate methods that can be used particularly with advanced consultants in training or with established professionals attempting to enhance consultation performance.

One of the possible reasons the field of applied sport psychology has not developed at a greater rate is the lack of attention placed on fostering future mentors. As described in chapter 1, sport psychology professionals have discussed many aspects of graduate training; however, implementation of a supervision process for developing counselors has been limited. The field of sport psychology needs to address the training of competent counselors and focus on teaching graduate students how to train the next generation of consultants. The current chapter will draw from diverse literature to highlight philosophies, theories, models, and methods of supervision that should be embedded within the development of future sport psychology counselors.

Philosophy, Theories, and Models of Supervision

Specialized training in supervision has become a necessary part of course curriculum within most counseling/psychology programs. Specifically, supervision courses are required in doctoral programs accredited by the Council for Accreditation of Counseling and Related Educational Programs (CACREP). Bernard and Goodyear (2004) suggested the clinical supervisor functions in a supportive and educational manner to promote the supervisee's professional development, and as a monitor to ensure client safety and welfare. Additionally, clinical supervision includes the following:

1. A review of ethical and legal requirements of the supervisee's practice.

2. Monitoring of the supervisee's activities in order to ensure services are provided safely and competently.

3. Verification that the supervisee provides clients with written notice of clinical supervision, including the name and telephone number of the clinical supervisor.

4. Verification that no conflict of interest exists between the supervisee and his or her clients.

5. Verification that no conflict of interest exists between the clinical supervisor and the supervisee.

6. Monitoring of supervisee's written documentation to ensure adequate clinical documentation.

7. Documentation written and maintained for at least seven years of all clinical supervision sessions, which includes the date and duration of each session; a comprehensive description of topics discussed; the name and signature of the supervisee; the name, signature, and telephone number of the clinical supervisor; and the designation of either individual or group supervision. (Lerner, 2005)

Rogers (1957) hypothesized that supervision should assimilate a model of psychotherapy. He believed that supervisors should display high levels of respect, empathy, warmth, self-disclosure, understanding, and unconditional positive regard, while demonstrating congruence and genuineness as an individual; however, most supervisors vary the levels at which they express these characteristics in different situations. For example, a supervisor might self-disclose in a given domain and not feel it appropriate to self-disclose in a different context. It is also important for the supervisor to be knowledgeable and experienced in therapy and supervision standards. Early meetings with a supervisee should provide the basic information that includes the client's developmental history, diagnosis, and treatment plans. These meetings set the stage for the relationship formed between a supervisor and supervisee and will lead to trust, openness, mutual understanding, communication, and collaboration.

Given these standards, specific goals should be set to address treatment issues, a supervisee's skills and experience, and a client's characteristics. These goals will help the supervisee develop learning strategies to more effectively solve client issues. Additionally, a collaborative pursuit of goals strengthens the working alliance between supervisor and supervisee.

Supervisors can also use a variety of different teaching techniques and modes of data collection and presentation, depending upon the goals of supervision. Brannon (1985) discussed a variety of teaching techniques that help a supervisor communicate information and knowledge:

- brainstorming that allows the free and open exploration of novel ideas in a supportive environment
- role play that provides individuals with various therapeutic outcomes and strategies for behavior modification
- modeling behavior that allows a supervisor to demonstrate specific behaviors to supervisees for future reference;
- guided reflection that allows a supervisor to replay processes and events during a therapist-client session in order to increase supervisee awareness and to improve data collection (pp. 30-32)

Another important factor in supervision is supervisor feedback. Freeman (1985) outlined certain guidelines for an individual delivering feedback to a supervisee. Feedback should be all of the following:

1. *Systematic:* Feedback is objective, accurate, consistent, and reliable. It should not be influenced by subjective variables.
2. *Timely:* Feedback is delivered as soon as possible after an encounter, dialogue or an exchange of information.
3. *Clearly understood:* Both positive and negative feedback are explicit and presented in a language the client can understand.

4. *Reciprocal:* Feedback is provided in a two-way communication pattern in which a suggestion is presented not as the only approach to the problem but as a potentially useful one.

Hess (1986) established a stage theory for supervisor development:

- Stage 1 (the beginning): Characterized by someone who has little, if any, formal training in supervision. The supervisee now becomes the supervisor, which can be confusing and unknown because this is the first attempt for this individual to guide and develop young professionals in the field. McColley and Baker (1982) found that beginning supervisors have problems with trainee resistance to supervision (26.7%), not knowing how to intervene (21.3%), not understanding the case (21.3%), and lack of knowledge of techniques and research literature (15-20%).

- Stage 2 (the exploration stage): Occurs when supervisors recognize the good and bad practices of supervision and can adjust their style based on the situation so that the supervisee can learn and grow properly. Ultimately, supervisors take on the qualities of professional supervisors (e.g., incorporating supervision literature into their practice and attending professional workshops and conferences).

- Stage 3 (the final stage): Confirmation of the supervisor's identity is expressed by the promotion to learn and grow by both the supervisor and supervisee and by the feeling of being respected as a professional within the field.

Supervision also involves the awareness of multicultural issues by both the supervisor and supervisee. It is important for both professionals to examine and address their own socio-cultural background in order to understand the impact this may have on the counseling and/or supervision process. Carney and Kahn (1984) developed a theoretical framework for cross-cultural counseling supervision that examines the role of the supervisor at each stage of development:

- Stage 1: The supervisee has little or no knowledge of ethnicity. The supervisor's role is to encourage the exploration of various cultures, including his or her own, within a structured and guided environment.

- Stage 2: The supervisee begins to increase awareness of ethno-cultural issues. The supervisor continues to educate the supervisee via specific literature and in vivo experiences while challenging the supervisee to further explore his or her sense of culture. It is important at this stage for the supervisee to increase understanding of diverse cultural backgrounds and personal attitudes and beliefs concerning these backgrounds.

- Stage 3: Represents an internal struggle of the supervisee in an attempt to resolve cultural differences that arise due to this exploration.

- Stage 4: Allows the supervisee to develop new self-identities that incorporate various aspects of diverse cultures. The supervisor works with the supervisee to engage in cross-cultural experiences. The final stage is characterized by having the supervisee take responsibility to promote cultural equality within his or her practice. The supervisor is now seen as a consultant that guides the supervisee toward areas that can elicit social change.

One of the earlier supervision models, developed by Hogan (1964), displayed a four-stage developmental process for supervision:

- Stage 1: The supervisee is insecure and dependent on the supervisor but highly motivated to learn. The supervisor's goal is to provide support and develop awareness in the supervisee.

- Stage 2: The supervisee struggles between dependency and autonomy, and the supervisor continues to provide support and guidance.

- Stage 3: The supervisee exhibits a greater sense of confidence and insight. The supervisor begins to challenge and confront the supervisee in this stage, since there is an increase in confidence and insight. This is easily accomplished by allowing supervisees to have more control over sessions and by asking them direct and indirect questions when they are consulting with athletes.

- Stage 4: The final stage is termed *master psychologist,* in which the supervisee has established personal autonomy and is established as a peer of the supervisor.

Stoltenberg (1981) expanded Hogan's (1964) model to include the cognitive aspects of supervisees as they develop during supervision. His counselor complexity model involves four stages on how the supervisor can create growth and change for the supervisee:

- Stage 1: Supervisors provide a structure for the supervisees to explore their autonomy. Specifically, the supervisor encourages risk taking, helps develop a theoretical orientation with the supervisee, and allows for questions to be asked and answered relating to the therapeutic process. The supervisee tends to imitate the supervisor and wants explicit guidance.

- Stage 2: The supervisee experiments with different theories and thus develops his or her own identity as a counselor. The supervisee strives for independence and increases assertiveness within the therapeutic relationship. The supervisor promotes autonomy and helps the supervisee acquire new skills and techniques.

- Stage 3: There is a sharing of ideas and collegiality develops. The supervisee has more empathy and less anxiety and has established a main theoretical orientation in order to work with a variety of clients. The supervisor is able to confront and challenge ideas that the supervisee brings to supervision, and a more collegial relationship is developed with the supervisee. The supervisor continues to decrease instruction, and there is a mutual sharing of ideas and insight.

- Stage 4: In the final stage, the supervisee is capable of independent practice and can integrate the standards of the counseling profession into his or her personal value system. The supervisor consults only at the request of the supervisee.

Sansbury developed a three-stage model that parallels traditional graduate training programs with its inclusion of a pre-practicum, a practicum, and an internship:

- *Pre-practicum* involves basic listening skills and understanding the role of a counselor. The supervisor provides feedback, assessment, reinforcement, and support and models appropriate counseling skills for the supervisee.

- *Practicum* establishes a supervisee's theoretical orientation, explores his or her case conceptualization abilities, and develops competence and ethical guidelines for the supervisee. The supervisor's role is to provide help in resolving cases, to confront the supervisee regarding treatment plans and interventions, and to instruct the supervisee to ask for help when needed.

- *Internship* helps broaden and refine the understanding of the supervisee's caseload, examines personal issues during supervision, and increases the learning process in order for the supervisee to be self-reliant.

Hess (1986) discussed a four-stage theory on how supervisees develop as counselors during the supervision process:

- Stage 1: The inception stage involves basic skill and role definitions, the setting of boundaries, and an elucidation of psychotherapy.

- Stage 2: Skill development is characterized by identification with a specific theoretical orientation and philosophy of human nature.

- Stage 3: The consolidation stage is the one in which skill refinement and competence emerge by virtue of continuing education courses/workshops, training, experience, and personal abilities.

- Stage 4: The final stage, mutuality, involves the supervisee becoming an autonomous professional who can create solutions to problems and convey these issues to others.

The Integrated Developmental Model (IDM) of supervision has been used in counseling and psychology for many years and is still one of the most important resources for practitioners in the field (Stoltenberg, McNeill, & Delworth, 1998). The model identifies three overriding developmental structures that provide markers in assessing professional growth for the supervisee: (a) self- and other-awareness (i.e., thought processes and changes in emotions for the supervisee), (b) motivation (i.e., supervisee's interest and effort), and (c) autonomy (i.e., changes in the supervisee's independence). Additionally, the IDM discusses eight domains of clinical activity that the supervisee encounters throughout the supervision process:

1. Intervention skills competence refers to the supervisee's level of confidence in creating and implementing an intervention program, which is dependent upon the theoretical orientation used and the supervisee's familiarity with it.

2. Assessment techniques examine the supervisee's level of confidence in using psychological assessments, which depends upon his or her training and experience in this particular arena.

3. Interpersonal assessment refers to keen judgment of the client/athlete dynamic.

4. Client conceptualization refers to the supervisee's ability to diagnose and understand the client's developmental/athletic history, overall characteristics, and presenting issue. Again, this depends on the supervisee's knowledge of the theoretical orientation implemented.

5. Individual differences allow the supervisee to explore the client's social and cultural diversity experiences.

6. Knowledge of theoretical orientation is necessary for supervisees to incorporate a variety of theories into their own practice.

7. Treatment plans and goals refer to the supervisee's understanding of how and when to use specific techniques in order to further the athlete/client's level of success.

8. Finally, professional ethics is an extremely important component for the supervisee, since there are various ethical codes (i.e., AAASP, APA, ACA) that must guide the supervisee throughout his or her professional development. It is necessary for the supervisor to explore how the ethical codes mesh with the supervisee's personal ethical development (Stoltenberg, McNeill, & Delworth, 1998).

The IDM outlines three distinct levels through which the supervisee progresses:

- Level 1: The supervisee's self and other awareness is limited, self-focus is high, and there is a basic ignorance of personal strengths and weaknesses. Inexperience as a counselor contributes to high levels of anxiety; however, motivation is heightened as the supervisee concentrates on acquiring the necessary skills. Autonomy is achieved through the structure and positive feedback given by the supervisor (Stoltenberg, McNeill, & Delworth, 1998).

- Level 2: The supervisee's self- and other-awareness focuses more on the client, because he or she is better able to understand the client, but the supervisee may become confused or enmeshed in regard to the therapeutic relationship. Motivation remains high, despite the complexity of therapy and supervision that can shake the supervisee's confidence and lead to confusion, despair, and vacillation. The supervisee fluctuates between dependency on and independence from the supervisor, which can involve the supervisee only requesting specific input rather than incorporating all feedback (Stoltenberg, McNeill, & Delworth, 1998).

- Level 3: Allows the supervisee to attain a higher level of responsibility and the ability to accept personal strengths and weaknesses within self- and other-awareness. Motivation is stable, and there is a push toward professional identity even though doubts arise during the supervisory relationship. In terms of autonomy, the supervisee knows when to seek consultation and has a firm belief in his or her own autonomous behaviors (Stoltenberg, McNeill, & Delworth, 1998). This level recognizes the supervisee as a "master" practitioner. A personalized understanding across all eight domains is in place and allows the incorporation of personal identity into professional life. Motivation remains stable, and the practitioner has a strong professional identity across all domains (Stoltenberg, McNeill, & Delworth, 1998).

The implementation of this model within the athletic environment was discussed recently (Tonn & Harmison, 2004). The complexities of working with athletes, especially in a team setting, often can lead to trainees feeling overwhelmed, uncertain, and intimidated. The IDM was applied by the supervisor in this case and proved to be useful in monitoring the supervisee's professional growth and skill development. Specifically, the supervisor initially followed a direct and behavioral approach by providing support and guidance to counter the supervisee's doubts and confusion about providing services, establishing relationships, clarifying her role with the team, and maintaining professional boundaries. At the outset, time spent in supervision centered mostly on the supervisor reinforcing desirable behaviors and correcting mistakes. Over time, as the supervisee lessened self-focus, increased awareness of others, and initiated more and more independence, the supervisor switched to a phenomenological approach. The supervisor focused on creating an environment that fostered personal growth and a sense of control in the supervisee.

The Supervisory Relationship

Many states have formalized the supervision process by mandating qualifications for clinical supervisors and requiring contractual arrangements between supervisors and supervisees. Qualities such as empathy, respect, self-disclosure, and challenge are relevant to a successful relationship, as it is important for the supervisor to provide professional growth, development, and welfare for the supervisee.

Trust is a major factor in the enhancement of the supervisory relationship. It is a sensitive task for the supervisor to balance between supportive and challenging interventions; the supervisor must provide guidance in order for the supervisee to feel secure enough to challenge himself or herself and accept the feedback from the supervisor (Proctor, 1994). Ultimately, the ethical concerns of supervision need to be discussed and adhered to so that trust can be established and developed.

Documentation

Supervisee documentation

There are specific considerations when documenting supervision meetings. Clinical supervision records should always include standard documentation, such as date and duration of each session, clinical description of each topic and identification of cases discussed, dated signature and phone number of the supervisor, and dated signature of the supervisee. Supervision records should be kept for at least seven years, but some states may require them to be maintained for a longer period of time. Additional information can include date and session number, client progress and problems, suggestions for further treatment, remedial plans for the supervisee, goals for supervision, and outcomes of evaluations. Harmison (2004) developed a log for the supervisee to complete that includes the setting in which the supervision took place, length and date of contact, type of contact, and a summary of the session. An example of the Harmison log is provided on the next page.

Evaluation of supervisee by supervisor

The supervisor must evaluate the supervisee to ensure the supervisee's rights are not violated or ignored in supervision. The supervisor must define successful completion of the training experience and what consequences will follow if the criteria are not satisfied on the part of either the supervisor or supervisee. During this evaluation process, the supervisor should establish a framework for dealing with grievances from all parties involved in the counseling environment.

Harmison's (2004) guidelines for supervisor evaluation of the supervisee on specific criteria that can enhance a successful consulting relationship are presented beginning on page 185.

MONTHLY PRACTICUM UPDATE

Practicum Student _____ Date_____

Supervisor _____ Month _____

Dates	Setting (e.g., office, on-site)	Type of Contact (e.g., face-to-face, e-mail, observation)	Length	Summary (e.g., issues discussed, interventions utilized)

Total amount of monthly contact

Briefly summarize your observations regarding the student's applied sport psychology knowledge, skills, and behaviors to this point.

SUPERVISOR EVALUATION OF
SUPERVISEE COMPETENCE

Supervisee: _____ Date: _____

Supervisor: _____ Semester: _____

Directions: Using the rating scales below, evaluate your student on each of the following sections by providing (a) an overall rating for each section and (b) an individual rating for each item. Circle NA only if the individual item is in no way applicable to you or your student's experience; otherwise, use the following 5-point scale:

1 = unsatisfactory   2 = below average   3 = satisfactory
4 = above average   5 = outstanding   NA = not applicable

I. Theoretical Foundations: Assess the extent to which the student can comprehend and apply core theory and research in sport-exercise psychology that serves as a foundation for practice.

Overall Rating (check one)   Evidences (Circle the number that best represents your opinion of the student.)

☐ 5 = Outstanding
☐ 4 = Above Average

1. Knowledge of relevant sport psychology theory and concepts.   1   2   3   4   5   NA

☐ 3 = Satisfactory
☐ 2 = Below average
☐ 1 = Unsatisfactory

2. Knowledge of relevant performance enhancement skills and technique.   1   2   3   4   5   NA

3. Ability to appropriately apply sport psychology theory and research to athletes and coaches.   1   2   3   4   5   NA

II. Helping Relationships: Assess the extent to which the student can effectively and ethically establish and maintain relationships in professional settings.

Overall Rating (check one)   Evidences (Circle the number that best represents your opinion of the student.)

☐ 5 = Outstanding
☐ 4 = Above Average

4. Ability to establish and maintain rapport.   1   2   3   4   5   NA

☐ 3 = Satisfactory
☐ 2 = Below average
☐ 1 = Unsatisfactory

5. Display of appropriate interpersonal warmth and compassion with others.   1   2   3   4   5   NA

6. Is aware of and maintains professional boundaries.   1   2   3   4   5   NA

7. Awareness of ethical and legal concerns (e.g., confidentiality).   1   2   3   4   5   NA

III. Individual Skills: Assess the extent to which the student can demonstrate an ability to appropriately assess and conceptualize case material and plan and implement interventions to individuals in sport-exercise settings.

Overall Rating (check one)

Evidences (Circle the number that best represents your opinion of the student.)

☐ 5 = Outstanding
☐ 4 = Above Average
☐ 3 = Satisfactory
☐ 2 = Below average
☐ 1 = Unsatisfactory

8. Ability to comprehensively assess case material for individual athletes.	1	2	3	4	5	NA
9. Ability to conceptualize and develop intervention plans for individual athletes.	1	2	3	4	5	NA
10. Ability to implement interventions with individual athletes in a skillful manner.	1	2	3	4	5	NA
11. Produces and maintains accurate records of client contact.	1	2	3	4	5	NA

IV. Group Skills: Assess the extent to which the student can demonstrate an ability to appropriately assess case material and develop and implement interventions to groups in sport-exercise settings.

Overall Rating (check one)

Evidences (Circle the number that best represents your opinion of the student.)

☐ 5 = Outstanding
☐ 4 = Above Average
☐ 3 = Satisfactory
☐ 2 = Below average
☐ 1 = Unsatisfactory

12. Ability to comprehensively assess case material for groups or teams.	1	2	3	4	5	NA
13. Ability to conceptualize and develop intervention plans for groups or teams.	1	2	3	4	5	NA
14. Ability to implement interventions with groups or teams in a skillful manner.	1	2	3	4	5	NA
15. Presents concrete, applied information to groups or teams in a meaningful and useful way.	1	2	3	4	5	NA

V. Normal and Abnormal Behavior: Assess the extent to which the student can identify and label psychopathology and developmental growth in sport-exercise settings.

Overall Rating (check one)

Evidences (Circle the number that best represents your opinion of the student.)

☐ 5 = Outstanding
☐ 4 = Above Average
☐ 3 = Satisfactory
☐ 2 = Below average
☐ 1 = Unsatisfactory

16. Knowledge of normal and abnormal behavior as it pertains to sport.	1	2	3	4	5	NA
17. Ability to identify and label developmental growth and psychopathology in athletes.	1	2	3	4	5	NA
18. Recognizes limits of competence and appropriately refers athletes to other professionals.	1	2	3	4	5	NA

VI. Sport Science: Assess the extent to which the student can comprehend and apply core theory and research of the physiological, motor, and psychosocial bases of behavior in sport exercise settings.

Overall Rating (check one)

- ☐ 5 = Outstanding
- ☐ 4 = Above Average
- ☐ 3 = Satisfactory
- ☐ 2 = Below average
- ☐ 1 = Unsatisfactory

Evidences (Circle the number that best represents your opinion of the student.)

19. Knowledge of relevant physiological, motor, and psychosocial aspects of behavior in sport.	1	2	3	4	5 NA
20. Ability to identify potential physical, technical, or social explanations for behavior in sport.	1	2	3	4	5 NA
21. Collaborates with coaches and other support staff where appropriate.	1	2	3	4	5 NA

VII. Research and Evaluation: Assess the extent to which the student can critically evaluate research and apply scientific methodology to analysis of case material.

Overall Rating (check one)

- ☐ 5 = Outstanding
- ☐ 4 = Above Average
- ☐ 3 = Satisfactory
- ☐ 2 = Below average
- ☐ 1 = Unsatisfactory

Evidences (Circle the number that best represents your opinion of the student.)

22. Knowledge of scientific methodology as it pertains to applying sport psychology.	1	2	3	4	5 NA
23. Ability to use theoretically and empirically sound interventions.	1	2	3	4	5 NA
24. Communicates in writing in a clear and scholarly manner.	1	2	3	4	5 NA

VIII. Diversity: Assess the extent to which the student can comprehend and value human diversity in professional settings.

Overall Rating (check one)

- ☐ 5 = Outstanding
- ☐ 4 = Above Average
- ☐ 3 = Satisfactory
- ☐ 2 = Below average
- ☐ 1 = Unsatisfactory

Evidences (Circle the number that best represents your opinion of the student.)

25. Knowledge of cultural factors as it pertains to participation in sport.	1	2	3	4	5 NA
26. Sensitivity to cultural and individual differences.	1	2	3	4	5 NA
27. Values and appreciates human diversity in sport.	1	2	3	4	5 NA

IX. Professional Identity: Assess the extent to which the student can value and demonstrate attitudes essential for continual learning and scholarly inquiry.

Overall Rating (check one)   Evidences (Circle the number that best represents your opinion of the student.)

28. Is responsible and conscientious when conducting professional activities.	1	2	3	4	5	NA
29. Demonstrates self-sufficiency and initiative.	1	2	3	4	5	NA
30. Is self-aware and self-reflective about his or her own behaviors.	1	2	3	4	5	NA
31. Is open to interpersonal feedback and supervisory input.	1	2	3	4	5	NA

Provide additional behavioral observations about the student's competence:

Practicum Student _____ **Date** _____

Supervisor _____ **Date** _____

Evaluation of supervisee by athlete

One of the best measures of supervisee "job performance" is when an athlete positively evaluates the practitioner. This feedback may come in many forms, such as a formal written evaluation form, a call back from the athlete requesting a continuation of work with the supervisee, word-of-mouth referral (another athlete seeks the services of the supervisee), and/or the fact that a coach or an athletic organization is interested in the services of the supervisee based on feedback they have received from athletes. The relationship developed between the athlete and practitioner is very important and based upon trust. The site evaluation document presented below is completed by the client in order to establish the strengths and weaknesses of the supervisee. The example that follows was developed by Harmison (2004).

Site Evaluation of Supervisee Competence

Please rate the student's competence using the following anchors:

1 = Unsatisfactory   2 = Below average   3 = Satisfactory   4 = Above average
5 = Outstanding   NA = Not applicable

I.   Theoretical Foundations

1. Had useful knowledge about mental skills training	1	2	3	4	5	NA
2. Was able to apply psychology to sport in a meaningful way	1	2	3	4	5	NA

II. Helping Relationships

3. Seemed open, flexible, and easy to collaborate with	1	2	3	4	5	NA
4. Proved to be trustworthy	1	2	3	4	5	NA
5. Demonstrated personal integrity and ethical conduct	1	2	3	4	5	NA

III. Individual Skills

6. Displayed compassion with athletes	1	2	3	4	5	NA
7. Was easy for individual athletes to relate/talk to	1	2	3	4	5	NA
8. Effectively helped individual athletes in their attempts to reach their goals	1	2	3	4	5	NA

IV. Group Skills

9. Fit in with the team	1	2	3	4	5	NA
10. Presented clear, practical, and concrete strategies to the team	1	2	3	4	5	NA
11. Was an effective consultant in helping the team strive for its goals	1	2	3	4	5	NA

V.   Normal and Abnormal Behavior

12. Seemed knowledgeable about healthy and dysfunctional human behavior	1	2	3	4	5	NA
13. Was a helpful resource for athletes with personal issues	1	2	3	4	5	NA

VI. Sport Science

14. Was knowledgeable about the physical, technical, and social aspects of sport	1	2	3	4	5	NA
15. Collaborated with coaches and other staff regarding athletes where appropriate	1	2	3	4	5	NA

VII. Research and Evaluation

16. Utilized interventions that seemed logical	1	2	3	4	5	NA

17. Communicated with athletes, coaches, and staff in a knowledgeable manner	1	2	3	4	5	NA

VIII. Diversity

18. Sensitive to cultural and individual differences	1	2	3	4	5	NA

19. Values and appreciates human diversity in sport	1	2	3	4	5	NA

IX. Professional Identity

20. Displayed appropriate professional behavior	1	2	3	4	5	NA

21. Was responsible and conscientious when working with the team	1	2	3	4	5	NA

22. Demonstrated self-initiative with athletes and coaches	1	2	3	4	5	NA

I would recommend this consultant to other athletes and coaches   ☐ Yes   ☐ No

Do you have any recommendations to improve the quality or effectiveness of the sport psychology consultation service being offered?

This type of honest feedback by the athlete provides both constructive criticism and productive supportive feedback to the supervisee from the actual client. It is important to let the athlete know that the supervisee wants honest feedback as part of the growth process. The supervisee, just like the athlete, wants to know what skills to improve upon in order to enhance performance.

Honest information from the person the supervisee worked with is a very important part of the supervisee's growth process because it is the only first-person feedback available.

Evaluation of supervisor by supervisee

It is the responsibility of the supervisor to provide the supervisee with continual performance appraisal and evaluation feedback throughout the supervision relationship. It is the role of the supervisor to supply the supervisee with continuous assessment concerning the adequacy of clinical services and overall development. Additionally, the supervisor should address any anxieties the supervisee may have that relate to the ability to offer direct services to clients. The supervisor should phrase the feedback in a way that conveys the strengths and positive qualities of the supervisee, while still discussing weaknesses and developmental opportunities for growth. Andersen, Van Raalte, and Brewer (1994) developed a feedback tool that allows for the evaluation of the supervisor. This 41-item inventory contains five sections:

1. Providing information and technical support (i.e., knowledge of sport psychology and record keeping)
2. Fulfilling supervisory responsibilities (i.e., addresses strengths and weaknesses of the supervisee),
3. Facilitating interpersonal communication (i.e., delivers the appropriate feedback),
4. Fostering student autonomy (i.e., encourage and motivate the supervisee), and
5. Providing a professional model (i.e., ethical behavior).

The feedback provided can assist the supervisor in assessing strengths and weaknesses identified by the supervisee, resulting in improvement in how the supervisor fulfills his or her role in the future.

Methods of Supervision

Many methods of supervision exist and each has strengths and weaknesses. We will briefly describe some of the common supervision methods used in applied sport psychology. Selection of appropriate methodology for consultant development may depend on a variety of constraints including, but not limited to, characteristics of the supervisee, time commitments of the supervisor, and resources available. Adoption of an eclectic supervision methodology that integrates the strengths and limits the weaknesses of each may be advisable.

Self-report. Possibly the most primitive of supervisions methods, self-report requires the supervisee to communicate to the supervisor not only the case conceptualization but also reflections on thoughts and feelings experienced during the session. This method of supervision assumes there is no systematic documentation occurring throughout the session; therefore, the quality of self-report can be contaminated by a variety of factors, including knowledge of theory, stage of professional development, emotional maturity, and recall and timing of documentation and communication. Inexperienced consultants may not benefit from this approach because they may not know where to focus their attention when reflecting on sessions. Any lag between sessions and recall may impact the accuracy of self-report. Similarly, emotions experienced within the session may have the opportunity to dissipate, or highly charged emotions may cause immediate self-reporting that blurs actual issues contained in the session. Moreover, the fact that supervisees miss mistakes they make or misconceptions they articulate cannot be discerned because no direct observation has occurred. Supervision without direct observation precludes the opportunity for independent judgment regarding the client's problem (Holloway, 1988). Although self-report may be extremely inexpensive in terms of time commitment, scheduling, and equipment needed, it is severely limited as a supervision method because supervisee insight is restricted; therefore, supervisee and client enhancement may be attenuated.

Case notes. To overcome some of the deficiencies of self-report supervision, supervisees can be encouraged to take in-session notes. These case notes can range from a simple outline of the temporal sequence of events to copiously detailed notes. The advantage of case notes is that they can activate recall of the session to increase accuracy of self-reporting. Unlike some of the objective methods of supervision described below, case notes may provide direct insight into supervisees' subjective experiences of consultation (Goldberg, 1985). Analysis of case notes provides insight into supervisee perceptions, conceptualizations, hypotheses, and conclusions. Implemented exclusively, case notes have similar disadvantages to self-report methods of supervision. Subjective material can be helpful; however, when lacking objective material to augment it, this data is limited by characteristics of the supervisee. Supervision, and thus supervisee development, may be limited by supervisee experience and knowledge. Furthermore, supervisees may distort or delete salient session material. For these reasons, exclusive use of case notes as a supervision method should only be utilized with advanced supervisees.

Audiovisual recording. Technological advancements have afforded new methods of supervision. Almost 70 years ago, counselors began using audio recordings to enhance psychotherapy (Covner, 1942a, 1942b; Rogers, 1942). More recently, video recordings have allowed supervisors to gain full objective access to sessions without actually being present in the room. Indeed, computer technology now allows supervisees to record sessions digitally (audio or visual) and simply e-mail the files to supervisors for feedback. Given this technology, former criticisms such as cost and storage are not valid anymore. Obviously, audiovisual recordings provide a great advantage via replay of the session. Supervisors are afforded the flexibility of listening to or viewing supervisee sessions that they cannot attend. Supervisees can revisit their sessions with augmented recall of flow and experience. Moreover, with the aid of recording (especially video), supervisees can self-critique their consulting including content, process, and nonverbal behaviors such as body positioning (e.g., leaning in), eye contact, and facial expressions, as well as voice inflection and pace. This method is particularly relevant for applied sport psychology because video feedback has inundated the athletic world. It is difficult to find collegiate athletic programs that do not engage in film sessions with their athletes.

Similarly, many individual sport instructors in such areas as tennis and golf utilize onsite digital video for immediate feedback and instruction.

Given the prevalence of video as a method to enhance learning in sport, it may be less likely that this method disrupts consulting sessions with athletes; however, one theoretical weakness of video recording is that it may heighten self-presentation concerns of either the client or consultant. To examine oneself from a third-person perspective is awkward. Furthermore, being evaluated in the performance of such an abstract skill as sport psychology consultation can provoke anxiety. Supervisors must acknowledge this response, which is likely pervasive with less experienced supervisees; however, as with other consulting skills, supervisors must help supervisees embrace situations outside their comfort zone as opportunities for growth. One possible method for reducing anxiety is to allow supervisees an opportunity to review their own sessions in private prior to sharing with supervisors.

Given that a sport psychology supervisee will often help athletes overcome anxiety, the hope is that performance anxiety is not a critical issue for the supervisee himself or herself. Possibly a more relevant weakness of video use is the amount of feedback to be taken in by a supervisee. When presented with video of themselves, supervisees are literally inundated with stimuli. Supervisors can alleviate the feeling of being overwhelming by highlighting areas on which to focus. Alternatively, supervisees can view videos multiple times with a distinct focal point on each occasion, much like a coach might review a play once to highlight defensive position and again to focus on offensive flow.

Interpersonal process recall. Kagan and colleagues (Kagan, 1980; Kagan & Kagan, 1997) developed interpersonal process recall (IPR) to augment the use of video in supervision. The concept is analogous to the golf instructor who video records her student's swing on the range and later guides the student through the swing step by step while displaying the recording on a monitor. Rather than view a video recording separately, supervisor and supervisee can "break down film" together in a safe, learning environment. In this method, supervisees are responsible for reporting on the session much like a play-by-play announcer calling a baseball game. Thoughts, feelings, hypotheses, and case conceptualizations can be articulated midstream by the supervisee. Additionally, supervisors can pause at teachable moments to help guide supervisees toward discovery of alternate questioning or conceptualization within sessions. IPR is advantageous as a method of supervision because it integrates objective information (video) with subjective interpretation (supervisee reflection). IPR has similar limitations as previous methods discussed in that supervisees must be relatively secure in critiquing themselves on video and receiving critique, and they must be experienced enough to be able to engage in deep reflection and recall, as well as case conceptualization. Another obvious weakness is the time commitment and scheduling constraints associated with IPR. Supervisor and supervisee must meet at a mutually convenient time to review the video. Additionally, to be most effective, the session may need to be previewed to determine important segments on which to focus. An hour session, if viewed in its entirety with pauses for reflection and teaching, could easily translate into two hours of supervision.

Group supervision. A common supervision method implemented to increase time efficiency is group supervision, defined as a situation "in which supervisors oversee a supervisee's professional development in a group of peers" (Holloway & Johnston, 1985, p. 333). Aside from increased time economy, Bernard and Goodyear (2004) identified several **advantages** of using group supervision:

- First, conducting supervision among a group can reduce the hierarchical nature of supervision because feedback is communicated as a discussion among colleagues rather than communicated down from an authority.

- Second, peer supervisees can learn from others without experiencing the situation first-hand (i.e., vicarious learning).

- Third, because of the number of peers in the group, it is likely that they will bring in a variety of clients and issues that may converge with or diverge from a particular supervisee's experience. In sport psychology, this is particularly insightful because one supervisee working with a baseball player may learn a different way of framing a similar issue experienced by a supervisee working with a fencer.

- Fourth, given the number of people in the supervision process, the variety of perspectives will be increased beyond what a single supervisor can provide.

- Fifth, group supervision may increase the quality of feedback because it can be discussed and communicated in ways that increase the likelihood of supervisee comprehension and internalization.

- Sixth, supervisors may get a broader understanding of each supervisee in the group because the supervisees will provide insight not only into their own cases but also into their peers' cases.

Bernard & Goodyear (2004) have suggested that limitations of group supervision can be reduced by implementing some **basic guidelines:**

- First, supervisors should attend to structuring the group to maximize the benefit for each supervisee. It may be particularly important to conduct group supervision with individuals who are similar in caseload, experience, and skill. Moreover, group size might expand the time allotted for each member to communicate during discussion in order to maximize learning.

- Second, supervisors must accentuate the rules of discussion to limit crossing boundaries of confidentiality. It may be necessary to not communicate names of athletes. Supervisors can embrace this method as an opportunity to reinforce ethical boundaries.

- Third, supervisors must structure the environment and pace the group to confront issues but not dwell on them so that discussions remain relevant for each supervisee.

- Lastly, as with any group, developing sport psychology consultants may engage in interpersonal dynamics that are maladaptive to supervisee development. Rather than view this as a limitation on group supervision, supervisors in sport psychology should embrace it as a challenge to reinforce sport psychology principles and principles of group dynamics. For instance, at a major university, it is possible for one supervisee to experience jealousy of a peer because of his or her work with a high-profile athlete. Group supervision provides the supervisor with a chance to engage developing sport psychology consultants in an atmosphere where he or she can highlight examples of group process as they occur.

Live observation. Supervisors will be able to acquire a comprehensive understanding of supervisees' sessions by observing live with no interaction. Rather than being limited to the scope of a camera lens in video recorded supervision, supervisors can take in the whole room from a dynamic perspective. For instance, a supervisor could focus solely on the body positioning of an athlete after confrontational questioning by a supervisee. Additionally, if observation occurs through a one-way mirror or through use of advanced technology (e.g., webcams), peer supervisees may be present with the supervisor, allowing for midstream teaching moments. Lastly, live observation may allow for immediate feedback from the supervisor and/or peer supervisees to the consultant. At the end of a session, the supervisor and supervisee can meet and discuss the consulting process and case conceptualization while everything is fresh in their minds.

Live supervision. Several methods of live supervision have been presented by Bernard and Goodyear (2004): bug-in-the-ear, monitoring, in vivo, walk-in, phone-in, and consultation. In each of these methods, supervisors observe supervisee sessions live and may interrupt to offer direction. The differences in these methods are centered on the technology used and the proximity of the supervisor (i.e., in the room, outside the room). Rather than focus in detail on these methods, we would like to offer a unique method of live supervision that differs slightly in form but vastly in function to the typical methods listed here. We believe the greatest learning in applied sport psychology consultation can occur in a team consultation environment. In vivo supervision may be the closest existing model of supervision in which the supervisor and supervisee are both present in a session, and when teachable moments occur, the supervisor is able to interject. In contrast to in vivo supervision, we recommend the supervisor interrupt a session when necessary to direct the consultation. This form of supervision is similar to a pilot/ co-pilot model of flying an airplane-at times, the co-pilot may need to take control of the plane. The supervisor may serve as the co-pilot, allowing the supervisee (pilot) to lead the athlete until too much turbulence is experienced, at which point the experienced supervisor asserts himself or herself and redirects the session.

There are several advantages of this supervision model:

- First, and foremost, the athlete does not experience any interruption or decline in sport psychology services. Athletes in general, and student-athletes in particular, do not have much time to waste serving as test dummies for graduate student development. By taking over the consulting controls, the supervisor can ensure that the athlete receives high-quality consultation within the flow of the session.

- Second, learning occurs through modeling. Supervisees are given the opportunity to observe an expert redirect a session to a more optimal path of self-discovery for the athlete. The supervisee is given a brief moment to perceive the change, adapt focus, and prepare to take control of the session when the supervisor relinquishes it to the supervisee.

- Third, the credibility of the supervisee remains intact. Within this model, the supervisor must be expert at asserting himself or herself into the session without criticizing the supervisee or highlighting mistakes. The supervisor is challenged to deflect attention away from the supervisee for a moment to redirect the athlete to the desired path. If done eloquently, the athlete leaves the consulting room with a sense of satisfaction in the progress he or she has made and a desire to return to two competent consultants for another session.

The model described above has been used successfully within the sport psychology training clinic for almost two decades at The University of North Carolina-Chapel Hill. We believe the advantages distinctly outweigh the limitations; however, it is important to discuss the limitations here. Obviously, the proposed model requires more time commitment from supervisors than any other method described in this book. For young, tenure-track faculty, it may seem impossible to implement such a system when the university may not reward them for it. Unfortunately, the time commitment cannot be relieved; however, we believe it is well worth it in the long run for two reasons:

- First, it enhances the quality of experience and training for supervisees, which will ultimately result in increased quality of service provision in the athletic community.

- Second, it can enhance the bonds between supervisor and supervisee, developing an enduring collegial relationship.

Another drawback to the proposed method is that supervisees require a great deal of emotional maturity, cognitive control, and resilience. It may be difficult for insecure individuals to observe a supervisor "take the reins" of a session because their thoughts may immediately jump to, "What did I do wrong?" We hope that this idea leads developing sport psychology professionals to a strong conclusion: We must be able to practice what we preach. Just as we will challenge athletes to let go of previous mistakes while performing, we must also let go and shift our attention toward the future. Sport psychology supervisees who may be threatened and debilitated by making a mistake in session may need to self-reflect before challenging an athlete on the same topic.

Advancing the Application of Sport Psychology

Through the development of systematic models of training, colleagues aspiring to practice sport psychology will have a higher probability of developing competence, confidence, and valuable experience *before* they engage in their first intervention with a client or team. It is hard to believe that systematic training and supervision models have not been implemented as a basic requirement in all sport psychology programs professing to prepare professionals for practice. It has been more than twenty years since AAASP was founded with a central goal directed toward advancing the practice and application of sport psychology. The structuring of graduate programs so that professionals interested in practicing have the appropriate supervisory experiences is long overdue. Achieving this educational and training goal should be transformed from a point of emphasis with major organizations such as AAASP and APA Division 47 to a point of implementation.

References

Andersen, M. B., Van Raalte, J. L., & Brewer, B. W. (1994). Assessing the skills of sport psychology supervisors. *The Sport Psychologist, 8,* 238–247.

Bernard, J. M., & Goodyear, R.K. (2004). *Fundamentals of clinical supervision* (3rd ed.). Boston, MA: Pearson Education.

Brannon, D. (1985). Adult learning principles and methods for enhancing the training role of supervisors. *The Clinical Supervisor, 3,* 27–41.

Carney, C. G., & Kahn, K. B. (1984). Building competencies for effective cross-cultural counseling: A developmental view. *The Counseling Psychologist, 12,* 111–119.

Covner, B. J. (1942a). Studies in phonographic recordings of verbal material: I. The use of phonographic recordings in counseling practice and research. *Journal of Consulting Psychology, 6,* 105–113.

Covner, B. J. (1942b). Studies in phonographic recordings of verbal material: II. A device for transcribing phonographic recordings of verbal material. *Journal of Consulting Psychology, 6,* 149–151.

Freeman, E. (1985). The importance of feedback in clinical supervision: Implications for direct practice. *The Clinical Supervisor, 3,* 5–26.

Goldberg, D. A. (1985). Process notes, audio, and videotape: Modes of presentation in psychotherapy training. *The Clinical Supervisor, 3,* 3–13.

Harmison, R. J. (2004, September). The pursuit of professional training via a master's degree in sport psychology. In R. J. Harmison (Chair), *Professional training in applied sport psychology: The quest for the golden fleece?* Symposium presented at the 19th annual meeting of the Association for the Advancement for the Applied Sport Psychology, Minneapolis, MN.

Hess, A. K. (1986). Growth in supervision: Stages of supervisee and supervisor development. *The Clinical Supervisor, 4,* 51–67.

Hogan, R. A. (1964). Issues and approaches in supervision. *Psychotherapy: Theory Research and Practice, 1,* 139–141.

Holloway, E. L. (1988). Instruction beyond the facilitative conditions: A response to Biggs. *Counselor Education and Supervision, 27,* 252–258.

Holloway, E. L., & Johnston, R. (1985). Group supervision: Widely practiced but poorly understood. *Counselor Education and Supervision, 24,* 332–340.

Kagan, N. (1980). Influencing human interaction-eighteen years with IPR. In A. K. Hess (Ed.), *Psychotherapy supervision: Theory, research and practice* (pp. 262–286). New York: Wiley.

Kagan, H. K., & Kagan, N. I. (1997). Interpersonal process recall: Influencing human interaction. In C. E. Watkins, Jr. (Ed.), *Handbook of psychotherapy supervision* (pp. 296–309). New York: Wiley.

Lerner, B. (2005). Supervision: What does it all mean? *AZCA Newsletter, 3,* 3–7.

McColley, S. H., & Baker, G. L. (1982). Training activities and styles of beginning supervisors: A survey. *Professional Psychology, 13,* 283–292.

Proctor, B. (1994). Supervision-competence, confidence, accountability. *British Journal of Guidance and Counseling, 22,* 309–318.

Rogers, C. R. (1942). The use of electrically recorded interviews in improving psychotherapeutic techniques. *American Journal of Orthopsychiatry, 12,* 429–434.

Rogers, C. R. (1957). Training individuals to engage in the therapeutic process. In C.R. Strother (Ed.), *Psychology and mental health* (pp. 76–92). Washington, DC: American Psychological Association.

Sansbury, D. L. (1982). Developmental supervision from a skills perspective. *The Counseling Psychologist, 10*(1), 53–57.

Silva, J.M. (1998). Athlete evaluation of sport psychology graduate student counseling ability and skills. Unpublished evaluation form. Chapel Hill, NC.

Stoltenberg, C. (1981). Approaching supervision from a developmental perspective: The counselor complexity model. *Journal of Counseling Psychology, 28,* 59–65.

Stoltenberg, C. D., McNeill, B. W., & Delworth, U. (1998). *IDM supervision: An integrated developmental model for supervising counselors and therapists.* San Francisco, CA: Jossey-Bass.

Tonn, E., & Harmison, R. J. (2004). Thrown to the wolves: A student's account of her practicum experience. *The Sport Psychologist, 18,* 324–340.

CHAPTER 7

Counselor
Self-Enhancement

A t its core, applied sport psychology is defined by its focus on enhancement. It is appropriate that the final chapter points the developing professional toward ongoing self-enhancement to maintain competence and professional vigor. Several suggestions are offered toward the aim of perpetual professional development. The authors discuss the benefits of becoming involved and maintaining active involvement in professional organizations. Additionally, as the evolution of sport psychology continues, the authors anticipate that AAASP certification may require engagement in continuing education workshops, thus they describe the benefits of this engagement. Apprentices learned in chapter 2 the importance of using application based on science. In this chapter, young applied professional are encouraged to maintain proximity to the scholarly community. The authors also highlight the role supervision can play in keeping consultants current in their knowledge and skills. Developing professionals will obtain strategies for broadening their horizons by understanding the importance of exposure to a variety of cultures, worldviews, and sports. New experiences open new avenues for conceptualizations and applications. Lastly, the authors advocate the importance of "practicing what you preach." Engaging in the principles that define our discipline and profession are critical for establishing credibility and genuineness. It is the authors' vision that this final chapter represent a beginning rather than an end-a beginning of self- and other-enhancement in the context of sport.

Preparation for Practice Comes Full Circle

The majority of this text has focused on how to prepare to practice sport psychology and how to gain entry into the field. The emphasis has been on a series of teaching and learning experiences that provide knowledge, technical skills, and a structure to base one's practice around. Investing the time and energy to properly prepare for entry into the practice of sport psychology is a significant accomplishment. After practice has begun, it is easy to become set in one's ways and to stick with what seems to work well for the consultant's style of interacting with athletes. Although experience is a great teacher and there is no substitute for hands-on experience, it is essential to understand that the science and practice of sport psychology continue to evolve and expand. Professionals in applied sport psychology have an ongoing responsibility to continually monitor themselves and seek experiences that will provide professional enhancement. In considering competence as a process and not a destination, sport psychology professionals recognize personal strengths as well as weaknesses and enjoy opportunities afforded through professional enrichment that can enhance the quality of service delivery. Elman, Illfelder-Kaye, and Robiner (2005) define professional development as a comprehensive process:

> Professional development is the developmental process of acquiring, expanding, refining, and sustaining knowledge, proficiency, skill, and qualifications for competent professional functioning that result in professionalism. It comprises both (a) the internal tasks of clarifying professional objective, crystallizing professional identity, increasing self-awareness and confidence, and sharpening reasoning, thinking, reflecting, and judgment and (b) the social/contextual dimension of enhancing interpersonal aspects of professional functioning and broadening professional autonomy. (p. 368)

Interpersonal functioning and thinking like a psychologist are two central components of professionalism. Interpersonal functioning refers to developing self- and social awareness in order to attain skills for relating effectively to others. This component includes developing an awareness and appreciation for multicultural issues and how they may affect consultation. Thinking like a psychologist refers to problem solving and consists of factors such as: "(a) critical thinking and logical analysis; (b) being conversant with and utilizing scientific inquiry and professional literature; (c) being able to conceptualize problems and issues from multiple perspectives; and (d) being able to access, understand, integrate, and use resources (e.g., empirical evidence, statistical approaches, technology, collegial consultation)" (p. 369). Clearly, sport psychology embraces similar aims in terms of professional development. In order to provide the best services to clients, sport psychology consultants should continually strive to enhance their skills. In the remainder of the chapter, we will recommend several mechanisms that will foster professional development and a refinement of practice skills.

Enrichment through Professional Organizations

An excellent method for maintaining close proximity with the state-of-the-art in sport psychology science and practice is to be actively involved in professional organizations. At a minimum, practicing sport psychology consultants should maintain membership in one or more of the following professional associations:

Association for the Advancement of Applied Sport Psychology (AAASP)

American Psychological Association (APA—Division 47)

North American Society for the Psychology of Sport and Physical Activity (NASPSPA)

International Society of Sport Psychology (ISSP)

American Alliance for Health, Physical Education, Recreation & Dance (AAH-PERD)

Canadian Society for Psychomotor Learning and Sport Psychology (SCAPPS)

British Association of Sport and Exercise Sciences (BASES).

These organizations offer many benefits; periodic newsletters and/or scholarly journals keep the counselor abreast of current news and findings in the field, and group functions promote professional development. Sport psychology consultants should routinely attend annual meetings of the organizations listed above. Moreover, professionals could involve themselves in committee work, special assignments and projects, or serve as a conference abstract reviewer for upcoming professional meetings.

Continuing Education Workshops

Another method for professionals to maintain proximity to modern sport psychology concepts and practice techniques is to engage in continuing education workshops offered in and outside of annual conferences. For instance, AAASP routinely offers several workshops, in advance of its annual meeting, conducted by leading sport psychology consultants and scholars. Currently, maintaining Certified Consultant-AAASP status requires either completion of continuing education hours or teaching a course within the sport psychology field. The sport psychology listserv, SPORTPSY, often contains messages announcing continuing education workshop opportunities. Importantly, workshops regarding a breadth of diversity ranging from empirical techniques to consulting techniques should be considered annually. Professional development may be further enhanced by developing and conducting such workshops at annual meetings or regional gatherings.

Engage in Research Practices

Engagement in research endeavors meets all the principles of professional development as noted by Elman, Illfelder-Kaye, and Robiner (2005). By definition, the scientific method is a systematic, logical, and critical thought process that expands our understanding of phenomena. Professionals who engage in scholarship are consistently challenged to critically examine theories, models, and concepts from which interventions are based. At minimum, applied sport psychology consultants should be conversant with current literature in the field. Refereed journals such as *Journal of Applied Sport Psychology, Journal of Sport & Exercise Psychology, The Sport Psychologist, Psychology of Sport & Exercise,* and *International Journal of Sport & Exercise Psychology* are specifically oriented toward sport psychology and allow consultants to maintain proximity to the current state of the discipline. With this knowledge, practitioners can make informed refinements to interventions being employed. Professional development can be enhanced further by actively engaging in the research process. Serving as a formal reviewer for a journal is a very beneficial way to stay current with the body of knowledge. Reviewers are charged with critically analyzing manuscript submissions; therefore, the nature of the position directly pertains to facets of professional development. Lastly, sport psychology professionals, both in and out of academe should consider conducting research projects and disseminating the results in the form of publications, position papers, and presentations. Full-time sport psychology consultants do not have a formal mandate nor do they have the incentive of academic sport psychology professionals for conducting research; however, full-time professionals can bring a realistic perspective to applied research based on their practical experience. There is a great need for applied research and a systematic examination of sport psychology in the "real world" with athletes of all ages.

Enhance Professional Development Through Supervision

Delivering and receiving supervision can enhance professional development in several significant areas. Serving as a supervisor for sport psychology consultants-in-training benefits both supervisee and supervisor. Supervision requires meticulous planning and focus that stimulates the supervisor to engage in different processing than when counseling (Bernard & Goodyear, 2004). Providing supervision can enhance communication skills, provide for self-awareness of professional identity, update ethical awareness, and practice determining standards of accountability (Elman, Illfelder-Kaye, & Robiner, 2005). Supervisors are challenged to think critically to consider cases from a different perspective than if they were serving as the primary consultant. For professionals in academia, supervision of graduate students may be embedded in daily professional activities as a required component of the position. Sport psychology consultants employed outside of academe are encouraged to consider providing supervision as a means to remain current and oriented toward professional development. All practicing sport psychology professionals can provide service to the field at large by providing structured and supervised internships that afford developing practitioners hours needed to become CC-AAASP. Additionally, sport psychology professionals should adopt the stance that their consulting competence is always a work in progress. Given this philosophy of personal growth, seeking supervision periodically can be thought of as a critical component for evaluation and identification of areas of weakness. Receiving critical feedback can help to develop interpersonal skills used in consultation. In essence, sport psychology practitioners, like all other professionals, should routinely seek objective external feedback to avoid professional stagnation.

Broaden Horizons

As stated by Elman, Illfelder-Kaye, and Robiner (2005), one aspect of development for which professionals should strive is expanding the perspectives used to conceptualize client issues. To increase perspective, consultants can focus on increased exposure to three distinct areas: theories of intervention, diverse world views, and new sports. Each of these is described in turn below.

Expose yourself to alternate theories of intervention. Throughout this text cognitive behavioral modification has served as the foundational theory for sport psychology training. Many other theories drawn from general psychology have demonstrated validity in applied sport psychology. This is a dynamic and evolving discipline, and as such, future theories are surely yet to be formulated. Trainees of sport psychology, like other disciplines, are frequently confined to the theoretical perspective of their mentors during training. Professionals can inform, shift, or crystallize their professional identity by learning the assumptions, premises, techniques, and outcomes of alternate theories of intervention. Considering alternate theories allows professionals to challenge their own assumptions and beliefs. The process requires critical assessment and self-reflection, which only strengthens professionals in the services they provide to athletes. In addition, problem solving may require solutions from various sources. For instance, cognitive behavioral strategies may be most effective for helping an athlete overcome attentional control; however, interpersonal strategies may be effective when examining suboptimal coach-athlete relations.

Study and learn diverse worldviews. One of the major benefits of sport is that it tends to serve as a common language that bonds many cultures. Indeed, the Olympics are routinely marketed as an opportunity for the "world to come together" to highlight the heterogeneity of cultures involved in sport; therefore, sport psychology consultants should not be surprised to provide services to athletes of a vast array of worldviews. Sue, Ivey, and Pedersen (1996) define a worldview as "how a person perceives his/her relationship to the world (nature, institutions, other people, etc.)" or "the way we make meaning in the world" (p. 7). Our attitudes, values, opinions, and conceptualizations affect our cognitions, decision-making, behaviors, and perceptions of events (Sue & Sue, 1990). Consultants and athletes alike are influenced by their religions, ethnicity, socioeconomic background, culture, and gender, to name a few characteristics. Mainstream psychology has been criticized for adhering to Western theories and assumptions when providing counseling services to individuals of diverse backgrounds. Sport psychology is not exempt from these concerns. Although it may be politically correct to avoid discussion of values and their foundation, it may be an important factor to consider in consultation. For instance, consider an athlete who firmly believes success and failure are in God's hands. It may be challenging to focus this athlete on aspects of performance within his or her control because the contingency between increased effort resulting in improved performance is not explicitly evident to this athlete. Indeed, cognitive behavior modification is very Eurocentric, emphasizing cause and effect and the future. Such an approach may be less powerful with athletes who emphasize an Eastern approach, focused on harmony, going with the flow, and the present. Consequently, professional development in sport psychology can be enhanced through exposure to diverse worldviews and value systems. Unfortunately, multicultural counseling and diversity training has been largely neglected in sport psychology as AAASP certification does not currently require such coursework or experience (Martens, Mobley, & Zizzi, 2000).

According to Kontos & Arguello (2005), all athletes should be considered within the context of their culture, which is determined by enculturation and acculturation. Whereas enculturation refers to an athlete's enmeshment with his or her ethnically based beliefs, values, and practices, acculturation refers to an athlete's adoption of the dominant culture's practices. Both enculturation and acculturation levels should be considered when providing sport psychology services. In short, multicultural considerations are necessary to take into account all aspects of an athlete's cultural involvement. Athletes who are highly enculturated may continue to adhere strongly to their native language, diet, and religious traditions, for instance. A prominent example familiar to Americans may be Yao Ming, a Chinese basketball player who moved to the United States to play for the Houston Rockets and responded to interviews during his rookie season in his native tongue. In contrast, individuals of international descent who grew up in the United States, who are therefore mostly detached from their ancestral languages and routinely listen to popular music, serve as good examples of high acculturation. Rather than making erroneous cultural assumptions and stereotypes regarding athletes, sport psychology consultants must be sensitive to enculturation/acculturation in their clients. Moreover, given the dynamic nature of these processes, sport psychology professionals must continually monitor evolving acculturation that may occur within each client.

A few scholars have suggested increasing cultural awareness as a means of professional training and development. Indeed, Parham (2005) suggested (a) an understanding of cultural context is essential for effective sport psychology service delivery, (b) diverse athletes should be treated as individuals and not as individuals of homogeneous groups, and (c) an understanding of alternate cultural and ethnic worldviews may free professionals from the constraints of Euro-American psychology. Parham recommended specific self- and other-reflective questions both prior to consultation and after consultation. During the pre-consultation phase, consultants are advised to ask themselves four intertwined questions:

1. "Do I possess the skills, knowledge, and abilities to respond appropriately and accurately to this request?"

2. "To what degree will my ethnicity, gender, age, and so on influence the work I do on behalf of my client?"

3. "What do I know concretely about this client I am about to see?"

4. "How will his or her ethnicity, gender, age, and so on influence our consultation relationship?" (p. 209).

These questions are designed to enhance awareness of cultural differences and influences that may impact consultation processes. After the sessions, consultants are encouraged to reflect on what they have learned about themselves and their clients as well as on how they have changed because of the cross-cultural consulting relationship.

Martens, Mobley, & Zizzi (2000) offered a few tangible methods to enhance professional development in terms of multicultural training:

• First, to increase awareness and sensitivity, sport psychology professionals are encouraged to experience culture shock by immersing themselves in alternate cultural gatherings. For example, a Caucasian consultant could attend a local African-American church. Alternatively, professionals can read literature from other cultures, listen to diverse forms of music, and view culturally oriented movies.

• Second, professionals are encouraged to increase their knowledge of cultural groups and racial and ethnic identity development.

• Third, awareness and knowledge should be augmented by practical application of sport psychology or authentic role-playing activities with clients of diverse cultures. Sport psychology professionals are encouraged to seek out opportunities to consult athletes of various ethnic backgrounds as a means of broadening and strengthening their professional competence.

- Lastly, professionals can develop multicultural understanding by actively seeking opportunities to supervise consultants of diverse cultures as well as cross-cultural dyads. These varied experiences will help to expand a sport psychology professional's consulting competence.

To this point, the focus of our discussion has been on ethnic diversity; however, many of the techniques and methods described for professional development can also be applied when working with diverse sexual orientations. Martens and Mobley (2005) review of the admittedly lacking body of literature regarding male homosexuality revealed four central themes regarding male homosexuality in sport. Sport is traditionally viewed as an arena to demonstrate masculinity. The demonstration of physical prowess dominates male sport; men who are strong, fast, and so on are traditionally also perceived as heterosexual; consequently, homosexuality-stereotyped as effeminate-appears largely out of place in the world of sport. This limited definition of male sport may result in contempt for homosexual athletes. Rather than accept this alternate worldview and lifestyle, some sport psychology consultants have articulated a bias toward homosexuality as a threat or a psychological disorder (Rotella & Murray, 1991). Obviously, consultants who hold these biases may impede progress of their clients. Not surprisingly, homosexual athletes are often forced to remain silent about their identity out of fear of being "outed." Regarding female homosexuality, similar issues emerge (Barber & Krane, 2005). Given that sport is framed as a test of masculinity, successful female athletes are often conveyed as "Amazon women" who are undesirable mates for men because they are too masculine. Athletes who cannot fully disclose to sport psychology consultants may not be able to fully investigate themselves. Lastly, fear of HIV and AIDS continues to permeate sport professionals' views as well as the perceptions of the general public.

Professional development in sport should also include diversity training relative to differences in sexual orientation. Paralleling the examples highlighted above to expand cultural awareness and understanding, sport psychology professionals must first self-reflect on their own beliefs and values regarding homosexuality. We must be cognizant of traditional American institutions such as Christianity, the military ("don't ask, don't tell"), and sport, which may have a profound impact on the way we perceive homosexual athletes. Sport psychology professionals are encouraged to experience culture shock by attending events of groups whose sexual orientations are other than their own. Additionally, active engagement in developing knowledge (e.g., books, workshops, classes, movies) regarding preconceptions about sexual orientation can be helpful in expanding a consultant's sensitivity and competence.

Given the traditions and stereotypes associated with and embedded in sport, developing consultants may feel extremely awkward approaching this topic. It may be perceived as easier to avoid the topic and attempt to provide services only to athletes who are "straight." We argue that this solution is not only antagonistic to the philosophy of humility and ongoing self-enhancement but it is also impractical. For example, suppose a consultant is faced with an athlete who articulates several problems communicating with teammates and coaches. Although the presenting issue may simply be differing communication styles, it may be a reflection of a deeper issue for the athlete because he does not feel a connection with his teammates and coaches because of his sexual orientation. Within a consulting dyad, discovery of the true depth of the interpersonal dysfunction may take several sessions to occur. Those who adopt a narrow stance regarding sexual orientation may be faced with a difficult ethical and moral dilemma: They do not want to work with a homosexual athlete, yet a good working relationship has already been developed with this person. We advocate active self-enhancement regarding awareness and understanding of sexual orientation to put sport psychology professionals in a position to handle similar situations ethically and with competence.

Study and learn new sports and their cultures. It is not surprising to find sport psychology trainees to be biased toward specific sports. More often than not, development in sport consists of specialized training in a particular or small number of sports. For example, a graduate student who played collegiate softball may feel more comfortable consulting with softball players. If formal training experiences do not challenge trainees to develop consultation skills in the context of unfamiliar sports, these consultants would be particularly advised to familiarize themselves with other sports upon graduation. In fact, we recommend that sport psychology consultants of all experience levels challenge themselves to learn about sports new to them and to try to have directly supervised experiences when working with athletes in sports that are unfamiliar to the consultants. The market demand for sport psychology services is not currently high enough to allow for specializations within sport psychology; therefore, any consultant wishing to attempt to make a living on consultation alone will need to be diverse enough to provide services to athletes who participate in a wide variety of sports. Given the likely diversity of sports represented by clients met in consultation, sport psychology practitioners will benefit by understanding the different norms and subcultures within various sports. A consultant not familiar with the social psychological dynamics of the sport the athlete participates in will be at a distinct disadvantage when attempting to provide consultation.

Engage in Physical Activity/Sport

As professionals linked either directly or indirectly to the general field of sport and exercise science, sport psychology consultants are probably more aware than the average person of the benefits of physical activity and sport. As detailed in the Surgeon General's Report on Physical Activity and Health (Centers for Disease Control and Prevention, 1996), regular physical activity reduces risk for cardiovascular disease, cancer, osteoporosis, diabetes, and depression, among others. Aside from general health benefits, regular exercise and engagement in sport are critical to the enhancement of the sport psychologist's consultation rapport. The clients a sport psychology counselor serves are often competitive athletes who center on physical training. At all levels, athletes integrate strength training, plyometrics, aerobic activity, technical skill development, and tactical strategy into their daily routines. Sport psychology professionals can benefit from adopting some of these behaviors to immerse themselves in the experience of being a competitive athlete.

Recent scholarship points toward enhanced credibility of sport psychology consultants based on physical appearance. Lubker, Watson, Visek, and Geer (2006) examined perceptions of Division I collegiate athletes regarding build and dress of performance enhancement consultants. As opposed to those with large build and academic dress, lean consultants in athletic clothing were perceived to be more knowledgeable of sport. More importantly, athletes reported higher likelihood to seek the services of these physically fit consultants. Consequently, sport psychology professionals may consider engaging in physical activity as a means of maintaining physical fitness to enhance their chances of being perceived as capable, knowledgeable, and credible by prospective clients.

We described empathy as one of the critical qualities of counseling earlier in the text. Rather than rely on imagination or previous experience, sport psychology professionals can engage in new exercise regimens implemented by strength trainers or be involved in city sport leagues to fully appreciate the experience from the athletes' perspectives. Oftentimes, sessions can be bogged down simply because the consultant does not fully understand the meaning of terms used by clients. Engagement may afford learning of new terminology that can enhance communication in sessions and help to increase efficiency of sessions. Active engagement goes beyond observation and requires professionals not only to grasp cognitive components of motor skills but also to learn to perform these skills. For example, to talk about not hesitating when attempting a header in a crowd in a close soccer match is different from understanding that statement from an experiential perspective. We are not suggesting that consultants must have physical experience in every sport before consulting with athletes; however, if physical involvement is reasonable (i.e., there are no physical barriers to involvement), we highly recommend it to gain additional first-person perspective. We have found that the vivid communication that evolves from authentic understanding of sport and exercise enhances credibility and trust, which ultimately increases rapport development with athletes.

Engagement in sport and exercise can also expand a consultant's clientele. Bruce Ogilvie (Ogilvie & Tutko, 1966), known as the father of applied sport psychology, openly discussed how he became involved with athletes in part because of his regular physical activity at a local facility where athletes were often present. Given that the majority of sport psychology professionals are employed in academia, it is recommended that these individuals work out in the recreation center to enhance visibility as an active person and to open communication avenues with sport and exercise participants. Similar avenues may be available for private consultants as well by enrolling and regularly exercising in the local gym, sport club, or a comparable alternative.

Implement Sport Psychology Principles in Your Own Life

Possibly the most important aspect of establishing and maintaining professional credibility in sport psychology is to "practice what you preach." Consultants who strongly advocate certain sport psychology principles to their athletes but do not implement these principles in their own lives convey a powerful message. Either these consultants do not believe in what they teach or they may not have the self-discipline or expertise to enact the principles they encourage. In either case, conflicting messages can be conveyed to athletes, causing confusion and even distrust. In a university setting where consultants' primary responsibility is teaching, there may be expanded opportunity for athletes to observe the consultants' behaviors outside of sessions. If these individuals routinely show up late and/or unprepared for classes or have difficulty coping with stress (e.g., faulty computer-projector interface, etc.), it may be difficult for clients to fully internalize and implement the same behaviors discussed in sessions. Although consultants with private firms may not experience the same amount of public exposure or contact with clients outside of sessions, lack of genuineness, reflected in not adhering to principles, can be detected by clients. Imagine a consultant focused on helping a client develop intrinsic motivation through setting process-oriented goals. How would this consultant be perceived if he or she complained about low teacher salary or got out of the office as soon as possible to make up for low wages? In sport psychology, as in many other domains, "Do as I say, not as I do" is not an acceptable philosophy.

The Circle Never Ends

Remember the day you found sport psychology? Do you remember how excited you were about this new field? Were you eager to join up and become a sport psychologist so you could get out there and practice? Did you think you were going to be able to connect with athletes like no one else before you? Remember that passion and energy you had for this field-how that energy had captured your imagination, all the possibilities you envisioned? Where are you now on that never-ending circle of professional life?

Many professionals young and old have become frustrated with sport psychology. Many prospective students and colleagues have left the field disappointed, disillusioned, and disenchanted. One of the major complaints is the lack of quality sport psychology graduate programs specifically focused on the education and training experiences necessary to become an AAASP Certified Consultant or to have a viable practice base. Over the years we have consistently heard from students, young professionals, and established professionals that they need a text that will provide the guidance needed to develop educational and training experiences that will enhance competence in sport psychology service delivery.

Throughout this text, we have offered a practical model for the training and development of professionals in the practice of sport psychology. This text is a point of departure, a first attempt to provide a guide to the training of future professionals in the practice of sport psychology. Each generation of sport psychology service providers should be better prepared than the last. The knowledge within the discipline and the progress made through practice experiences should be transmitted to each new generation in training and to each past generation of service providers who continue their education and training experiences.

The science and practice of sport psychology can be exhilarating because consultants are faced with the challenge of helping physically fit, skilled, energetic individuals in their pursuit of optimizing personal and team performance. What other profession demonstrates such a convergence between goals of client and the service provider? Collectively, our experiences leave us very optimistic about future generations of sport psychology professionals. Young professionals in sport psychology have demonstrated a desire for professional self-enhancement and improved graduate education and training programs. It is an exciting and evolutionary time to be actively involved in applied sport psychology training and professional development. Those who invest significant amounts of their energy to the practice of sport psychology, those who are in the field every day, must step forward and help advance applied sport psychology and the provision of services to athletes, teams, and coaches. As one small step forward, we hope this text will contribute to the continued evolution of this field. There certainly are persistent issues that challenge the viable practice of sport psychology, but these issues can be resolved (Silva, 1989; 1996). The advancement of a field is a never-ending goal.

References

Andersen, M. B. (1993). Questionable sensitivity: A comment on Lee and Rotella. *The Sport Psychologist, 7*, 1–3.

Barber, H., & Krane, V. (2005). The elephant in the locker room: Opening the dialogue about sexual orientation on women's sports teams. In M. B. Andersen (Ed.), *Sport psychology in practice* (pp. 265–285). Champaign, IL: Human Kinetics.

Centers for Disease Control and Prevention (1996). *Surgeon general's report on physical activity and health.* Retrieved May 10, 2005 from http://www.cdc.gov/nccdphp/sgr/pdf/chap4.pdf.

Elman, N. S., Illfelder-Kaye, J., & Robiner, W. N. (2005). Professional development: Training for professionalism as a foundation for competent practice in psychology. *Professional Psychology: Research and Practice, 36,* 367–375.

Kontos A. P., & Arguello, E. (2005). Sport psychology consulting. *Athletic Insight: The Online Journal of Sport Psychology, 7.* Retrieved May 19, 2006, from http://www.athleticinsight.com/Vol7Iss3/LatinAmerican.htm.

Kontos A. P., & Breland-Noble, A. M. (2002). Racial/ethnic diversity in applied sport psychology: A multicultural introduction to working with athletes of color. *The Sport Psychologist, 16,* 296–315.

Lubker, J. R., Watson, J. C., Visek, A. J., & Geer, J. R. (2006). Physical appearance and the perceived effectiveness of performance enhancement consultants. *The Sport Psychologist, 16,* 446–458.

Martens, M. P., & Mobley, M. (2005). Straight guys working with gay guys: Homophobia and sport psychology service delivery. In M. B. Andersen (Ed.), *Sport psychology in practice* (pp. 249–263). Champaign, IL: Human Kinetics.

Martens, M. P., Mobley, M., & Zizzi, S. J. (2000). Multicultural training in applied sport psychology. *The Sport Psychologist, 14,* 81–97.

Ogilvie, B. C., & Tutko, T. A. (1966). *Problem athletes and how to handle them.* London: Pelham.

Parham, W. D. (2005). Raising the bar: Developing an understanding of athletes from racially, culturally, and ethnically diverse backgrounds. In M. B. Andersen (Ed.), *Sport psychology in practice* (pp. 201–215). Champaign, IL: Human Kinetics.

Rotella, R. J., & Murray, M. M. (1991). Homophobia, the world of sport, and sport psychology consulting. *The Sport Psychologist, 5,* 355–364.

Silva, J. M. (1989). Establishing professional standards and advancing applied sport psychology research. *Journal of Applied Sport Psychology, 1,* 160–165.

Silva, J. M. (1996). A second move: Confronting persistent issues that challenge the advancement of applied sport psychology. *Journal of Applied Sport Psychology, 8,* S52.

Sue, D. W., Ivey, A. E., & Pedersen, P. B. (1996). *A theory of multicultural counseling and therapy.* Pacific Grove, CA: Brooks/Cole.

Sue, D. W., & Sue, D. (1990). *Counseling the culturally different: Theory and practice.* New York: Wiley.

ABOUT THE AUTHORS

John M. Silva, Ph.D. is a professor of sport psychology in the Department of Exercise and Sport Science at the University of North Carolina at Chapel Hill. He received his Ph.D. from the University of Maryland, and the M.S. and B.S. from the University of Connecticut. Dr. Silva was the founding president of the Association for the Advancement of Applied Sport Psychology (AAASP), currently the largest sport psychology association in the world, and was the inaugural editor of the *Journal of Applied Sport Psychology,* the first nonproprietary sport psychology journal in the United States. He is co-editor of two sport psychology textbooks, including the widely used *Psychological Foundations of Sport* published in 2002, and is a fellow in AAASP, a certified AAASP consultant, a member of the APA, the USOC Sport Psychology Registry, and a Research Consortium Fellow. A faculty member at Chapel Hill since 1981, Dr. Silva has served as the director of the sport psychology

graduate program and director of the sport psychology laboratory. Dedicated to the development of students, he formed three sport psychology clinics as part of the sport psychology graduate training program at Carolina. These directly supervised clinics provided master's students with hands-on counseling experiences with collegiate athletes. Dr. Silva has served as a sport psychology consultant for athletes and teams for over 25 years. He has provided consultation and on-site services to athlete's competing in national, international, and world competitions. Discussion of his work and research has appeared in *The New York Times, The Washington Post, Psychology Today, NCAA News, USA Today,* and *The Chronicle of Higher Education,* in several national wire releases, and on national television. Invited lectures include the 1984 Los Angeles Games Olympic Scientific Congress, the 1985 World Sport Psychology Congress in Copenhagen, Denmark, a series of invited lectures in 1985 in Sweden, the 1988 Olympic Scientific Congress in Seoul, South Korea, lectures at East German and Soviet sport psychology institutes in 1989, a 1990 address to the Spanish Olympic Organizing Committee and National Governing Bodies in Madrid, Spain, a 1995 keynote at the International Congress for Sport Science in Komotini, Greece, a 1999 invited address in Osaka, Japan, and numerous invited addresses at sport psychology conferences including the Coleman Griffith Memorial Lecture at AAASP in 1995 and an invited presentation on the future of sport psychology at the AAASP 20th Anniversary Conference in 2005. In 2000 he was elected to the USA Team Handball Board of Directors and has served on its Sports Medicine Committee since 1987. From 1995 to the present he has chaired or co-chaired the USA Team Handball Sport Science and Technology Committee. Dr. Silva has coached over a dozen Carolina students who have become USA Team Handball National Team players including two members of the 1996 USA Team Handball Olympic team. He coached the Women's South Team in the 1993 Olympic Festival and the Men's South Team, which won the Gold Medal in the 1995 Olympic Festival. In December 2003 he was awarded the USOC, USA Team Handball Volunteer Coach of the Year Award. In 2004, 2005, and 2006 he coached Carolina Team Handball men's team to three consecutive USA Team Handball Collegiate National Championships. The Carolina Team also won the bronze medal at the 2006 USA Team Handball Open Tournament in the Elite Division.

Jonathan N. Metzler is Assistant Professor of Health & Kinesiology and Co-Coordinator of the sport psychology graduate program at Georgia Southern University. Jon has published manuscripts in the *Journal of Applied Sport Psychology*, the *Journal of Sport & Exercise Psychology*, *Measurement in Physical Education and Exercise Science*, and *Structural Equation Modeling* and has delivered presentations at several multinational professional meetings. His research has focused primarily on achievement motivation, emotion in sport, coaching behaviors, and psychometrics. He also serves as associate editor for the Journal of Coaching Education. Jon has delivered sport psychology services to intercollegiate, Olympic, and professional athletes including some who participated in NCAA Division I National Championships and the Olympics. A member of the Association for the Advancement of Applied Sport Psychology since 1998, Jon has served as student regional representative and on the Graduate Training, Organizational Outreach, and Accreditation Committees.

Bart Lerner, Ed.D., is the dean of the Arizona School of Professional Psychology, and chair of the MA Professional Counseling and Forensic Psychology Programs at Argosy University in Phoenix, Arizona. He is a Licensed Professional Counselor in Arizona and an AAASP Certified Consultant. His areas of interest include youth sport education, performance enhancement training, self-confidence, psychological aspects of injury and rehabilitation, substance abuse issues, supervision and training, and graduate training in sport psychology.

INDEX